007250 Centre 1

We have had _ C...
training, but I ...
with the doll becaus...
with too many for St...
back screeched incredibly
just was incredibly
"I was to the same
took me — I recognis
hospital — I recognis

THE
WISDEN
BOOK OF
CRICKET
QUOTATIONS

THE
WISDEN
BOOK OF
CRICKET
QUOTATIONS

Edited by
David
Lemmon

Macdonald
Queen Anne Press

A QUEEN ANNE PRESS BOOK

© David Lemmon 1990

First published in Great Britain in 1990 by
Queen Anne Press, a division of
Macdonald & Co (Publishers) Ltd
Orbit House
1 New Fetter Lane
London
EC4A 1AR

A member of Maxwell Macmillan Pergamon Publishing Corporation

Picture credits
The Mansell Collection vii, 1, 46, 62, 126, 157
Hulton-Deutsch 93, 113

British Library Cataloguing in Publication Data
The Wisden book of cricket quotations − 2nd ed.
   1. Cricket
   I. Lemmon, David
   796.35'8

   ISBN 0-356-17650-9

Typeset by Brian Smith Partnership, Bristol
Printed and bound in Great Britain by
Billing & Sons Limited, Worcester

CONTENTS

INTRODUCTION

The doubts that one has about writing an introduction are brought about by the doubts that one has as to whether or not anyone ever reads an introduction. I say this because I was at pains to point out in the introduction to the first edition of the *Wisden Book of Cricket Quotations* that all quotations included in the volume had their origin in literature, and that each quotation could be verified by reference to the original, the written word. One commentator chose to ignore this and criticised the book for not including folklore, legend and apocryphal story. He will again be disappointed, for the same criterion is applied to this second edition as was applied to the first, and the sayings attributed to the young Fred Trueman or to Javed Miandad in the outfield at Adelaide have no place here as they had no place in the first edition.

That first edition has long been out of print. It comprised just over 1,000 quotations which were classified in 12 sections. In this edition, more than half of the quotations used in the first volume have been discarded, and the total number included has been doubled. The quotations are now classified in seven groups and are, I hope, more meaningful.

What I have tried to do, particularly in the earlier sections, is to balance comments and opinions against each other, so, for example, in the first section, Observations and Attitudes, Julian Mitchell's assertion that 'cricket is a fundamental part of the capitalist conspiracy' is followed by Harold Rhodes' complementary comment that cricket mirrors 'the social and economic times in which we live'. Sometimes adjacent quotations will not complement but contradict each other so that when Stacy Aumonier suggests that sportsmanship epitomises the game, 'one doesn't take advantage of a mistake. It isn't done', Herbert Farjeon can counter this by claiming that 'sharp practice in our national game is probably a good deal more common than most Englishmen would care to admit'.

As in the first volume, when I turned to Bernard Darwin for support, the strengths and weaknesses of such a compilation as this are that they are dependent to some extent on a personal taste, but I have tried to be as wide-ranging as possible, and the number of authors referred to, like the number of quotations, has doubled.

Sentences earn their inclusion for their pithiness, succinctness, literary elegance or simply because they are recognised as *bon mots*, but also included are comments which have some social significance, as in the once great debate over gentlemen and players, or because they draw our attention to some fact which might otherwise have passed unnoticed.

I have bowed to pressure in making the final section, The Masters, take up half the book. Those who were warm in their praise for the first edition still hinted that they would like to see more about Botham, Woolley or Hammond, and at least something about Sobers. So much more has become available in the past six years as to make this possible, and there is, I trust, now a full representation of comments on the great.

It must not be felt that a large number of quotations from a particular author or book indicates an esteem for that author or book above all others. It is often that he has written the type of book or story that lends itself readily to quotation. For example, Stacy Aumonier is well represented on the strength of one story because it is full of pertinent phrases; Mike Brearley, on the other hand, is represented by only four quotations. Many will find this surprising, for Brearley has been recognised as one of the outstanding writers on the game in recent times, yet a close examination of his work reveals that it is narrative and analytical in style. He describes how Willis took his wickets at Headingley in 1981; he is concerned with technique, tactic and result, not the emotion, response or atmosphere that the result created.

To cite a parallel, it is interesting to note that the actor Peter Barkworth, in his splendid one-man show on the work of Siegfried Sassoon, did not draw upon *The Flower Show Match*, much as he loved it because he could find nothing there that he felt he could get his teeth into.

Inevitably, of course, there are writers who stand above the rest – Arlott, Swanton, Cardus, Altham, Peebles, James, Robertson-Glasgow – but I have tried also to be more modern in approach. My recent reading suggests to me that some of our contemporary writers have not been given the credit they deserve and some of the ancients more than they deserve, and I hope I have achieved a balance. Favourites will be apparent. I have not lost my admiration for A E Knight although I reduced the number of quotations by which he is represented by more than half.

As I mentioned earlier, the number of authors represented in the collection has doubled, and I am happy that I have been able to go beyond the bounds of cricket literature to include the words of playwrights like Alan Ayckbourn, Julian Mitchell, John Mortimer and Bettine Mankelow, of a theatre critic and cricket-lover like Michael Billington, of an actor like Lord Olivier, and of novelists like Talbot Baines Reed and Dorothy L Sayers as well as those who were included in the first edition and who have been retained.

I must express a debt of gratitude to anthologists David Rayvern Allen, John Bright-Holmes and Benny Green who, by their work, have made so much more material readily available, and I am happy that all three are included in their own right in this volume. I also remain indebted to *The Bibliography of Cricket* compiled by E W Paddick for The Library Association. Again, no serious work on cricket could be completed without reference to this marvellous work.

Much has changed in the past six years, but my feelings as I drew close to completing this work were as they were in 1983. I felt myself in the position of a selector. The selection will not please all. Some will feel slighted or even aghast. All one can do is to stand firm again and hope that one has chosen a winning side.

David Lemmon
Leigh-on-Sea
1989

OBSERVATIONS AND ATTITUDES

I tend to believe that cricket is the greatest thing that God ever created on earth.

1   I tend to believe that cricket is the greatest thing that God ever
     created on earth.

                                                    Harold Pinter
                            Pinter on Pinter in *The Observer* (1980)

2   *Judd:* I wasted my youth on *Wisden.*

                                                  Julian Mitchell
                                          Another Country (1982)

3   I was brought up to believe that cricket is the most important
     activity in men's lives, the most important thread in the fabric
     of the cosmos.

                                             Bernard Hollowood
                                     Cricket on the Brain (1970)

4   Patient, dramatic, serious, genial,
     From over to over the game goes on,
     Weaving a pattern of hardy perennial,
     Civilisation under the sun.

                                                  Gerald Bullett
                    Village Cricket in *News from the Village* (1952)

5   If you have a love for the game of cricket, whether you are a
     player, an ex-player, or simply an onlooker, many will be the
     pleasures in your life.

                                                    Keith Andrew
                                     The Handbook of Cricket (1989)

6   Cricket to us, like you, was more than play,
     It was a worship in the summer sun.

                                                  Edmund Blunden
                                      Pride of the Village (1925)

7   Capital game – smart sport – fine exercise – very.

                                                  Charles Dickens
                                         Pickwick Papers (1837)

8 *Judd:* What I really *hate* about cricket is, it's such a damned good game.

> **Julian Mitchell**
> *Another Country* (1982)

9 *Toby:* They've started this filthy floodlit cricket with cricketers wearing tin hats and advertisements for contraceptives on their boots.

> **Alan Ayckbourn**
> *A Gardener in Love, Intimate Exchanges* (1982)

10 The one-day game, the idea of never-dull, action-packed cricket with all the homey atmosphere of speedway racing and the amenities of a Wimpy Bar, is Mickey Mouse cricket, but nobody will mention it.

> **Stanley Reynolds** (1975)
> Reprinted in *The Guardian Book of Cricket* (1986)

11 One-day cricket has debased the currency, both of great finishes and of adjectives to describe them.

> **Matthew Engel** (1984)
> Reprinted in *The Guardian Book of Cricket* (1986)

12 Cricket never was and never can be a game of continuous excitement or of great achievement every day. The quiet hours, the simple strivings, are as much a part of the attraction as the unforgettable moments of high drama. Cricket is a composite joy, a blending of the modest and the magical.

> **J M Kilburn**
> *Cricket Decade* (1959)

13 Casting a ball at three straight sticks and defending the same with a fourth.

> **Rudyard Kipling**
> Quoted by Sir Neville Cardus in *Cricket* (1930)

14 Cricket is an altogether too sacred thing to him to be tampered with on merely religious grounds.

> **H G Wells**
> *Certain Personal Matters* (1898)

15   Cricket and church were alike holy. The flight of the ball, the
swift, graceful movements of the men, the swing of the bat,
were as full of praise as were the hymns we sang.

Alison Uttley
Carts and Candlesticks (1948)

16   His lightest interest was cricket, but he did not take that lightly.
His chief holiday was to go to a cricket match, which he did as
if he was going to church; and he watched critically, applauded
sparingly, and was darkly offended by any unorthodox play.

H G Wells
The History of Mr Polly (1910)

17   *Prodnose:* They don't play cricket in Russia.
Myself: I know, but this man learned it over here.
Prodnose: What on earth for?
Myself: He thinks it might be introduced into Russia, to take
the place of religion, as it does here.

'Beachcomber'
Morton's Folly (1933)

18   Reading poetry and watching cricket were the sum of my world,
and the two are not so far apart as many aesthetes might
believe.

Philip Lindsay
Don Bradman (1951)

19   Cricket seems to me to be richer in potential, deeper in its
emotional and cerebral possibilities and wider in artistic scope
than all games.

Bernard Hollowood
Cricket on the Brain (1970)

20   The whole of cricket was a confidence trick.

A C H Smith
Extra Cover (1981)

21   'Cricket,' said Raffles, 'like everything else is a good enough
sport until you discover a batter . . .'

E W Hornung
Raffles, The Amateur Cracksman (1899)

22   *Julian:* You know I want you, honestly I do. It's just that I
         was always brought up to have a sense of honour and
         going to bed with another man's wife . . .
     Stella: It's not cricket.
     Julian (earnestly)*:* No, it certainly isn't cricket.
     Stella: But it's much more fun, isn't it?

Bettine Mankelow
Couples (1981)

23   To this day I have never been present at a cricket match though
     this odd activity is hard to escape when you have a TV and a
     family that thinks God wears white flannels.

James Cameron (1982)
Reprinted in *The Guardian Book of Cricket* (1986)

24   We were not seriously devoted to tennis, but found it our
     hardiest weapon against cricket – the game, we wrote, in
     which the selfishness of the few did not excuse the boredom of
     the many.

Robert Graves
Goodbye to All That (1929)

25   In the cricket season I learned there was a safe and far-away
     place on the field called 'deep' which I always chose. When
     'Over' was called I simply went more and more 'deep' until I
     was sitting on the steps of the pavilion reading the plays of
     Noel Coward, whom I had got on to after Bulldog Drummond.

John Mortimer
Clinging to the Wreckage (1982)

26   To stand upright during so many hours of an extreme heat; to
     take a violent exercise without any need; to run deliberately a
     grave danger not less than that which one is obliged to
     encounter on a field of battle – all this is folly of the most
     profound. I cannot believe that there is really some pleasure at
     all in it.

Anatole Gonjon (1884)
Quoted by Kenneth Gregory in *In Celebration of Cricket* (1978)

27   I'm not at all surprised the French have never understood this
     game, whose players cannot be *serieux* when their honour is at
     stake.

Geoffrey Moorhouse
The Best-Loved Game (1979)

28   If the French *noblesse* had been capable of playing cricket with their peasants, their chateaux would never have been burned.

> **G M Trevelyan**
> *English Social History* (1944)

29   In spite of recent jazzed-up one-day matches, cricket to be fully appreciated demands leisure, some sunny warm days, and an understanding of its finer points – and as it depends more than any other ball game on varying conditions, on the state of the pitch, on weather and wind and light, it multiplies its fine points. Though it is often considered a 'gentlemanly game', an idea supported by its leisurely progress and breaks for lunch, tea, cool drinks on the field, we must remember that many of its greatest performers came from the industrial North, which also supplied, until our own time, large numbers of its most knowledgeable and keenest spectators.

> **J B Priestley**
> *The English* (1973)

30   In those days, before it became scientific, cricket was the best game in the world to watch, with its rapid sequence of amusing incidents, each ball a potential crisis!

> **G M Trevelyan**
> *English Social History* (1944)

31   I first fell under the spell of cricket, as every other small boy will have done, by batting and bowling on the nearest available space the moment I got home from school.

> **Geoffrey Moorhouse**
> *The Best-Loved Game* (1979)

32   To some people cricket is a circus show upon which they may or may not find it worth while to spend sixpence; to others it is a pleasant means of livelihood; to others a physical fine art full of plot, interest and enlivened by difficulties; to others in some sort it is a cult and a philosophy, and these last will never be understood by the *profanum vulgus,* nor by the merchant-minded nor by the unphysically intellectual.

> **D L A Jephson**
> *A Few Overs* (1913)

33   Cricket as a passion is distinctly contagious.

> **David Frith**
> *England v Australia* (1981)

34   Cricket, however, has more in it than mere efficiency. There is something called the spirit of cricket, which cannot be defined.

Lionel, Lord Tennyson
Sticky Wickets (1950)

35   Things never turn out at cricket as one expects.

Talbot Baines Reed
The Fifth Form at St Dominic's (1887)

36   It was a great game, and exciting and dramatic and even at times tragic − but funny it emphatically was not.

Sir J C Masterman
Fate Cannot Harm Me (1935)

37   Cricket is no excuse for ignorance.

Barry Perowne
Raffles of the MCC (1979)

38   Culture seems to make for humility − and with it, effeminate traits; and humbleness and effeminacy are not the things a great cricketer can afford to be.

G A Faulkner
Cricket: Can It Be Taught? (1926)

39   *Cunningham:* And one's passions are so random and unreliable − cricket scores one minute, Swinburne the next.

Julian Mitchell
Another Country (1982)

40   Long ago I discovered there was more to life than cricket: and more to cricket than runs and wickets.

David Foot
Cricket's Unholy Trinity (1985)

41   The joy, the tension and exhilaration, and the happiness those Sundays brought into our lives served as a cushion, I am sure, for the sterner life which was ahead for all of us.

Learie Constantine
The Changing Face of Cricket (1969)

42   Cricket is quite a gentle, harmless game, but he is a lucky man who has not to sweat some blood before he's done with it.

J C Snaith
Willow the King (1899)

43   There can be raw pain and bleeding where so many thousands see the inevitable ups and downs of only a game.

C L R James
Beyond a Boundary (1963)

44   My fortune in cricket was to play when the first-class game was free and fast-flowing and with a county as concerned to play attractive and sporting cricket as to win.

H A Pawson
Runs and Catches (1980)

45   Before 1914 it was beauty that counted in cricket — elegance of strokes, stylishness of bowling action, quixotry in captaincy. The gallant gesture was just as important as the mammoth score, the picturesque as the efficient.

W J Edrich
Cricket Heritage (1948)

46   I caught glimpses of white-clad figures striding purposefully to and fro, heard men's voices calling each other in tones of authority and urgency, as if life had suddenly become more serious, as if battle were in prospect.

L P Hartley
The Go-Between (1953)

47   I remember walking to the cricket ground with our team, sometimes trying to feel, and sometimes trying not to feel, that I was one of them; and the conviction I had, which comes so quickly to a boy, that nothing in the world mattered except that we should win.

Ibid.

48   Cricket at the highest level has never been simply a demonstration of sporting excellence: it has always been about winning and losing.

James P Coldham
F S Jackson (1989)

49   It is a brave pastime, a game for soldiers, for each tries to
strike the other with the ball, and it is but a small stick with
which you ward it off. Three sticks behind show the spot
beyond which you may not retreat. I can tell you that it is no
game for children, and I will confess that, in spite of my nine
campaigns, I felt myself turn pale when the first ball flashed
past me.

Sir Arthur Conan Doyle
Adventures of Gerard (1903)

50   Cricket is an ancient pastime: it ripened sweetly, it has endured
nobly.

Thomas Moult
Bat and Ball (1935)

51   Dear, lovely game of cricket that can stir us so profoundly, that
can lift up our hearts and break them, and in the end fill them
with pride and joy.

Sir Neville Cardus
Good Days (1934)

52   Nothing that the law-makers or the law-breakers or the MCC or
the Board of Control or any conferences or county committees
or pressmen or captains or players can do to it or have done to
it over the years − nothing can affect cricket's basic worth or
irresistible attraction.

Ben Travers
The Infatuee in *The Cricketer's Bedside Book* (1966)

53   For the game is everlasting only in so far as we keep returning
to it for delights put into it by countless boys of all ages.

Sir Neville Cardus
Cricket (1930)

54   For a game of cricket is at work from the first ball to the last
in shaping an outline and design for itself; sometimes the design
degenerates into dullness and incompetence and a man may
waste his time in looking for subtlety in the motive that
prompts a batsman to pat a half-volley carefully to mid-off, but
design there always is and there is interest even in the tracing of
the course and impulse of its failures.

Dudley Carew
To the Wicket (1946)

55   For cricket is an art in itself. A batsman who is dull and stolid, dour and ungainly, gives little to the game. A great cricketer must be an artist and express himself in his strokes. If he can put all the exhilaration, all the beauty, all the humour and dignity which make up life into his cricket, then he is truly a great player.

Margaret Hughes
All on a Summer's Day (1953)

56   He was an admirer of the bullfight, and he had once drawn my attention to the fact that only cricket and bullfighting had inspired any considerable literature.

Dal Stivens
The Demon Bowler and Other Cricket Stories (1979)

57   Cricket is first and foremost a dramatic spectacle. It belongs with the theatre, ballet, opera and the dance.

C L R James
Beyond a Boundary (1963)

58   I had devoted too much of my life to this utterly irrational game. I would chuck the whole thing and take to Strindberg for amusement.

A A Thomson
Cricket My Happiness (1955)

59   As there is nothing in the whole range of poetry or prose with which to point a parallel, it must be allowed that beside a perfectly-timed boundary hit, on a hard ground, from fast bowling, all other delights of this life are as nothingness.

J C Snaith
Willow the King (1899)

60   Oh, goodness, what a clinking game cricket was! Splendid even to watch.

Hugh de Selincourt
The Cricket Match (1924)

61   O, Wind, if Membership Card comes, can Spring be far behind.

Roy Hattersley (1983)
Reprinted in *The Guardian Book of Cricket* (1986)

62   Out with your flannels, gloves, and bats,
And play the finest game on earth!

Norman Gale
The Bigot (1890)

63   Temple and I talked of the ancient raptures of a first of May
cricketing-day on a sunny green meadow, with an ocean of a
day before us, and well-braced spirits for the match.

George Meredith
The Adventures of Harry Richmond (1871)

64   Give me a day of drenching May,
Give me a ball to bowl,
Give me a pitch, I'll count me rich,
And you can have the whole
Terrestrial earth for what it's worth,
Including the North Pole!

Herbert Farjeon
Bitter Sweet in *Cricket Bag* (1946)

65   I've known grown men to lose their appetite for breakfast at
the mere mention of rain on the radio.

Nico Craven
Waiting for Cheltenham (1989)

66   Cricket's all right in spite of the newspapers, but the trouble is
that three-quarters of us don't know how to use our own gifts.

Dudley Carew
The Son of Grief (1936)

67   Last Munday youre Father was at Mr Payns and plaid at
Cricket and come home pleased anuf, for he struck the best
Ball in the game and whished he had not anny thing else to do
he wuld play Cricket all his life.

Mary Turner (1739)
Quoted by Sir Neville Cardus in *Cricket* (1930)

68   You do well to love it, for it is more free from anything sordid, anything dishonourable, than any game in the world. To play it keenly, honourably, generously, self-sacrificingly, is a moral lesson in itself, and the classroom is God's air and sunshine. Foster it, my brothers, so that it may attract all who can find time to play it; protect it from anything that would sully it, so that it may grow in favour with all men.

Lord Harris
Letter to *The Times,* 2 February, 1931, variously quoted

69   And the reward of it all? Of that we may be certain: the joy of health and strength harnessed to an art and to a venture, the friends that it brings to us, even if on the field of play they are foes, and when you take off your pads, whether for the day, for the season, or after long years for good, the memory of troubles halved and joys doubled, because both have been shared with them.

H S Altham
The Importance of Coaching in *The Gillette Book of Cricket and Football* (1963)

70   English cricket may be compared to an imposing edifice. The spacious foundations are formed by village matches. On that is raised the charming ground-floor of club cricket. The more austere and less irresponsible superstructure of county encounters appears majestic but serene. The cupola consists of Test matches and is so elevated as to excite ambitious aspirations, but also so bleakly exposed as to lose recreative consciousness.

Sir Home Gordon
Club Cricket in England in *The MCC 1787 – 1937* (1937)

71   Hail, Cricket! glorious manly, British Game!
First of all Sports! be first alike in Fame!

James Love
Cricket (1744)

72   'But it's more than a game. It's an institution,' said Tom.
'Yes,' said Arthur, 'the birthright of British boys, old and young, as *habeas corpus* and trial by jury are of British men.'

Thomas Hughes
Tom Brown's Schooldays (1857)

73   Against the increased tempo of modern life cricket must be regarded as rather a slow-moving activity. Nevertheless I believe that cricket represents something traditional in the English way of life which will always command enough support to keep its head above water.

H S Altham
Evidence to Lord's Tribunal (1959) quoted in *Lord's 1946 – 1970* (1971)

74   Cricket is the senior, most widespread, and deeply-rooted of English games.

John Arlott (1968)
Reprinted in *The Guardian Book of Cricket* (1986)

75   Cricket achieved its unique place in the English scene because its champions were admired for themselves. They were men of dignity who stood in the eyes of their countrymen for a code of conduct.

E W Swanton
A History of Cricket, Volume Two (1962)

76   The game of cricket, philosophically considered, is a standing panegyric on the English character: none but an orderly and sensible race of people would so amuse themselves.

Rev James Pycroft
The Cricket Field (1851)

77   If you have a right ambition you will desire to excel all boys of your age at cricket.

Lord Chesterfield
Letters to His Son (1774)

78   Oh, I am so glad you have begun to take an interest in cricket. It is simply a social necessity in England.

P G Wodehouse
Piccadilly Jim (1917)

79   Should every county cricket ground be closed and never another shilling of gate-money leave our pockets, cricket would still be in England's lifeblood drawing its undismayable devotees from every section of the nation: the cricket that has such a hold on the young that they take their bats to bed with them, and on the old that they cannot see half a dozen urchins in the street, with only a lamp-post for stumps without pausing for a minute or two to watch; the cricket that stirs up such a turmoil of hopes and fears in our breasts that to consult the barometer can be almost an anguish.

E V Lucas
English Leaves (1933)

80   Cricket is pre-eminently the breakfast-time sport, recognised and enjoyed all over the world, though nowhere quite so deeply nor so frequently as in England.

John Arlott
The Boundary Book Second Innings (1986)

81   By its nature and constituents a Cricket Week is an institution peculiarly English, for it connotes the very essence and quiddity for an English countryside in summer and the deep-rooted democratic devotion to a national game which eliminates all mere social and intellectual distinctions.

Lt-Col C P Hawkes
Bat, Ball and Buskin in *The MCC 1787 – 1937* (1937)

82   It is astonishing that cricket should have taken root in the English climate. It almost makes me believe that our summers have grown worse over the past few centuries, though people who have studied the evidence say it is not so.

Alan Gibson
A Mingled Yarn (1975)

83   It wasn't cricket; it wasn't cricket that an elderly gnome-like individual with a stringy neck and creaking joints should, by dint of hard-work and superior cunning, reverse the proverb that youth will be served. It was an ascendancy of brain over brawn, of which, like a true Englishman, I felt suspicious.

L P Hartley
The Go-Between (1953)

84   Cricket was not merely a game – a great and noble game – it was the embodiment of everything that was best in the British, it was something above politics, a bridge that crossed the divides separating the races.

James P Coldham
F S Jackson (1989)

85   Cricket is a very humanising game. It appeals to the emotions of local patriotism and pride. It is eminently unselfish; the love of it never leaves us, and binds all the brethren together, whatever their politics and rank may be.

Andrew Lang
Introduction to Richard Daft's *Kings of Cricket* (1893)

86   Cricket is simply the most catholic and diffused, the most innocent, kindly and manly of popular pleasures, while it has been the delight of statesmen and the relaxation of learning.

Ibid.

87   The whole edifice of Christian virtues could be raised on a basis of good cricket.

Edward Cracroft Lefroy
Quoted in W A Gill's *Edward Cracroft Lefroy: His Life and Poems* (1897)

88   Cricket is a liberal education in itself, and demands temper, justice and perseverance. There is more teaching in the playground than in the schoolrooms and a lesson better worth learning often. For there can be no good or enjoyable cricket without enthusiasm – without sentiment, one may almost say; a quality that enriches life and refines it; gives it, what life more and more is apt to lose, zest.

Andrew Lang
In K S Ranjitsinhji's *The Jubilee Book of Cricket* (1897)

89   Cricket is essentially a co-operative sport – it is confined to no class: it is *best* practised where it is most *fused*.

'Quid' (R A Fitzgerald)
Jerks in from Short Leg (1866)

90   'Ah! That's the beauty of cricket!' declared old John heartily, wiping his face all over with a large handkerchief, 'that's the glorious beauty of cricket. Every single man-jack of us helped, one way or another to win that game.'

Hugh de Selincourt
The Cricket Match (1924)

91   The side was what mattered to everyone and when you get that attitude cricket can be a very happy game.

Ray Illingworth
Yorkshire and Back (1980)

92   *Major:* But for God's sake, man! We didn't realise what the state of the game would be. Can you stand there with English blood in your veins and desert a cricket team – with two runs to win?

R C Sherriff
Badger's Green (1930)

93   He was a man who, even then, in the early 1940s, was clearly sliding out of fashion, a man for whom life was a cricket pitch, a thing of straight bats, stiff upper lips, and keeping one's end up on a sticky wicket.

Brian Glanville
Up She Jolly Goes in *Love is Not Love* (1985)

94   High and low, rich and poor, greet one another practically on an equality, and sad will be the day for England if Socialism ever succeeds in putting class v class and thus ending sports which have made England.

Lord Hawke
Recollections and Reminiscences (1924)

95   The tone suggests some justification for the friends who said that Hyndman, a cricketer, had adopted Socialism out of spite against the world because he was not included in the Cambridge XI.

Barbara Tuchman
The Proud Tower (1966)

96   I played cricket the first season, but resigned because the team seldom consisted of the best eleven men available; regular players would be dropped to make room for visiting gentry.

Robert Graves
Goodbye to All That (1929)

97   Cricket symbolises the class war, and to avoid identification both sides dress in white.

Alan Plater
From the novel by Christopher Mullin, *A Very British Coup* (1988)

98   Cricket, we have shown, was originally classed among the games of the lower orders; so we find the yeomen infinitely superior to the gentlemen even before cricket had become by any means so much of a profession as it is now.

Rev James Pycroft
The Cricket Field (1851)

99   During the Middle Ages cricket was popular but frowned on by those engaged in raising military forces: it interfered with the practice of archery.

Ivor Brown
A Book of England (1935)

100   *Bennett:* The proletariat is forced to labour in the field, while the bourgeoisie indulges in the pleasures of batting and bowling. The whole system derives from the lord of the medieval manor's wholly unjustified 'right' to the unpaid labour of villeins at haymaking and harvest.

Julian Mitchell
Another Country (1982)

101   *Bennett:* Cricket is a fundamental part of the capitalist conspiracy.

Ibid.

102   Cricket may be only a game but it has usually mirrored the social and economic times in which we live.

Harold Rhodes
The Harold Rhodes Affair (1987)

103   Changing social conditions and the growing encroachment of
       commercial promotions may have secured the game's economic
       salvation but inevitably they have diminished its original spirit
       and character.

                                                    Gerald Pawle
                                                 R E S Wyatt (1985)

104   Tragically the onset of war changed the outlook of cricketers;
       an equalitarian society was to arrive; and there would be an
       increase in professionalism and of 'professionalism': the
       amateur would disappear and the game would change,
       sometimes for the better but sometimes it would change so
       much that it would no longer be cricket.

                                             Anthony Woodhouse
                                   The History of Yorkshire CCC (1989)

105   Cricket is certainly a very good and wholesome exercise, yet it
       may be abused if either great or little people make it their
       business.

                                        Gentleman's Magazine (1743)
                      Reprinted in *The Badminton Library – Cricket* (1904)

106   It has become tougher, more brutal, more combative and is a
       game where the letter has taken over from the spirit of the law.

                                                  Henry Blofeld
                                       One Test After Another (1985)

107   The sportsman has ceased to be a hero. To achieve heroic
       status, the hero must put something ahead of his own personal
       interests.

                                                 Michael Davie
              The Packer Revolution (1977) reprinted in *The Observer on
                                                      Cricket* (1987)

108   Controversy has always been part of cricket. It titillates and
       enlivens the human fabric. Much of it is unseemly but we are
       inclined to relish it in retrospect.

                                                     David Foot
                                     Cricket's Unholy Trinity (1985)

109   At Baron's Lodge there was no suggestion, as there was at so many schools, that skill at cricket implied moral excellence or that the game itself was a proving ground for life.

Simon Raven
Close of Play (1964)

110   The cricket world, surely, is as crazy and as inconsistent as the outside one.

Jack Fingleton
Brightly Fades the Don (1949)

111   The wonder is that such a lot of good cricketers evolved from a world so clouded with misconceptions.

C B Fry
Life Worth Living (1939)

112   Is there life after cricket? First go through cricket, to earn the right to this unknown passage. Your discovery may be socially incommunicable: an unplayable wicket.

Marvin Cohen
Stranger's Gallery (1974)

113   Often in this our life do we begin by cursing men and end by loving them. A sense of the common fallibility of all flesh makes us kin. No man is lovable who is invincible.

Sir Neville Cardus
Good Days (1934)

114   Still is a cricket field a sphere of wholesome discipline in obedience and good order; not to mention that manly spirit that faces danger without shrinking, and bears disappointment with good nature.

Rev James Pycroft
The Cricket Field (1851)

115   If a cricketer wants safety and security then let him go into a bank and work. If he's going to play cricket then let him enjoy the game and entertain the public.

Margaret Hughes
All on a Summer's Day (1953)

116   The key to the health and prosperity of the game is embedded not in rules and regulations but in the hearts and minds of the cricketers of today.

E W Swanton
A History of Cricket, Volume Two (1962)

117   A game is exactly what is made of it by the character of the men playing it. New laws, new ways of preparing wickets, new schemes of reckoning championships — these external things do not matter.

Sir Neville Cardus
Good Days (1934)

118   The real fault of the amateurs is that they do it all for nothing; they must be enjoying themselves, and we cannot bear it.

J C Squire
Introduction to *Cricket* (1930)

119   *Caldicott:* That German officer looked a lot like old Dickie Randall. You know him, used to bowl slow leg-breaks. He played for the Gentlemen once — caught and bowled for a duck as I remember.
Charters: You think he's a traitor then?
Caldicott: But he played for the Gentlemen!
Charters: Ah, but only once.

Frank Lauder and Sidney Gilliat
A Night Train to Munich (1940)

120   Whatever the authorities may say to the contrary, cricket is nowadays increasingly run by the players both on and off the field.

Henry Blofeld
One Test After Another (1985)

121   It was perhaps a trivial thing, but it epitomised the game we played. One does not take advantage of a mistake. It isn't done.

Stacy Aumonier
The Match in *Miss Bracegirdle and Other Stories* (1923)

122   Sharp practice in our national game is probably a good deal more common than most Englishmen would care to admit.

Herbert Farjeon
Cricket Bag (1946)

123   A Kent player sat down to get wind after a run, his bat in his ground but with his seat of honour out, and for a moment let go the handle, and the wicket-keeper stumped him out! He was very angry and said he would never play again; however, he did play the return match at Canterbury, where he was put out in precisely the same manner.

Rev James Pycroft
The Cricket Field (1851)

124   In one word, there is no game in which amiability and an unruffled temper is so essential to success, or in which virtue is rewarded half as much as in the game of cricket.

Ibid.

125   *Miles:*   I don't want to leave it here while I'm on the field. Can't risk that.
Rowena: Well, I must say, that's terrific spirit, isn't it? The great comradeship of cricket. Nobody trusts anybody. Is that why they all rush off the field at the end of Test matches? To see if anyone's stolen their watches.

Alan Ayckbourn
A Cricket Match, Intimate Exchanges (1982)

126   Among cricketers, the pleasure is heightened by the conviction that their pastime is untainted by vulgarity and cruelty; and that their fair countrywomen may witness of prowess of a brother, a lover or a husband, without a blush, or the painful sense of impropriety.

Frederick Lillywhite
On Cricket in *The Young Cricketer's Guide* (1850)

127   For my own sake too I wished that time might stop; that I might stand for ever in the sun, while the trees rustled and the young voices laughed along the terrace, and watch my darling so beautiful and happy at his play.

Simon Raven
Fielding Gray (1969)

128 There's a breathless hush in the Close to-night —
Ten to make and the match to win —
A bumping pitch and a blinding light,
An hour to play and the last man in.
And it's not for the sake of a ribboned coat
Or the selfish hope of a season's fame,
But his captain's hand on his shoulder smote:
'Play up! play up! and play the game!'

Sir Henry Newbolt
Vitai Lampada in *Admirals All and Other Verses* (1897)

129 *Headmaster:* You shall be taught to wash and bowl straight and
wipe your dirty noses.

John Mortimer
A Voyage Round My Father (1970)

130 . . . The school clock crawled, but cricket thoughts would fill
The last slow lesson-hour deliciously
(Drone on, O teacher: you can't trouble me)
'Kent will be out by now' . . . (Well if you choose
To keep us here while cricket's in the air,
You must expect our minds to wander loose.)

Thomas Moult
Names (1924)

131 Now in Maytime to the wicket
Out I march with bat and pad:
See the son of grief at cricket
Trying to be glad.

A E Housman
A Shropshire Lad (1896)

132 No one who has never experienced it can ever appreciate the
tense joy of a cricketer when he comes out to begin a match.

Stacy Aumonier
The Match in *Miss Bracegirdle and Other Stories* (1923)

133 It was jolly to be in flannels and to feel the sun on one's skin,
for the day promised to be hot.

Ibid.

134   For all who were playing and watching there was nothing in mind beyond the next ball, the challenge of the moment, the absorption in good-natured contest. Time stood still in a distillation of delight.

J M Kilburn
Thanks to Cricket (1972)

135   Every ball now was bowled to an accompanying deep attentive hush and each stroke or item of fielding greeted with applause.

William Godfrey
Malleson at Melbourne (1956)

136   Cricket in high summer played with the mind of the true lover of it conscious the whole while that all this happy life is about him − that cricket is just a corner in the teeming garden of the year.

Sir Neville Cardus
The Summer Game (1929)

137   I am sure the Almighty never intended that cricket should be . played in anything but golden sunshine, especially if the wicket was doing a bit.

Ray Illingworth
Yorkshire and Back (1980)

138   Cricket is the greatest outdoor game in the world. He who plays it in the right spirit learns endurance, is taught to keep his temper under trying circumstances, gives up his own selfish interests for the sake of the general good, and practises himself in undergoing a hard day's work, when eye and hand and foot are hard put to it, to overcome rivals in healthy combat.

Bishop Henry Montgomery
The History of Kennington and its Neighbourhood (1889)

139   In the very breadth of its humanity, its sweet simplicities, its open-air fragrance and charm, the game of cricket appeals to nearly all men.

A E Knight
The Complete Cricketer (1906)

140   The cricket that we love as people the wide world over is the
sum-total of all the personal skill and character which have
been put into it by great men who have played it and who, by
giving to the technique and form some turn or push of their
own, have kept development alive and in touch with people,
decade after decade.

> **Sir Neville Cardus**
> *Good Days* (1934)

141   But after all it's not the winning that matters, is it? Or is it?
It's − to coin a word − the amenities that count: the smell of
the dandelions, the puff of the pipe, the click of the bat, the
rain on the neck, the chill down the spine, the slow, exquisite
coming on of sunset and dinner and rheumatism.

> **Alastair Cooke** (1951)
> Reprinted in *The Guardian Book of Cricket* (1986)

142   For cricket, of whatever kind, is still at its best in the country;
and the agrarian country sides, though seldom the most
efficient and never the richest, are usually the pleasantest to
watch.

> **J C Squire**
> Introduction to *Cricket* (1930)

143   Few things are more deeply rooted in the collective imagination
of the English than the village cricket match. It stirs a romantic
illusion about the rustic way of life, it suggests a tranquil and
unchanging order in an age of bewildering flux, and it
persuades a lot of townsfolk that that is where they would
rather be.

> **Geoffrey Moorhouse**
> *The Best-Loved Game* (1979)

144   I doubt if there be any scene in the world more animating or
delightful than a cricket match; − I do not mean a set match
at Lord's Ground for money, hard money, between a certain
number of gentlemen and players, as they are called − people
who make a trade of that noble sport, and degrade it into an
affair of bettings, and hedgings, and cheatings, it may be, like
boxing or horse-racing; nor do I mean a pretty *fete* in a
gentleman's park, where one club of cricketing dandies
encounter another such club, and where they show off in
graceful costume to a gay marquee of admiring belles, who
condescend so to purchase admiration, and while away a long
summer morning in partaking cold collations, conversing

occasionally, and seeming to understand the game — the whole being conducted according to ball-room etiquette, so as to be exceedingly elegant and exceedingly dull. No! the cricket that I mean is the real solid old-fashioned match between neighbouring parishes, where each attacks the other for honour and a supper, glory and half-a-crown a man.

Mary Russell Mitford
Our Village (1824 – 32)

145   Having, the other day, once again spent an afternoon in watching a village match, I am again perplexed by the passion for that game which is displayed by those who cannot shine at it.

E V Lucas
Only the Other Day (1936)

146   Village pride is reflected in the richness of the turf, the excellence of the wicket, and the aspect of the pavilion whose smooth green plots and whitened curbs give it the trim natty air of a coastguard station.

Don Davies (1943)
Reprinted in *The Guardian Book of Cricket* (1986)

147   If village cricket is not what it was, it has certainly not lost its modesty.

Norman Shrapnel (1956)
Reprinted in *The Guardian Book of Cricket* (1986)

148   Although village cricket is loosely built around the laws of cricket, its adherence to them is subject to wide interpretations, and subtle variations, and is more characteristic in the breach than in the observance.

Robert Holles
The Guide to Real Village Cricket (1983)

149   Village cricket was one of the nation's institutions which suffered severely because of the First World War. The game simply stopped, and for a variety of reasons. Some thought it unpatriotic to play.

Gerald Howat
Village Cricket (1980)

150   The game, whether it is called first-class or otherwise, is
       CRICKET, and any measure can only be a half-measure which
       aims at differentiating between the classes of cricket.

K S Ranjitsinhji
The Jubilee Book of Cricket (1897)

151   There is as much difference between the first-class cricketer and
       the ordinary club-man as there is between a professional actor
       and the gifted amateur.

J C Snaith
Willow the King (1899)

152   And although she and Richardson played with all the
       truthfulness the situation could bear, it was like Edrich and
       Compton going in to bat against a Minor Counties attack. Of
       course, they scored all round the wicket. Of course, they made
       centuries. But then so could many other people have done in
       similar circumstances.

Michael Billington
Peggy Ashcroft (1988)

153   All cricketers are cricketers, none the less so for not being
       'first-class', which is no more than a statistical distinction.

John Arlott
An Eye for Cricket (1979)

154   I know of nothing more painful in this world than to see some
       of our Saturday afternoon local cricket games.

A E Knight
The Complete Cricketer (1906)

155   This cricket is a great and glorious game. It is played by grand
       fellows.

Fred Root
A Cricket Pro's Lot (1937)

156   Since cricket became brighter, a man of taste can only go to an
       empty ground, and regret the past. Or else watch a second-class
       county match, and regret the future.

C P Snow
Death Under Sail (1932)

157 Now the joys of this game are chiefly these;
A blazing sun and a gentle breeze;
A close-cut field and a shady spot
To ruminate over the runs you've got;
A clear, clean eye and a steady hand,
A nerve of steel, and a cheerful band
Of fellow cricketers, one and all.
Ready to welcome what'er befall.

A E Chadwick
The Joyous Game (1926)

158 But what care I? It's the game that calls me –
Simply to be on the field of play;
How can it matter what fate befalls me,
With ten good fellows and one good day!

A A Milne
The First Game (1910)

159 Together we impell'd the flying ball:
Together waited in our tutor's hall:
Together joined in cricket's manly toil.

Lord Byron
Cricket at Harrow in *Hours of Idleness* (1807)

160 One thing that struck me at once was the fellowship of first-class cricketers. It was a fellowship into which one was immediately included by playing county cricket and by no other means. Until you played you were out: once you had played you were in. You were called by your first name by all in this fellowship from that point on.

T C Dodds
Hit Hard and Enjoy It (1976)

161 Volumes might be written on the cricket lunch and the influence it has on the run of the game; how it undoes one man, and sends another back to the fray like a giant refreshed; how it turns the brilliant fast bowler into sluggish medium, and the nervous bat into the masterful smiter.

P G Wodehouse
Mike (1909)

162   It is good to bowl with action high
Or to smite the leather hard and far,
But it's better to wear the proper tie
And to keep your end up at the bar.

Donald Hughes
The Short Cut (1957)

163   On a normal cricket tour hospitality can be kept within
reasonable bounds by firm and tactful management.

Gerald Pawle
R E S Wyatt (1985)

164   Touring is bad enough when a cricketer is playing, fully
involved in the thick of it, but it takes a special kind of passive
equanimity to sit contentedly on the sidelines for three months,
watching others playing and receiving the garlands of success,
especially if one feels that omission is arguably due more to
personal rather than cricketing motives.

Frances Edmonds
Another Bloody Tour (1986)

165   Village cricketers are too kindly to drop you with abruptness at
the end of your career.

Eric N Simons
Friendly Eleven (1950)

166   The game itself might be compared to other more generous
liquors: exhilarating and exciting is it, like champagne;
beneficial, cordial and fortifying to the system even as port; or
it may be better likened for its infinite variety to that nectarious
compound of all that is exquisite in beverage – the old-
fashioned punch, as graphically described by John Nyren in his
'Cricketer's Guide'.

Charles Box
The English Game of Cricket (1877)

167   A game of cricket is a variety show which, on a good day, will
put many different talents on view: magicians of spin and
masters of pace, acrobatic close-fielders and, in the outfield,
athletes with prodigious throwing arms.

Allen Synge
Cricket: The Men and the Matches that Changed the Game
(1988)

168 But cricket is full of glorious chances, and the goddess who presides over it loves to bring down the most skilful players.

Thomas Hughes
Tom Brown's Schooldays (1857)

169 In every game there is a moment of destiny, a moment when fortune hesitates which way she will incline, when the genius of the match is poised and is ready to follow the side which has the courage and intelligence to take charge of her.

Dudley Carew
To the Wicket (1946)

170 Only a drama that is allowed to unfold over five days could permit such a twist in the plot so wild as to be almost unthinkable.

Paul Fitzpatrick
Leeds (1981) reprinted in *The Guardian Book of Cricket* (1986)

171 In the game of cricket, where all enter chivalrously into the game, neither is greater nor less than the other. There is no monopoly for a gifted four; it affords scope for every diversity of talent – bowling, fielding, wicket-keeping, free hitting, safe and judicious play, and good generalship; in one of these points many a man has earned an honourable distinction though he may be inferior in the others.

Temple Bar (1862)

172 If in sporting terms greatness can be defined as the ability to outplay all around you, then cricket must surely provide one of the most searching tests.

Peter Walker
Cricket Conversations (1978)

173 I was a firm believer in predestination, and I used to improvise superstitions of my own in connection with the cricket matches I played in.

Siegfried Sassoon
The Flower Show Match in *Memoirs of a Fox-Hunting Man*
(1928)

174   Cricket was never intended to be a negative game, and temporary negativism is only tolerable as a necessary though melancholy prelude to positivism.

Philip Trevor
Strand Magazine (1928)

175   The central theme was to hit the ball hard and enjoy it, and play beautiful cricket. It was a humbling experience that the nearer I came to achieving my aim the more I was aware of my inadequacies and imperfections.

T C Dodds
Hit Hard and Enjoy It (1976)

176   What's bred in the bone will come out at cricket − if only men will trust to their own impulses and not seek to find a formula, a dependable way of getting things done efficiently.

Sir Neville Cardus
Cricket (1930)

177   Few of the great players are deep theorists on cricket, probably because the game has come to them too naturally to need any very close analysis.

E W Swanton
Denis Compton: A Cricket Sketch (1948)

178   All good things done well are beautiful. There is much more in a fine off-drive or a well-bowled ball than the resulting four or wicket.

K S Ranjitsinhji
The Jubilee Book of Cricket (1897)

179   Defeat was glory in such a struggle − victory, indeed, made us only 'a little lower than angels'.

John Nyren
The Young Cricketer's Tutor (1833)

180   Cricket heroes outlive the matches they play. There is little reason why it should be different; that is the way of pastime and sport.

Christopher Lee
From the Sea End (1989)

181   And are the penmen players all?
Did Shakespeare shine at cricket?
And in what hour did Bunyan wait
Like Christian at the wicket?

G K Chesterton
Lines on a Cricket Match

182   Flush'd with his rays, beneath the noontide sun,
In rival bands, between the wickets run,
Drive o'er the sward the ball with active force,
Or chase with nimble feet its rapid course.

Lord Byron
Cricket at Harrow in *Hours of Idleness* (1807)

183   The umpires were stationed behind the wickets; the scorers were
prepared to notch the runs; a breathless silence ensued.

Charles Dickens
Pickwick Papers (1837)

184   There, beside her in a lawn-coloured frock with narrow black
edges, he had watched the game, and felt the old thrill stir
within him.

John Galsworthy
To Let in *The Forsyte Saga* (1922)

185   Heavenly weather really. If life was always like that. Cricket
weather. Sit around under sunshades. Over after over. Out.
They can't play it here. Duck for six wickets. Still Captain
Buller broke a window in the Kildare Street Club with a slog to
square leg.

James Joyce
Ulysses (1922)

186   And from here and there came the sounds of the cricket bats
through the soft grey air. They said: pick, pack, pock, puck:
little drops of water in a fountain slowly falling in the
brimming bowl.

James Joyce
Portrait of the Artist as a Young Man (1916)

187   Condemned to stay at home, he had at once begun to take his
       bats from their corners and was seen to be in one of the
       gardener's sheds estimating their oiliness.

Charles Morgan
Portrait in a Mirror (1929)

188   They knew that cricketers should be ardent, alert.

Ibid.

189   Cricket, having been created and evolved, has achieved its
       purpose, produced one lovely thing, and ought to die.

C P Snow
Death Under Sail (1932)

190   Drinking the best tea in the world on an empty cricket ground
       – that, I think, is the final pleasure left to man.

Ibid.

191   The summer evening shadows fell on the village ground, the
       traffic died away, the harsh contours of functional architecture
       became blurred. Peace descended.

Gerald Howat
Village Cricket (1980)

192   It is a game for gentle men;
       Entirely wrong that man's spare rib
       Should learn the mysteries of spin.

Vernon Scannell
Wicket Maiden

193   Cricket has always been one of her passions and Harry
       Andrews remembers captaining a side against a women's team
       led by Peggy. The gentlemen batted left-handed and bowled
       under-arm and the pre-arranged plan was that the scores would
       finish level. The highly competitive Robert Shaw, then making
       his mark in the company, would have none of this and swiped
       endless sixes. But, in the end, the Ian Botham of English acting
       was caught in the deep by Angela Baddeley.

Michael Billington
Peggy Ashcroft (1988)

194   There are three kinds of cricket-match girls: the girl who knows
all about the game, who scores her brother's runs and keeps his
bowling analysis, and takes not her eyes from the wickets while
any play is to be seen; the girl who is in the state of interested
bewilderment; and the girl who watches the game with her
back.

E V Lucas
Lord's and Ladies in *Willow and Leather* (1898)

195   And may not the knowledge that such eyes are upon them
impel the cricketers to finer heroism?

Ibid.

196   Looking back it is amusing that a few diehards were aghast to
learn that ladies would be admitted into the pavilion but the
younger element were frankly delighted, and it was
acknowledged as a proper and sensible arrangement.

Tom Watson
Ibis Cricket, 1870 – 1949 (1950)

197   None of them was at all interested in cricket, but they never
ceased, when men were present, to ask questions about it.

Charles Morgan
Portrait in a Mirror (1929)

198   She played her forward stroke, she swayed, she confidently
toppled.

Ibid.

199   One of the cricketers brought his girlfriend out. It was an
expensive trip and the gesture was both endearingly kind, and
touchingly generous. It might, on reflection, have been even
more kind and touchingly generous had he brought his wife
instead.

Frances Edmonds
Another Bloody Tour (1986)

200   *Spooner:* How beautiful she was, how tender and how true.
Tell me with what speed she swung in the air, with
what velocity she came off the wicket, whether she
was responsive to finger spin, whether you could bowl
a shooter with her, or an off-break with a leg-break
action. In other words, did she google?

Harold Pinter
No Man's Land (1975)

201   Women will always play for the love of the game and there will
        be no professional female cricketers. At the same time, the
        enjoyment of the game must go hand in hand with skill, ability
        and flair.

Rachael Heyhoe Flint and Netta Rheinberg
Fair Play (1976)

202   Some women's cricket at club level is played solely for
        enjoyment and is perhaps better not seen by the public – but
        then so is some men's cricket for that matter.

Ibid.

203   The rich diversity of clubs and players has always been an
        important aspect of cricket's attraction.

E W Swanton
Sort of a Cricket Person (1972)

204   Cricket, like the novel, is great when it presents men in the
        round, when it shows the salty quality of humanity.

John Arlott
Cricket (1953)

205   'Cricket,' he once remarked, 'was intended to be played
        between 22 sportsmen for their own pleasure; it was never
        meant to be the vehicle for international competition, huge
        crowds and headline news – otherwise it wouldn't have been
        given a code of laws with such gaps as you could drive through
        with a coach and horses.'

B H Lyon
Quoted by John Arlott in *An Eye for Cricket* (1979)

206   I can think of many energetic and successful business men who
        would be contributing much more to the public service were
        they playing county cricket well for six days in the week.

Sir J C Squire
Introduction to *Cricket* (1930)

207   It had often occurred to him that many who went to watch
        cricket without any understanding of its intricacies eventually
        deserted the game in favour of the simpler appeal of soccer
        because there was no readily available way they could learn
        about an infinitely more subtle art.

Gerald Pawle
R E S Wyatt (1985)

208 We have had long periods of failure before, we are having one now, and shall have them again, but we have also had long periods of success and, if we cannot beat our friends this year, we will at least learn our lesson from them and be grateful to them for teaching it to us.

Anonymous
England v Australia, Lord's (1921) reprinted in *The Observer
on Cricket* (1987)

209 The future lies with the young cricketers of today and the misfortune is that they have so few sound models to copy.

Ibid.

210 You see, cricket had something against it, rather like tennis, which few played. It was played better by the English.

Tony Lewis
Playing Days (1985)

211 Cricket is the queerest game,
Every stroke is just the same
Merely whacking at a ball;
Nothing else to see at all.
Then there comes some big surprise
When I chance to close my eyes.

Anonymous

212 And finally should you ever reach the dizzy heights of county cricket always reserve your best efforts for Saturdays. You will then get your name in the papers twice, on Sunday and Monday.

J C Clay
Glamorgan CCC Year Book (1936)

213 When I see a young man who has an expensive and pretty hair-do, I have doubts as to his ability to reach Test standard.

Ted Dexter
A Walk to the Wicket (1985)

214 I know I shall never forget the sensation of waiting in the England dressing room to go in next.

Tony Lewis
Playing Days (1985)

215   It was on the scoreboard – England: A R Lewis. All my life at home, England has been the opposition.

Ibid.

216   Now is the time of the cricketer's plenty – June and July. Let him cherish every moment as it passes; never will he be so young again.

Sir Neville Cardus
Cricket (1930)

217   While tons of ephemera has been sacrificed through carelessness, stupidity or sheer expediency, the game of cricket has weathered the ravages of time better than many other branches of human activity.

David Frith
The Golden Age of Cricket, 1890 – 1914 (1978)

218   There is nothing I have detested more than the way in which elder men have said that their young days had the best. Cricket is constantly in flux.

Sir Home Gordon
Background of Cricket (1939)

219   In one way we county cricketers of the early sixties were the cheated generation. We had been brought up on Hutton, Compton, Edrich, Washbrook, Evans, Bedser and queued up to watch the 1948 Australians, clamoured into county grounds with thousands of others, and now when we ourselves had made the grade there was no one watching.

Tony Lewis
Playing Days (1985)

220   It was an end and a beginning: the end of the 1947 season – a happy, record-breaking, historic and gloriously sunny summer. It was the beginning of a memory – a gentle nostalgia which, ever since, has haunted those who shared it, whether as players, or among those who crowded, sweating and thirsty, forgetting rationing, revelling in the simplicity of cricket played in peace.

John Arlott
Vintage Summer, 1947 (1967)

221 There were a few people dotted around the ground, ones and twos here and there. I suppose most of them look forward all winter to their season's cricket.

Peter Roebuck
It Never Rains (1984)

222 County cricket in the 1930s had shared in the social and economic implications of the Depression. On the positive side, a cricketer might reflect that he was lucky to be in work when hundreds of thousands were not. On the negative side, he was playing a game in which survival and his wage-packet depended upon continuing personal ability and the financial security of his club.

Gerald Howat
Cricket's Second Golden Age (1989)

223 The golden age is always well behind us; we catch sight of it with young eyes, when we see what we want to see.

Sir Neville Cardus
Cricket (1930)

224 Nothing that truth can do will ever destroy the value of the original illusion. It is important that we should not forget that this game above all others demands for its true perspectives the light of the imagination.

Ronald Mason
Sing All a Green Willow (1967)

225 Like few other sports of the field, cricket is played very much with the mind. Only the unimaginative player escapes the tensions. Many, whatever their seeming unconcern, retreat into caverns of introspection.

David Foot
Harold Gimblett (1982)

226 This game preys on doubt. It is a precarious game. Form, luck, confidence are transitory things. It's never easy to work out why they have so inexplicably deserted you.

Peter Roebuck
It Never Rains (1984)

227   It is a cussed game. It can show you glimpses of beauty in a
       stroke perfectly played, perhaps, and then it throws you back
       into the trough of mediocrity. Only the most phlegmatic or
       those who don't give a damn or those with unshakeable belief
       survive these upheavals easily.

Ibid.

228   Perhaps cricket is more like boxing than any other sport in the
       way it transcends mere technical mastery and requires hidden
       gifts of timing and judgement as well as strength of character.

Ibid.

229   The best of games, yes, it is still that, at least for those who
       have taken to it and respect it (not 'love' it. I distrust anyone
       who says he 'loves' cricket).

Alan Gibson
Growing Up with Cricket (1985)

230   Even if it is foolish to pray about cricket, there is no doubt
       that many of us succumb, especially when we are young.

Ibid.

231   A time will come, a time will come,
       When the people sit with a peaceful heart,
       Watching the beautiful, beautiful game,
       That is battle and service and sport and art.

Arnold Wall
A Time Will Come (1948)

232   In 1969 half a million people, young people, assembled in a
       public park to hear a pop group. The most sedate crowd at
       cricket could have taught them nothing about decent behaviour.
       These young people do not need, nor do they want, cricket.

Rowland Bowen
Cricket: A History (1970)

233   I have always liked the idea of cricket. A day sitting in a deck
       chair in the sun, preferably with at least one similarly inclined
       companion to while away the longueurs between overs, seems to
       me a very civilised way of spending one's time. If the game
       becomes exciting, so much the better, though anyone who
       thinks that cricket can or should be consistently exciting fails, I
       think, to understand the game's appeal.

Tim Heald
The Character of Cricket (1986)

234   I wish you'd speak to Mary, Nurse,
    She's really getting worse and worse.
    Just now when Tommy gave her out
    She cried and then began to pout
    And then she tried to take the ball
    Although she cannot bowl at all.
    And now she's standing on the pitch,
    The miserable little Bitch!

Hilaire Belloc
The Game of Cricket

235   On the whole, I preferred the guardianship of my nurse. For the simple reason that she never objected to my taking with me my own small home-made bat and my own small, hard indiarubber ball.

'A Country Vicar'
The Happy Cricketer (1946)

236   At times I do get despondent with what I see on the field. The players don't look very happy, there aren't many characters around and many see it as a job of work. If they only knew that in a few years' time when their careers are over, they'll miss the game and perhaps then they'll wish they'd enjoyed it more.

E J Smith
'Tiger' Smith (1980)

237   Don't take it too much to heart. We all play the game seriously, I know. Indeed, cricket was never intended to be a pantomime. But whenever and wherever we are on the field, we can remember that first and last cricket is a game.

M D Lyon
Cricket (1932)

238   Ours is a slow-moving game and as such holds up a clearer mirror to character than most. We want to admire the stars for what they are as well as for what they do − which is why the exhibitionist antics of a few in recent times, giving the worst of examples to the young watchers on television, are so particularly abhorrent.

E W Swanton
From Grace to Botham − A Century of Cricket Fame (1980)
reprinted in *As I Said at the Time* (1983)

239   Some players, I am authoritatively informed, have won their
       places in league teams simply on the strength of their ability to
       shout and gesticulate eloquently.

M D Lyon
Cricket (1932)

240   As far as cricketers are concerned, however, there seems to
       have grown up a tradition that they must be treated as
       something divine. The whole subject must be discussed with
       bated breath in case the wrath of one of the little tin gods
       should be invoked.

Ibid.

241   The truest of all axioms about cricket is that the game is as
       good as those who play it. If one looks in certain directions this
       might be a disquieting thought in one or two respects just at
       the moment.

E W Swanton
Sort of a Cricket Person (1972)

242   Because this game of ours is a lasting one. It will endure to all
       eternity, come wars or earthquakes. Since it is of all Man's
       athletic inventions by itself the Greatest and Best Game
       invention of all – a Game that can and will stand any and all
       of the adverse criticism which those who do not understand its
       very ABC can bring to bear upon it.

E H D Sewell
Overthrows (1946)

243   A gentle game, cricket. It attracts gentlemen, scholars, vicars,
       cobblers, mild men of many hues. Not much strain or stress, a
       pleasant afternoon in green pastures, basking in the warm rays
       of the sun. A time of ease, a time to unwind from the cares of
       life. A time for reflection, a time to recite the poems of one's
       youth, a time to revel in the pleasing sound of leather on
       helmet.

Peter Roebuck
Slices of Cricket (1982)

244   Cricketers have become slaves of fashion, reflecting life in a
       much changed Britain. The embarrassing habit of embracing
       each other whenever a wicket falls is the most jarring. In my
       time bowlers expected wickets and took them in their stride.

E M Wellings
Vintage Cricketers (1983)

245   Cricket put its clock back more than a century when admitting bookmakers to its grounds in the sixties. The past contains much that is far more worthy of restoration.

Ibid.

246   My first belief is that cricket reached its peak before the Great War.

Ibid.

247   The Golden Age is behind us. But then it always was.

Benny Green
A History of Cricket (1988)

248   Epochs in a game like cricket do not generally succeed each other with abruptness, but rather melt one into the next with imperceptible grace.

Ibid.

249   I am far from being one of those who find no virtue in present-day cricket and cricketers − whose pleasure in the game is wholly centred in times past.

E W Swanton (1973)
Reprinted in *As I Said at the Time* (1983)

250   To all who love cricket, and to the Coarse Cricketer in particular, the winter is always long.

Spike Hughes
The Art of Coarse Cricket (1954)

251   Anything in shocking bad taste used to be described as 'not cricket'. I think we can now safely explode that myth. Cricket still retains its civilised vestiges but good manners are largely submerged in the rough and tumble of professionalism. Incorrigibly the thought intervenes that the old courtesy was always a polite veneer to hide or diminish the worst excesses of gamesmanship.

Alan Hill
The Family Fortune (1978)

252   It was as though Father Time had come down with a scythe to take a turn at the wicket. He left behind a whiff of office hours and the faint trail of gold so alien to the cricket field.

L P Hartley
The Go-Between (1953)

253   I see them in foul dug-outs, gnawed by rats,
      And in the ruined trenches, lashed by rain,
      Dreaming of things they did with balls and bats.

> **Siegfried Sassoon**
> *The Dreamers* (1917)

254   Memories of matches lost and won,
      Of summer afternoons and sun,
      Of many a doughty innings played,
      Of catches missed and catches made.

> **Alfred Cochrane**
> *The Master's Match* (1889 – 1914) in *Later Verses* (1918)

255   Recorded centuries leave no trace
      On memory of that timeless grace.

> **John Arlott**
> *On a Great Batsman*

256   But for an hour to watch them play,
      Those heroes dead and gone,
      And pit our batsmen of today
      With those of Hambledon!
      Our Graces, Nyrens, Studds and Wards
      In weeks of sunny weather,
      Somewhere upon Elysian swards,
      To see them matched together!

> **Alfred Cochrane**
> *Hambledon* in *Later Verses* (1918)

257   It is little I repair to the matches of the Southron folk,
      Though my own red roses there may blow;
      It is little I repair to the matches of the Southron folk,
      Though the red roses crest the caps, I know.
      For the field is full of shades as I near the shadowy coast,
      And a ghostly batsman plays to the bowling of a ghost,
      And I look through my tears on a soundless-clapping host
          As the run-stealers flicker to and fro,
            To and fro:
      O my Hornby and my Barlow long ago!

> **Francis Thompson**
> *At Lord's* in *Collected Poetry* (1913)

258 I wish I were young again, and on my way to the wicket to score my first century for Middlesex at Lord's.

> **H W Lee**
> *Forty Years of English Cricket* (1948)

259 If this was to be my last appearance — and that was the odds-on probability — I would have liked it to end rather more memorably. Most of all, I think I would have liked to finish with a bat in my hand, not wandering off the field at the end of a particularly frustrating day with a lot of people still confused by the finale.

> **Geoffrey Boycott**
> *The Autobiography* (1987)

260 I went to the crease for what I intended to be the very last time in my life. It is no longer fun standing in the field on an arthritic, stiffening knee.

> **Tony Lewis**
> *Playing Days* (1985)

261 I was very anxious not to go on too long and become an object of sympathy, as many of us do.

> **Sir Jack Hobbs**
> *My Story* (1935)

262 In the end it is only the camaraderie of the team, the lifelong friendships which you forge, and the opportunity for interesting sorties outside the grind of the cricket grounds which make the experience worthwhile.

> **Bill O'Reilly**
> *'Tiger' O'Reilly* (1985)

263 I realised that while I might not be burning to play the game, I should still be burning to remain a part of it.

> **Pat Pocock**
> *Percy* (1987)

264 The game we have not strength to play
Seems, somehow, better than before.

> **A E Knight**
> *The Complete Cricketer* (1906)

265   I can speak from personal experience when I state that there are few things more sad than having to leave one's XI because of the relentless force of *Anno Domini*.

Lord Hawke
Recollections and Reminiscences (1924)

266   Allowance, too, must be made for the deep, concealed, yet aching sadness of men doomed by age to be lookers-on merely at the game, when everything in them but their bodies − *hinc illae lacrimae!* − longs to be playing themselves.

Hugh de Selincourt
On the Village Green in *MCC 1787 – 1937* (1937)

267   So egotistical, so tenacious in his grip upon the game, is your ageing cricketer.

Eric N Simons
Friendly Eleven (1950)

268   I turned and walked through the stile, out of that home of joyous memories, out of our cricket field with all it held for me of life and laughter and rich recollections, out of the greatest game.

Ibid.

269   From this day on cricket for me would be pure spectacle, something that went on without me, influenced in no way whatsoever by my personality and will.

Ibid.

270   Imperial Summer bows her golden head −
The Wickets are laid low, the Bails are shed.

George Francis Wilson
Summer's Ending in *Cricket Poems* (1905)

271   When the cricket season was over I felt a deep sense of sadness. It was like the end of harvest.

Alison Uttley
Carts and Candlesticks (1948)

272   . . . the curving flight
Of sixes; the perennial delight
Of stolen runs; the lovely panther-leap
Of one fantastic catch.
All these are ours, to keep
And talk of on some bleak December night.

Dorothy Spring
Last Match

273   They vanish, these immortal players, and we suddenly realise
with astonishment that years have passed since we heard a
passing mention of some of them. At one point they seem as
much a part of the permanent scheme of things as the sun
which glows upon their familiar faces and attitudes and the
grass which makes the background for their portrait; and then,
bless us, it is time for even them to go.

Edmund Blunden
Cricket Country (1944)

274   Yet all in public, and in private, strive
To keep the ball of action still alive
And, just to all, when each his ground has run,
Death tips the wicket, and the game is done.

James Love
The Game of Cricket (1744)

275   Even as we pitch our wicket, flickering near
Are shades of men who found this cricket dear,
And sealed their happy venture ere we came.

Thomas Moult
Prelude to Summer Days in *Some Cover Shots* (1924)

276   There is no talk, none so witty and brilliant, that is so good as
cricket talk, when memory sharpens memory, and the dead live
again – the regretted, the unforgotten – and the old happy
days of burned-out June revive. We shall not see them again.
We lament that lost lightness of heart, 'for no man under the
sun lives twice, outliving his day', and the day of the cricketer
is brief.

Andrew Lang
Introduction to Richard Daft's *Kings of Cricket* (1893)

277   Has there ever been a game in the history of the world so
lovingly waffled over as cricket?

Stanley Reynolds (1975)
Reprinted in *The Guardian Book of Cricket* (1986)

PREPARATION, PRACTICE AND PITFALLS

In form and appearance it can be gentle, even idyllic, yet violence is always there.

278   I cannot remember when I began to play cricket. Respect for the truth prevents me from saying I played the first year of my existence, but I have little hesitation in declaring that I handled bat and ball before the end of my second.

W G Grace
Cricket (1891)

279   I should like to say that good batsmen are born, not made; but my long experience comes up before me, and tells me that it is not so.

Ibid.

280   It has often occurred to me as being curious indeed that many a good player has preferred to think that cricket is a game that cannot be taught.

G A Faulkner
Cricket: Can It Be Taught? (1926)

281   You must begin to learn to bat almost as a baby.

M D Lyon
Cricket (1932)

282   My own view is that a great bowler must be born with certain physical and mental qualities specially suited to bowling, and that he cannot ever become a great bowler without tremendous concentration, much hard work and an ability to practise, practise and then practise some more.

M S Nichols
Bowling (1937)

283   Like every other artist, whether it be in music, drama, art, literature, and I venture to add cricket, fame cannot be achieved without that long dreary drudgery of preparation, so that what is difficult becomes almost second nature.

Ibid.

284   Coaching which is good, simply sharpens up a player, as wide travel and experience will.

A E Knight
The Complete Cricketer (1906)

285   This right, this best, has been slowly discovered and verified by
       a kind of *evolution,* lasting through many years in the
       experience of thousands of players, who have learned that on
       the whole, *this* was the only correct thing to do in the present
       circumstances.

'An Old Hand'
A Book About Cricket (1924)

286   Out of the thousands of batsmen who have played cricket, it
       would be difficult to find two who stand exactly alike.

A E Knight
The Complete Cricketer (1906)

287   To stand ideally is either to inflict upon yourself a form of
       astigmatism or of painful neck wrenching.

Ibid.

288   He was hardly an encouraging sight with his sallow complexion,
       sloping shoulders and over-large pads. Un-English was hardly
       the word for it.

Anthony Couch
The Unspeakable in Gloucestershire in *Memoirs of a Twelfth
Man* (1984)

289   My definition of a foreigner is someone who doesn't
       understand cricket.

Ibid.

290   A nail-can or a kerosene tin, or if, as often happened, the older
       boys had monopolised all the stray 'tins', the trunk of a
       eucalyptus-tree for a wicket, a piece of stick (round or square,
       what mattered it?) for a bat, and a small indiarubber ball
       comprised our cricket tools.

George Giffen
The Golden Age of Australian Cricket (1898)

291   I was hungry for cricket, but my school didn't play it so I was
       limited to scratch games in the park and playing in the street
       under gas lamps.

E J Smith
'Tiger' Smith (1981)

292   As a very tiny boy, I always loved the game. As soon as the sun began to shine and one could feèl the warmth, my thoughts turned to cricket.

Herbert Strudwick
Twenty-five Years Behind the Stumps (1926)

293   Cricket was in my blood and I was mad about it, but I never seemed to do anything right.

Maurice Tate
My Cricketing Reminiscences (1934)

294   When I was growing up, playing against adults while I was still in short trousers, I was never coached.

Viv Richards
Cricket Masterclass (1988)

295   During the years I have been in cricket I do not think I have come across more than half a dozen players in the top class of whom it could be said with truth that they have been coached there.

'Patsy' Hendren
Big Cricket (1934)

296   We were never coached. We used to practise in the streets of Signal Hill, where some of us would be hauled off to jail by the police if we were caught playing on the road. It was on one of these streets that I learned to play fast bowling.

Basil D'Oliveira
Time to Declare (1980)

297   My first game of cricket was played in the street when I was four years of age. The pavement was our pitch, the front wall of a house the back-stop and a biscuit-tin the wicket.

M A Noble
The Game's the Thing (1926)

298   I cannot remember when I was not keen on cricket, and I used to practise often before breakfast in my night-shirt on a marble gallery which made a perfect wicket, bowled to by one Killebree (the patois for 'humming bird'), a native boy who did all sorts of jobs about the house and garden, and who assured my father that I should be a good bat when I grew up.

Sir Pelham Warner
Long Innings (1951)

299   For the reason, perhaps, that I was a little more advanced in
my ideas on cricket than most of the boys who played at
school, I was at the expiration of two years 'barred' from the
school team.

W W Read
Annals of Cricket (1896)

300   Those very early days, when I used to toddle around the Hove
ground, were very important ones for me. I was all the time
learning to enjoy cricket, and my father's good humour was a
source of encouragement.

Jim Parks
Runs in the Sun (1961)

301   Before we were old enough to practise at the nets with the
Burslem men, we played most of our cricket on waste land that
had been trampled flat by the clogs and boots of generations of
miners.

Bernard Hollowood
Cricket on the Brain (1970)

302   We played long after dusk, until in fact the black ball was
unidentifiable against the black pitch and the night sky.

Ibid.

303   I used to watch net practice exhibited on a tennis lawn by two
of the best local cricketers. I could see from a top window in
our house. I can remember the peculiar attraction, amounting
to a thrill, of the sound of willow against hard leather.
Psychologists will note that this thrill released some instinctive
impulse in the small boy, who for the life of him could not
have restrained himself from running down the garden the first
time, and always afterwards, whenever he heard that sound, to
watch the game over the thick quickset hedge.

C B Fry
Life Worth Living (1939)

304   All cricketers in their teens, aye, and afterwards, who wish to
improve their batting will do themselves a great deal of good by
swinging Indian clubs.

E H D Sewell
Well Hit! Sir (1947)

305   You have to keep working at cricket – whatever the standard
      in which you play – otherwise someone else will come along
      who plays it better and take your place.

Viv Richards
Cricket Masterclass (1988)

306   It is not surprising that a boy who loved cricket should have
      copied the methods of a father who was a good cricketer.

John Arlott
Maurice Tate (1951)

307   It is no sinecure being the son of a famous sportsman.
      Somehow, even subconsciously, one becomes aware of the
      hopes and aspirations of parents at a tender age.

Dudley Nourse
Cricket in the Blood (1949)

308   Early opportunities arose in my life for coaching. I did not
      avail myself of them.

Ibid.

309   Cricket had begun to consume me by the age of ten.

Bob Willis
Lasting the Pace (1985)

310   As cricket became more and more of a passion for me, school
      became less and less of a pleasure.

Ibid.

311   Only on a cricket pitch did I feel I was expressing myself
      adequately.

Ibid.

312   It was a bitter disillusionment when, after several months of
      high expectation, I made my first appearance outdoors. My
      performance was a caricature of its true potential.

I A R Peebles
Spinner's Yarn (1977)

313   Don't practise on an opponent's ground before match begins.
      This can only give them confidence.

Sir J M Barrie
Allahakbarries CC (1899)

314   The youngster who is unlucky enough to be reared on bad pitches against a hard ball is understandably apprehensive.

Trevor Bailey
Sir Gary (1976)

315   I remember little about early coaching. I did not like nets. I never did like them subsequently. I would use a net if I wanted to correct a fault or was out of form. Otherwise, it seemed to me that it encouraged a looseness of method which would be found out in competitive cricket.

Peter May
A Game Enjoyed (1985)

316   Of course, the trouble with Benson was that he never taught his company anything but cricket.

George Bernard Shaw
Quoted by J C Trewin in *Robert Donat* (1968)

317   It was rumoured that a sound bowler or a dependable half-back had a better chance of becoming a Bensonian than a good actor.

Hesketh Pearson
Sir Frank Benson in *The Last Actor-Managers* (1950)

318   Everyone felt that Shakespeare was safe in the hands of one who could play cricket, tennis, football and hockey so well.

Ibid.

319   Good all-rounder, played for England, soccer for the Corinthians but . . . well . . . it was such a drawback his being a mummer by profession.

David Rayvern Allen
Quoting a remark made of C Aubrey Smith in *Sir Aubrey* (1982)

320   He had seen the timid Music Club fielding with their feet to avoid bruising artistic fingers, watched Grand Theatre actors with their long-drawn, resonant appeals and learning their lines in the outfield.

Dennis Castle
Run out the Raj (1975)

321   They gallop like unbroken fillies, all jolly laughter in white, not caring when one has humbled another and reduced him to the purdah of the pavilion.

Ibid.

322   What is cricket to us if there is no disgrace in defeat, the loser
       to be shunned by his father, and banished from his tribe?

Ibid.

323   If we play the British, they must be made to feel beaten,
       cowed.

Ibid.

324   In our family if you were a boy you played cricket. If you
       didn't, there was something wrong with you, although, in fact,
       it was impossible not to play.

David Steele
Come in Number 3 (1977)

325   When you slammed the ball straight back past the bowler at the
       open end it would go dangerously close to the window of a
       nearby house. But that in itself was a useful discipline. It meant
       you had to keep the ball down and drive properly.

Ibid.

326   Lunchtime food was completely ignored, our hunger was only
       for cricket − even if it did get us into trouble with our
       teachers! As a result I confess I am no academic.

Malcolm Marshall
Marshall Arts (1987)

327   The full implications of the religious teaching may have passed
       me by, but there was one overriding compensation which made
       those three hours absolutely compulsory. We played cricket.
       Needless to say, I never missed Sunday School, bible in one
       hand and cricket ball in the other.

Ibid.

328   If you push someone forward as a sportsman or as an academic
       he can very easily, whatever his gifts and effort, lose contact
       with the rest of his year.

Chris Cowdrey
Good Enough? (1986)

329   I loved cricket too much to turn aside from it and take up the
       only other profession I considered worthwhile: that of medicine.

Brian Close
Close to Cricket (1968)

330   I am a frustrated cricketer and love all the sounds and ritual
       that go with the game. Possibly one of these days, a bat made
       from one of my willows will make a century somewhere, maybe
       in a Test or county match or perhaps on one of those charming
       village greens before the developers finally get them all.

                                              Sir Michael Balcon
                                        A Lifetime of Films (1969)

331   [MacLaren] . . . seems to have felt for Oxbridge cricketers a
       degree of respect attributable only to his own lack of a
       university education.

                                               David Kynaston
                                        Archie's Last Stand (1984)

332   Ranji travelled in the sixth coach and Fry and Jackson in the
       seventh (but W G Grace, although captain of Sheffield's XI,
       was not thus honoured, his lack of public school and university
       background seemingly making him less socially acceptable than
       the three young Varsity Blues).

                                             Anthony Meredith
                                   The Demon and the Lobster (1987)

333   Resentment towards the intruding amateurs undermined team
       spirit.

                                                         Ibid.

334   Club cricketers must learn to hit the ball really hard if they are
       ever to play county cricket. They must cultivate as many
       scoring strokes as possible. With the current scientific approach
       to the game, many strokes are automatically taken away from
       the batsman in the middle.

                                                 Bill Andrews
                                   The Hand That Bowled Bradman (1973)

335   Some are born with silver spoons in their mouths. I was born
       in Pudsey. You can't be luckier than that if you want to play
       cricket.

                                               Ray Illingworth
                                         Spinner's Wicket (1969)

336   Night after long night I tore skin off my back knocking against
the jagged coal edges as I reached and dug and shovelled and
half straightened-up, my back screaming, my sides aching. I got
used to it. I had to. Cricket was my outlet.

Harold Larwood
The Larwood Story (1965)

337   Cricketers will tell you that when they report back for pre-
season training there will be a biting east wind, gusting from
strong to gale force, usually laced with a little cold rain or sleet
in much the same way as a cook might add salt to taste.

Ray East
A Funny Turn (1983)

338   Fitness training consisted of lengthy games of soccer between
the capped and uncapped players. Matches lasted for as long as
it took the capped players to win.

Ibid.

339   Everybody knew everybody else and the match seemed to
provide the excuse for an old boys' reunion only interrupted by
the cricket.

Ibid.

340   We were breakfasted, lunched, dined and generally feted, and
when we took the field we received a tremendous ovation, the
natives being most enthusiastic. Cricket has become more than
a game.

Sir Pelham Warner
England v Australia (1912)

341   No professional drunkard has ever made a great professional
cricketer, nor ever will.

'Quid' (R A Fitzgerald)
Jerks in from Short Leg (1866)

342   Temperance in food and drink, regular sleep and exercise, I
have laid down as the golden rule since my earliest cricketing
days.

W G Grace
The Badminton Library − Cricket (1904)

343   In order to slim, he drank cider, although latter-day dieticians might look askance at a GP supping scrumpy to reduce his waistline.

Eric Midwinter
W G Grace (1981)

344   Let me say, however, that I never smoked until my day's cricket was done, and never drank anything except water for lunch when playing in a match.

Lord Hawke
Recollections and Reminiscences (1924)

345   Fitness, however, is half of cricketing success.

Learie Constantine
The Young Cricketer's Companion (1964)

346   A bad digestion, caused by silly feeding, makes other spots in front of the eyes, and you will be at a double disadvantage.

H M Herman
How's That? (1937)

347   Always lead a regular life. Get used to going to bed at the same time every night. It is easy to wake when you want to. Just tap your head on the pillow seven times before going to sleep. You will find that you will wake up at seven o'clock to the tick.

Ibid.

348   I always insist that my team be in bed before breakfast.

Colin Ingleby-Mackenzie
Many a Slip (1962)

349   Despite his sociable temperament, Bill had cut out the parties during the Test matches, and this contributed to the tension he was under.

Ralph Barker
The Cricketing Family Edrich (1976)

350   In winter he read cricket and practised shots in his cottage. Many a time I have passed his window and seen him inside pasting the daylights out of some imaginary bowler. His sole topics of conversation were the seasons that had gone and the seasons that were to come.

R T Johnston
Cricket in the Blood in *Century of a Lifetime* (1956)

351   I was still in good health, but I could not conceal from myself the fact that I had lost my old sharpness of judgement at the crease and a good deal of my agility in the field.

R T Johnston
Century of a Lifetime in *Century of a Lifetime* (1956)

352   I have been sacked four times by Somerset County Cricket Club, twice as a player and twice as a coach.

Bill Andrews
The Hand That Bowled Bradman (1973)

353   Nerves play more havoc than even the most devastating fast bowler on the other side.

Lord Hawke
Recollections and Reminiscences (1924)

354   These players had a limited vocabulary. It was a psychological war on the nerves of the batsmen.

Brigadier M A Green
Sporting Campaigner (1956)

355   I have long believed that the most important element in the playing of big cricket is temperament.

G A Faulkner
Cricket: Can It Be Taught? (1926)

356   A fast bowler may well say that he does not want to maim batsmen, but he knows that every time he delivers that ball there is a chance of causing serious injury.

Mike Denness
I Declare (1977)

357   Lillee said in a television interview, quite clinically illustrating his point, that there were certain parts of the body which he aimed to hit when bowling short to a batsman.

Ibid.

358   I don't think cricket fans really want to see a lot of people being hit on the head or going down with broken ribs.

Ibid.

359   The knowledge that one needed to move very fast to keep one's body intact was not a pleasant way to spend a day in the sunshine, and there were times for all of us when a few weeks in frozen England seemed quite a palatable alternative to yet another session of ducking the stream of short balls.

Keith Fletcher
Captain's Innings (1983)

360   A little occasional pain is one of the chances of cricket, and one takes it as cheerfully as one can.

Sir Arthur Conan Doyle
Memories and Adventures (1924)

361   You have a bat with which to defend yourself. What more do you want?
    I will answer:
    I want a tin hat, a chest protector, a fencing mask and −
and a revolver for the bowler.

M D Lyon
Cricket (1932)

362   It is not in the best interests of cricket, which still should remain a game: not a war, or a business, or a dog fight.

Ibid.

363   Cricket is at times a dangerous game. If legislation is needed to make it less so, there are proper times and places for considering it.

Bruce Harris
Jardine Justified (1933)

364   Sometimes an unlucky boy will drive his cricket ball full in my face.

Samuel Johnson
The Rambler, Number 30 (1750)

365   The ball hit him in the mouth, driving his lips through his teeth, and in writing him a letter of sympathy I could not help adding that I should advise him in future not to put his head where his bat ought to be.

Lord Harris
A Few Short Runs (1921)

366   He played his cricket on the heath,
The pitch was full of bumps:
A fast ball hit him in the teeth,
The dentist drew the stumps.

Anonymous
Stumps Drawn!

367   I took off my boot and tried to put it [the shoulder] in at once, but couldn't manage it, although I had someone to sit on his head and others to hold him down. He was very sweaty from bowling, I couldn't get a firm grip on his arm, so he had to go to hospital to have it done. I am certain to this day that had he kept still it would have saved a lot of trouble. Poor fellow, I don't think he ever bowled again.

S M J Woods
My Reminiscences (1925)

368   Both actually ducked into balls which would otherwise have done no damage.

E M Wellings
Vintage Cricketers (1983)

369   The situation looked very ugly, and I am convinced that it only wanted one man to put a foot over the pickets for murder to have been done.

Maurice Tate
My Cricketing Reminiscences (1934)

370   A Test match is there to be fought and won, not played with in an amused and off-hand manner.

Ronald Mason
Ashes in the Mouth (1982)

371   The batsman defeated by legitimate means ought to have no complaint, nor ought he to be in any danger of serious injury.

I A R Peebles
Straight from the Shoulder (1968)

372   There have been innumerable instances of sharp practice in the history of cricket, mostly trivial and usually laughable, to be grouped under the tolerant heading of 'gamesmanship'.

Ibid.

373 Isn't it rather odd that despite all the clouts and swipes, that there are, year in and year out, so few pavilion windows broken?

E H D Sewell
Overthrows (1946)

374 Everyone must from time to time bow to the needs of the team, whether it be by taking risks or visiting the sponsor's tent.

Peter Roebuck
Slices of Cricket (1982)

375 And there are some — only a few, to be sure — who shout as the bowler is running up, the batsman concentrating.

William Pollock
Talking About Cricket (1941)

376 Cricket, however, used to be a fight for supremacy. The tendency nowadays is to spar for an opening.

Philip Trevor
Cricket and Cricketers (1921)

377 Cricket is a game, a game of social enjoyment. It is not a fit subject for an inquest, which must be, or at any rate should be, a very serious affair.

Ibid.

378 Cricket is a subtle game. In form and appearance it can be gentle, even idyllic, yet violence is always there.

Mihir Bose
A Maidan View (1986)

379 It is institutionalised anger. Firmly within certain prescribed rules.

Ibid.

380 I shall never believe that cricketers — regardless of their nationality — are perpetually involved in bickering, brawling or breaches of the peace.

W H Ferguson
Mr Cricket (1957)

381   'I say, are you going to eat that roll?' Jennifer seized it without waiting for his answer and, with a strong throw learned on the cricket field at Benenden, hit Christopher Kempenflatt on the forehead.

John Mortimer
Paradise Postponed (1985)

382   *Rowena:* These Headmaster's XIs, you know. All these middle-aged wrecks rolling around on the field being crippled by small boys.

Alan Ayckbourn
A Cricket Match, Intimate Exchanges (1982)

383   As in life so in death lies a bat of renown,
Slain by a lorry (three ton);
His innings is over, his bat is laid down:
To the end a poor judge of a run.

George McWilliam
Epitaph

384   And if you thrive before you die
Till a hundred years be past,
They'll say he 'scored a centurie,
And his bails are off at last.'

Frederick Gale
An Old Cricket Hymn

385   *Moon:* Sometimes I dream of revolution, a bloody *coup d'etat* by the second rank – troupes of actors slaughtered by their understudies, magicians sawn in half by indefatigably smiling glamour girls, cricket teams wiped out by marauding bands of twelfth men.

Tom Stoppard
The Real Inspector Hound (1968)

ART AND CRAFT

It is so much easier to get runs with the pen than with the bat.

Fig. 1.—THE BATSMAN IN
POSITION.

Fig. 2.—"THE DRAW."

Fig. 3.—THE BOWLER.

Fig. 4.—THE WICKET-KEEPER.

386   To be able to compete on equal terms with the best of his contemporaries is perhaps the finest accolade that can be paid to any cricketer.

John Shawcroft
The History of Derbyshire CCC (1989)

387   I always felt very fortunate to be a professional cricketer, to be paid for doing something I loved and which was a hobby.

Bob Taylor
A Personal View in *The History of Derbyshire CCC* (1989)

388   Then ye returned to your trinkets; then
        ye contented your souls
With the flannelled fools at the wicket or
        the muddied oafs at the goals.

Rudyard Kipling
The Islanders

389   The cricket player is not an actor on a stage, merely a personality to be lost in the creation of a poet's brain or a playwright's mind; he is himself the poet and the playwright.

A E Knight
The Complete Cricketer (1906)

390   We would not say a word against the personal character of the English professional cricketer, for the great majority of this class are honest, hard-working and sober men. We only say that it is not in the interests of cricket that any branch of the game should be left entirely in their hands.

Hon R H Lyttleton
The Badminton Library − Cricket (1904)

391   There are no more excellent fellows than the modern cricketer: no better sportsmen and no better company.

E W Swanton
Cricket and the Clock (1952)

392   A straight bat in cricket and a straight bat in life, then the runs will come, boys, the runs will come!

Brian Glanville
Up She Jolly Goes in *Love is Not Love* (1985)

393   It is so much easier to get runs with the pen than with the bat.

J C Snaith
Willow the King (1899)

394   No one turned up more regularly at the nets, and none listened
more avidly to the advice of the senior members. Yet it was all
to no purpose.

R T Johnston
Century of a Lifetime in *Century of a Lifetime* (1956)

395   Cricket is a most precarious profession; it is called a team game
but, in fact, no one is so lonely as a batsman facing a bowler
supported by ten fieldsmen and observed by two umpires to
ensure that his error does not go unpunished.

John Arlott
An Eye for Cricket (1979)

396   *Miriam:* I don't know if I prefer Rog to have a good innings or
a bad one. If it's a good one, he relives it in bed, shot
by shot, and if it's a bad one, he actually replays the
shots until he gets it right. He can make a really good
innings last all winter.

Richard Harris
Outside Edge (1979)

397   Half the joy of cricket is playing the innings over again in your
mind afterwards.

Christopher Hollis
Death of a Gentleman (1943)

398   The two points that struck him most were that the other wicket
seemed nightmarishly close to be bowled at from, and there
were apparently about 30 fielders.

E F Benson
David Blaize (1916)

399   The bowler has ten aides in the field, but they are helpless to
act until that swift cut and thrust, that intensely private
moment between batsman and bowler, is done. This numerical
advantage of players to the bowling side, however, creates a
situation which is almost unique to cricket. It makes batting,

consequently the scoring of runs, an act of defiance by one man against a vastly superior force who control the ball at all times, except in that split second when it touches the bat.

Geoffrey Moorhouse
The Best-Loved Game (1979)

400   When you go in to bat, it is not that you dread aught special and particular. You would cheerfully endure anything rather than your present ordeals. You are not afraid of getting a 'duck'. On the contrary, you'll be almost happy if you get one. It is the mere sensation of an impending something, you know not what, that plays skittles with your impressionable nature.

J C Snaith
Willow the King (1899)

401   The ground flies up into my face, the sky lies at my feet, as I stand awaiting my first ball, holding with stiff, nervous fingers my bat, in what may be called the 'first position' of cricketers – bolt upright, with my person carefully curved out, and away from it, like Cupid's bow.

Helen Mathers
Comin' thro' the Rye (1875)

402   When the batsmen were not actually beaten by the spin they were out making desperate shots for fear of what the ball might do next.

David Lacey (1982)
Reprinted in *The Guardian Book of Cricket* (1986)

403   He would run till he burst, or stand still till he hardened into marble, if only he could keep this miracle from coming to an end. He was a poor bat, but a cricketer.

Dorothy L Sayers
Murder Must Advertise (1933)

404   . . . would have been a very fine batsman indeed if he could only have achieved the necessary co-ordination between hand and eye; the whisky got in the way of that.

John Moore
Brensham Village (1946)

405   His record, take it all in all,
Was not a very great one;
He seldom hit a crooked ball
And never stopped a straight one.

Anonymous
The Rabbit

406   It is as well for us to remember when we are watching the best
batsmen that, however easy it may all look, they do not achieve
their success without toil and sweat and that there are times
even with the greatest when they must seem to themselves, as
we humble performers so frequently seem to ourselves, to be
batting with a broomstick, with a barn door for a wicket.

E W Swanton
Denis Compton: A Cricket Sketch (1948)

407   He once practised for some match till he appeared to all the
bowlers about Lord's to have reduced batting to a certainty:
but when the day came, amid the most sanguine expectations of
his friends, he made no runs.

Rev James Pycroft
The Cricket Field (1851)

408   The margin of error between middle and edge of a cricket bat
is, after all, only two inches. That is a truth which never enters
a batsman's mind when he is in form; when he is off, it can
become an obsessive hazard.

John Arlott
Jack Hobbs (1981)

409   Like all cricket devotees I have many, many times shared with
all around me that infectious, 'breathless hush' tension as a
batsman, however well-set, however self-possessed, has to face
up to the obligation of scoring that hundredth run.

Ben Travers
94 Declared (1981)

410   Scores didn't count, and they don't with some of the great
batsmen. It's what you do and how you do it that matters.

Dal Stivens
The Demon Bowler and Other Cricket Stories (1979)

411   So let me go what'er befall,
       And I will make a score;
       I should not love thee, dear, at all,
       Loved I not batting more.

Alfred Cochrane
To Lucasta in *Collected Verses* (1903)

412   They had only one standard by which to measure the merit of
       an innings, and that was its actual duration in time.

Rex Warner
Escapade (1933)

413   Figures are not entirely conclusive, especially short-term figures,
       but it is difficult to avoid their significance if a man produces
       them year after year against every type of opponent and under
       all conceivable conditions.

Sir Donald Bradman
Farewell to Cricket (1950)

414   Batting is an unrivalled variety show in itself.

Allen Synge
Cricket: The Men and the Matches that Changed the Game
(1988)

415   What wonderful contrasts this great game of cricket attends in
       that a man who defied the cream of English bowling for seven
       hours, can, only a fortnight later, play an innings lasting one
       second.

D J Knight
England v Australia, Third Test (1926) reprinted in *The
Observer on Cricket* (1987)

416   I believe that every great batsman is a special organism; it must
       be so, for they are very rare, as rare as great violinists − I
       doubt if I have known many more than a dozen.

C L R James
Beyond a Boundary (1963)

417　His footwork alone was enough to make you go into rhapsodies. He moved close to the ball with his head right over it. There was never the waste of a movement. He played as Mozart must have played the pianoforte — 'like flowing oil', was how he said it should be done.

Dal Stivens
The Demon Bowler and Other Stories (1979)

418　Batting is one of those things which demand first and foremost a thorough belief in oneself. It need not be aggressive, but it must be there.

P G Wodehouse
Mike (1909)

419　If a batsman is obliged to wait with his pads on for more than half an hour he is normally reduced to the condition of frog-spawn, and this state will accompany him on the field of play and last for at least a couple of overs, which are seldom survived.

Robert Holles
The Guide to Real Village Cricket (1983)

420　Let us try to see what the duty of a batsman is when he goes to the wicket. Above everything else he must try to put self in the background.

F A H Henley
The Boys' Book of Cricket (1933)

421　The moment had come, the moment which he had experienced only in dreams. And in the dreams he was always full of confidence, and invariably hit a boundary. Sometimes a drive, sometimes a cut, but always a boundary.

P G Wodehouse
Mike (1909)

422　Even as the wicket rattled he was playing the stroke again, and with academic correctness, in his own mind.

E W Hornung
Chrystal's Century in *Old Offenders and a Few Old Scores*
(1923)

423   He was not a great cricketer, none of us were, but he had a
       good eye, the heart of a lion, and he loved the game.

Stacy Aumonier
The Match in *Miss Bracegirdle and Other Stories* (1923)

424   He blocked the doubtful balls, missed the bad ones, took the
       good ones, and sent them flying to all parts of the field.

Charles Dickens
Pickwick Papers (1837)

425   He did not feel in the least reckless; his recklessness in his
       cricket as in his life was a product of defeatism and of
       detestation of himself, but now the mood of the conqueror was
       on him, and a distant, impersonal part of his mind sat back
       and approved of his accomplishments.

Dudley Carew
The Son of Grief (1936)

426   It is a liberal cricket education to make runs, even against the
       worst bowling in the world.

E W Hornung
Chrystal's Century in *Old Offenders and a Few Old Scores*
(1923)

427   The worst player in the world, with his eye in, may resist
       indefinitely the attack of the best bowler; after all, a ball is a
       ball and a bat is a bat; and if you once begin getting the one
       continually in the middle of the other, and keeping it out of
       harm's way, there is no more to be said and but little to be
       done.

Ibid.

428   You concentrate on the difficult thing, bring it off, preen
       yourself a little, relax, and the fellow at the other end does you
       with his arm ball.

A C H Smith
Extra Cover (1981)

429   Hell has no fury like a cricketer who fancies some slight has
       been made on his prowess.

R T Johnston
Century of a Lifetime in *Century of a Lifetime* (1956)

430   That Bill's a foolish fellow,
He has given me a black eye.
He does not know how to handle a bat
Any more than a dog or cat.
He has knock'd down the wicket
And broke the stumps,
And runs without shoes to save his pumps.

William Blake
An Island in the Moon

431   Out – beyond question or wrangle!
Homeward he lurched to his lunch!
His bat was tucked up at an angle,
His great shoulders curved to a hunch.

Sir Arthur Conan Doyle
A Reminiscence of Cricket (1922)

432   In cricket, as spectators know,
There's an unwritten law,
Whatever way a batsman's out,
He's never leg before!

F B Wilson
Leg Before in *Sporting Pie* (1922)

433   They do not bowl me off my pad,
No catches from my glove are had:
The hated 'leg before' is banned
In matches played in Fairyland.

E B V Christian
Dreams That I Dream in *At the Sign of the Wicket* (1894)

434   I dream of many a glorious drive,
I feel the cut that goes for five:
I hear the crowd's applauding roar
That follows oft a hit for four.

Ibid.

435   There are easier things in the world than stopping a fast yorker.

P G Wodehouse
Mike (1909)

436   In conclusion, never treat a straight ball with contempt,
        however badly bowled.

W G Grace
The Badminton Library − Cricket (1904)

437   Perhaps the happiest scoring mood is that of a man, keen
        careful, tinged with anxiety to do well, but conscious of his
        power.

A E Knight
The Complete Cricketer (1906)

438   Ideally, the best batsman is he who can get the most runs in the
        most beautiful way in the quickest time.

Ibid.

439   You might say that balance and timing add up to rhythm, and
        that is the rhythm which the unsophisticated spectator is
        appreciating when an especially delicious stroke evokes murmurs
        of 'Lovely, sir, lovely!'

E W Swanton
Denis Compton: A Cricket Sketch (1948)

440   The great thing about hitting is, not to be half-hearted about it;
        but when you make up your mind to hit, to do it as if the
        whole match depended upon that particular stroke.

W G Grace
Cricket (1891)

441   A true batsman should in most of his strokes tell the truth
        about himself.

Sir Neville Cardus
Cricket (1930)

442   I do not believe so implicitly, as some cricketers and writers
        upon cricket do, in watching the bowler's hand. I prefer to
        watch the ball, and not anticipate events.

W G Grace
W G − Cricketing Reminiscences and Personal Recollections
(1899)

443   If you have legs, in the name of goodness use them. Spring out of your confined territory, and drive forward with all your might, with all your strength and with all your skill.

> **Nicholas Wanostrocht**
> *Felix on the Bat* (1845)

444   A professional batsman cannot bat as he likes, and the man who does not bat as he likes does not bat as well as he can.

> **Philip Trevor**
> *Strand Magazine* (1928)

445   Give me the batsman who squanders his force on me,
Crowding the strength of his soul in a stroke.

> **E V Lucas**
> *The Song of the Ball* in *Willow and Leather* (1898)

446   Even the most misanthropic critic must succumb to the smacking concussion of the full-blooded hit, to the fascination of the red ball rocketing into the blue sky, with its whirring flight of a driven partridge and its final crash as it lands on roof or window.

> **Hon T C F Prittie**
> *Mainly Middlesex* (1947)

447   I found myself reflecting on the blessings and curses of the natural aptitudes, those which bestow an innate athleticism, a ball sense, that seemingly effortless power that denotes perfect timing, that physical co-ordination which is quite instinctive and, though cultivated, can never be taught.

> **Ted Dexter and Clifford Makins**
> *Testkill* (1976)

448   Unlike tennis players who enjoy a knock-up on court, the Test batsman, even after net practice, is still forced to use the first few overs in the middle as a warm-up.

> *Ibid.*

449   Any fool can play forward, but it is only the good player who can score off forceful back strokes.

> **A C MacLaren**
> *The Young Batsman* in *The Cricketer* (1921)

450   It is commonly remarked of really great batsmen that the better the bowling the better they play, which means, as a rule, that only the very best batsmen have many scoring strokes against bowling of the highest class.

G W Beldam and C B Fry
Great Batsmen: Their Methods at a Glance (1905)

451   The great batsman lifts us out of our utilitarian selves; we admire his work for its beauty, not merely for its value in runs.

Sir Neville Cardus
An Innings of Hammond in *The Summer Game* (1929)

452   Among all the curious charges which have come upon cricket none is more to be regretted than the decline of hitting to leg; and it may be surprising that one of the explanations is the niceness of modern manners.

E V Lucas
A Hundred Years of Trent Bridge (1938)

453   The more elderly were reminded of how cricket used to be played and especially how the ball used to be driven before the game's descent, as many would lament, to an age of over-sophistication and a dreary philosophy of safety first.

E W Swanton (1950)
Reprinted in *As I Said at the Time* (1983)

454   A batsman who cannot make runs on turf after rain and sun and wind is only half a batsman.

E H D Sewell
Well Hit! Sir (1947)

455   The hardest tests in batting are to play fast bowling on a fiery wicket and spin bowling on a sticky one.

Sir Pelham Warner
Lord's 1787 – 1945 (1946)

456   Run, run, run, the ball's a-rolling,
Scarcely to the boundary she'll go;
And the throwing's getting wild, and the wicket-keeper's riled,
So we'll try and steal another for the throw.

Horace G Hutchinson
Song

457   Barnes went up to Barlow and said, 'Bowling at you is like
bowling at a stone wall!' The name stuck to Barlow, who,
though not the first to play slow cricket, was literally the first
'stonewaller' on the cricket field.

W G Grace
W G – Cricketing Reminiscences and Personal Recollections
(1899)

458   And the clock's slow hands go on,
And you still keep up your sticks;
But oh for the lift of a smiting hand,
And the sound of a swipe for six!
Block, block, block,
At the foot of thy wickets, ah, do!
But one hour of Grace or Walter Read
Were worth a week of you!

George Francis Wilson
On W Scotton, *Cricket Poems* (1905)

459   A field of outsiders are always going in to bowl at the Public
Service, and we block the balls.

Charles Dickens
Little Dorrit (1857)

460   Seriously, there is no case against the genuine stonewaller. No
lover of the game has a ghost of a reason for protesting against
true and natural obstinacy at cricket.

Sir Neville Cardus
The Time Spirit in *The Summer Game* (1929)

461   Today, dull batting has become so universally applied an
accusation that one is apt to forget that cricket is the
professional's livelihood, and for him the price of failure may
be penury.

Hon T C F Prittie
Mainly Middlesex (1947)

462   Oo am I to be put off my stroke, Mum, becos
      a few 'ooligans boos?
An Englishman's crease is 'is castle; I shall
      stay 'ere as long as I choose.

Hubert Phillips
An Englishman's Crease in *The Playtime Omnibus* (1933)

463   I still love to be out in the middle, taming the bowlers. Yet I
       know that class bowlers would get me out if I tried to hit them
       around as I used to.

                                                    Viv Richards
                                          Cricket Masterclass (1988)

464   You cannot prosper as a batsman unless you have a
       fundamentally correct technique.

                                                          Ibid.

465   Every position has its special charm.
       You go in first and find as a reward
       The wicket at its best; you go in later
       And find the fielders slack, the bowling loose.

                                                      A A Milne
                          An Average Man in *The Day's Play* (1910)

466   Since the glamour of cricket generally surrounds the batsman it
       is batting partnerships that have earned the most lasting
       renown, and in the nature of things the names best known and
       remembered are those who have gone in first together.

                                               E W Swanton (1974)
                         Reprinted in *As I Said at the Time* (1983)

467   Around the most illustrious of opening partnerships there
       lingers a romantic flavour.

                                                          Ibid.

468   The best partnerships rest on close mutual understanding, to
       say the least. No doubt differences may arise occasionally, but I
       never heard of a successful partnership on the field that was
       regularly at odds off it.

                                                          Ibid.

469   Closer, the bowler's arm swept down,
       The ball swung, pitched and darted,
       Stump and bail flashed and flew;
       The batsman pensively departed.

                                                    John Arlott
                                      Cricket at Worcester (1938)

470   We lose our wicket most frequently not by pace from pitch or
       great break or even huge swerve, valuable as such possessions
       are to a bowler: these qualities in bowling may complete our
       defeat or render it more certain; but we have been beaten
       essentially by our own defective judgement.

A E Knight
The Complete Cricketer (1906)

471   Bowlers and wicket-keepers, however brilliant, cannot by the
       nature of their work captivate the spectator in quite the same
       way as the greatest batsman.

E W Swanton
A History of Cricket, Volume Two (1962)

472   So used are the batsmen to being on top that when a form of
       attack is evolved to put bowlers on terms again up rises a wail
       of protest.

Bruce Harris
Jardine Justified (1933)

473   In the game of cricket it has always been customary to accord
       more adulation to batsmen than to bowlers.

I A R Peebles
Talking of Cricket (1953)

474   For years now everything has been done with an eye to the
       batsman, and unless the quality bowler is encouraged by the
       possibility of receiving a fair reward for his labours, no one can
       blame him for giving up the thankless task in disgust.

C G Macartney
England v Australia, Leeds (1938) reprinted in *The Observer on
Cricket* (1987)

475   The public in the main pay to see batting rather than bowling;
       and the tendency always is to make the bowler a mere means to
       the run-getter's spectacular end.

Bruce Harris
Jardine Justified (1933)

476   Bowling is the basis of cricket, for in the natural order of
       conflict defence can only develop according to the shape and
       quality of the attack.

E W Swanton (1947)
Reprinted in *As I Said at the Time* (1983)

477 Bowlers, in the future as in the past, will be applauded and rewarded far less than batsmen.

Phil Edmonds
100 Greatest Bowlers (1989)

478 The art of bowling is an incommunicable natural gift which can be perfected to almost any degree by practice.

S M E Kempson
Quoted by K S Ranjitsinhji in *The Jubilee Book of Cricket* (1897)

479 It has been said that bowlers, like poets, are not made.

I A R Peebles
Talking of Cricket (1953)

480 How remarkable it is that a bowler who appears so harmless from the pavilion seems terrifying and demoniacal when he comes tearing down the crease towards you!

Stacy Aumonier
The Match in *Miss Bracegirdle and Other Stories* (1923)

481 If you are going to win matches, it is largely your bowlers who will do it.

F A H Henley
The Boys' Book of Cricket (1933)

482 Give me the bowler whose fingers embracing me
Tingle and throb with joy of the game.

E V Lucas
The Song of the Ball in *Willow and Leather* (1898)

483 Even Test match bowling all over the world is so basic that it may be said to have gone right through the floor into the bargain basement.

Learie Constantine
The Young Cricketer's Companion (1964)

484 The bowler's job is to attack the batsman's wicket.

Ibid.

485   I never saw such a bowler,
       To bowl the ball in a tansey,
       And to clean it with my handkercher
       Without saying a word.

William Blake
An Island in the Moon (1787)

486   You see the moral: cover every strumpet in London if you've a
       mind to, it don't signify so long as you can take wickets.

George Macdonald Fraser
Flashman's Lady (1977)

487   The bowler's real target is the batsman, and *not* the stumps.
       His job is very like that of a general in war. Once or twice in a
       lifetime a general possesses such superiority in all arms that his
       enemy stands no chance whatsoever. But in 99 out of every 100
       engagements he must scheme to deceive the enemy commander,
       and lure him to his doom.

Christopher Sly
How To Bowl Them Out (1948)

488   It is worth observing here that whereas in old days bouncers
       were usually intended to disturb the batsman and were aimed to
       pass over the stumps today they are often aimed to intimidate,
       on the line of the body. The end still defies solution.

E W Swanton
'Gubby' Allen (1985)

489   Bodyline was not an incident, it was not an accident, it was not
       a temporary aberration. It was the violence and ferocity of our
       age expressing itself in cricket.

C L R James
Beyond a Boundary (1963)

490   In their disregard of anybody being hit and hurt some West
       Indians appeared callous and reminded me of bully boys.

J E Fingleton
Batting from Memory (1981)

491   His murderous bowling reduced heroes to panic: they just
       waved him good-bye and ran: and when he came in to bat men
       covered their heads and retired piecemeal to the boundaries.

Laurie Lee
Cider with Rosie (1959)

492   I have never known many professionals who relished it, because, as their bread-and-butter depends on their playing, they naturally do not want to be knocked out.

Lord Hawke
Recollections and Reminiscences (1924)

493   To bowl fast is to revel in the glad animal action, to thrill in physical power and to enjoy a certain sneaking feeling of superiority over mortals who play the game.

Frank Tyson
A Typhoon Called Tyson (1961)

494   High velocity in bowling has always meant initiative for the bowler, and ever since cricket was first played, whether casually or on an organised basis, the man with the ball has had the choice of exercising guile or straight-out aggression.

David Frith
The Fast Men (1975)

495   There seems one certainty: men have been firing cricket balls with evil intent at other men since long before young Neville Cardus was boiling type in a printer's works.

Ibid.

496   Bowling which does not get men out, like batting which brings no runs to the score, is an art abused.

A E Knight
The Complete Cricketer (1906)

497   Genuinely fast bowling, too, finds out batsmen short of the highest class because their reactions are not quite quick enough to deal with it.

John Arlott
An Eye for Cricket (1979)

498   I have often thought what a pity it is – how much better a life I would have had, what a better man I would have been, how much healthier an existence I would have led, if I had been a cricketer instead of an actor. But it was not to be.

Lord Olivier
My Life in Cricket in *The Twelfth Man* (1971)

499   In my mind I was already beginning to shape the first century
that I would make for the first XI . . . and I was clean bowled
by Douglas Bader. He ended my cricketing career.

Ibid.

500   It was with an air of resolution and confidence that the opening
batsmen went to the wicket, and their confidence was increased
when they observed that Sir Fielding Average was proposing to
open the bowling himself, an action which correspondingly
depressed the feelings of his own side.

Rex Warner
Escapade (1933)

501   And bowler, to you a caution or two,
To save your own side from disaster;
Don't mind if you're hit, tempt the batsmen a bit,
And vary your slows with a faster;

Anonymous
A Song of Cricket

502   The secret of fast bowling is rhythm, and all who achieve high
speed know of those magical days when everything clicks that
much more smoothly.

E W Swanton
'Gubby' Allen (1985)

503   I bowled three sanctified souls
With three consecutive balls!
What do I care if Blondin trod
Over Niagara Falls?
What do I care for the loon in the Pit
Or the gilded earl in the Stalls?
I bowled three curates once
With three consecutive balls.

Norman Gale
Cricket Songs (1896)

504   A gentleman's a-bowling
And down the wickets go!

Harrow School Song

505   A herd of boys with clamour bowled
And stumped the wicket

Alfred, Lord Tennyson
Quoted by John Arlott in *Cricket* (1953)

506 Cricket proper began with the length ball – because length means a curving flight. And the sight of a ball moving through the air awakens the sense of beauty. And where there is no beauty there is no cricket.

Sir Neville Cardus
Cricket (1930)

507 The bowler being human is but clay, to be moulded by the works of his hand and brain, by the time and experience which agglutinate them, but, having the innate gift, he is not bound up with the bands of our rules and regulations. A man is either a bowler or he is not a bowler.

A E Knight
The Complete Cricketer (1906)

508 Bowling, like everything worth doing, takes a lot of careful practice before it can be expected to meet with success.

A G Steel
The Badminton Library – Cricket (1904)

509 The teaching of bowling is an art so difficult that pages of weighty instruction and learned diagrams have gone almost for nothing.

R C Robertson-Glasgow
Cricket Prints (1943)

510 Intervals of whatever kind are, as every cricketer knows, the best of change bowlers.

Sir Jack Hobbs
The Test Match Surprise (1926)

511 Bowling consists of two parts: there is the mechanical part, and the intellectual part. First you want the hand to pitch where you please and then the head to know where to pitch, according to the player.

Rev James Pycroft
The Cricket Field (1851)

512 Bowling is a very delightful art, if you can play go-as-you-please with it; but from the grim drudgery of its prolonged effort nine out of ten professionals shrink.

A E Knight
The Complete Cricketer (1906)

513   Of all members of the cricket family, the bowler is the supreme
head. He is as the trunk from which even the greatest branches
depend; he is the great soldier at the flank upon whom the
goodly company wheels.

Ibid.

514   The bowler is a more delicate plant, less certain to rear, and
shorter-lived than the batsman.

I A R Peebles
Talking of Cricket (1953)

515   There is a final drop of venom which transforms a good bowler
into a great one.

Hon T C F Prittie
Mainly Middlesex (1947)

516   Having exhausted himself by his own ferocity, he lost his pace
and became more erratic than usual and was taken off, after an
expensive over; in favour of a gentleman who bowled
leg-breaks.

Dorothy L Sayers
Murder Must Advertise (1933)

517   As with bat so with ball,
And bygone hours come back,
When he was honoured with the call
To open the attack:
Alas! this compliment is gone,
Captains and creeds are strange,
And all too rarely he goes on
Till sixth or seventh change.

Alfred Cochrane
Verba non Facta in *Later Verses* (1918)

518   Persistence, muscle, luck and, of course, some skill, make up
the average seam bowler.

A V Bedser
Over and Out in *The Cricketer's Bedside Book* (1966)

519 The medium-pacer is the linchpin of English county cricket, a fact which mystifies people overseas, where such kind are regarded as cannon fodder for batsmen and in terms of importance about as useful as cold water at a banquet.

Peter Walker
Cricket Conversations (1978)

520 In passing I ought to stress that the ball does not always do the expected. If it does not swing or cut, the batsman is as much deceived as the bowler is gratefully surprised.

A V Bedser
Cricket Choice (1981)

521 Every ball that he bowled had brain behind it, if not exactness of pitch.

A G Macdonell
England, Their England (1933)

522 Every young spinner turned into a colourless medium-pacer constitutes a crime against a beautiful game.

David Frith
The Slow Men (1984)

523 The game minus slow bowling is like bread without butter, or even worse French cuisine without the sauces.

Trevor Bailey and Fred Trueman
The Spinners' Web (1988)

524 It is the slow spin bowler who is the arch-deceiver, almost the 'futurist' of the bowling art.

M S Nichols
Bowling (1937)

525 The value of a good bowler is often overlooked by some spectators, and his success is attributed too readily to bad batting.

Hedley Verity
Bowling 'em out (1936)

526   He shakes his head meditatively, as though the contemplation of the diabolical cunning of bowling a slow ball after four faster ones was almost too much to believe, as though it was a demonstration of intellectual callisthenics that this generation could not appreciate.

Stacy Aumonier
The Match in *Miss Bracegirdle and Other Stories* (1923)

527   Slow bowlers had better things to do in those days than make up the numbers on the field and spin a good yarn off it.

Nico Craven
Waiting for Cheltenham (1989)

528   The greatest slow bowlers, Rhodes, Blythe, Grimmett and Verity, have been the poker-players of the cricket field, disguising beneath a bland and perfectly simulated indifference the real depth and cunning of their designs.

Hon T C F Prittie
Mainly Middlesex (1947)

529   The mechanics of spinning a cricket ball are straightforward enough.

Benny Green
A History of Cricket (1988)

530   Leg-spinners pose problems much like love,
Requiring commitment, the taking of a chance.

Alan Ross
Watching Benaud Bowl in *Australia '63* (1964)

531   In any class of cricket, good leg-spin is the hardest to play. It's the type of bowling which separates the men from the boys.

Dal Stivens
The Ring-In in *The Demon Bowler and Other Cricket Stories* (1979)

532   I sometimes feel there are more leg-spinners in cricket fiction than in real cricket nowadays.

John Bright-Holmes
Lord's and Commons (1988)

533 Gone were the days when finger-licking spinners could follow a
rainbow and expect to find a sticky wicket glued to the ground
for their benefit.

Nico Craven
Waiting for Cheltenham (1989)

534 There is something so tempting to an inexperienced player in
seeing a ball chucked up in the air slowly and simply, it looks
so very easy to hit, so peculiarly guileless, that a wild slog is
frequently the result, too often followed by disastrous
consequences.

A G Steel
The Badminton Library − *Cricket* (1904)

535 Lobs are the most dangerous, insinuating things in the world.
Everybody knows in theory the right way to treat them.
Everybody knows that the man who is content not to try to
score more than a single cannot get out to them. Yet nearly
everybody does get out to them.

P G Wodehouse
Mike (1909)

536 Fielding is the only branch of the game in which, if one tries
hard enough, one can be sure of success.

K S Ranjitsinhji
The Jubilee Book of Cricket (1897)

537 No player is really a cricketer at heart if he doesn't look
forward to running about on a beautiful turf on any kind of
day.

G A Faulkner
Cricket: Can It Be Taught? (1926)

538 Collectively and individually fielding is largely a matter of
thought and discipline.

I A R Peebles
Talking of Cricket (1953)

539 Several players were stationed to 'look out', in different parts
of the field, and each fixed himself into the proper attitude by
placing one hand on each knee, and stooping very much as if

he were 'making a back' for some beginner at leap-frog. All the
regular players do this sort of thing; indeed it is generally
supposed that it is quite impossible to look out properly in any
other position.

Charles Dickens
Pickwick Papers (1837)

540   Sunburned fieldsmen, flannelled dream,
Looked, though urgent, scarce alive,
Swooped, like swallows of a cream
On skimming fly, the hard-hit drive.

John Arlott
Cricket at Worcester (1938)

541   It is surprising that the famous nurseries of amateur cricketers,
the great English Public Schools, with all their advantages, so
rarely produced fielders of more than average ability.

K S Ranjitsinhji
The Jubilee Book of Cricket (1897)

542   It is a disgrace. It shows an execrable attitude of the mind. A
slack, careless fielder needs the stick: he cannot possibly have a
right and proper spirit.

Ibid.

543   There is no doubt that the quality of fielding in England, like
the quality of mercy in the *Merchant of Venice,* is not strained.
Not merely is it not strained; it is not even sieved.

Learie Constantine
The Young Cricketer's Companion (1964)

544   There's no doubt that the general level of fielding has improved
during my time, and I don't mean only in county cricket.

E W Swanton (1973)
Reprinted in *As I Said at the Time* (1983)

545   The throwing today is marvellously good, and fielders are
prepared to hurl themselves about to save four runs in a way
that scarcely happened.

Ibid.

546   Conduct on the field has become, in its own sly way, as loose as that as some of the people who pay for tickets.

> **Benny Green**
> *A History of Cricket* (1988)

547   Fielding is the greatest fun in cricket. After all, it is the only full-time job in the game.

> **H M Herman**
> *How's That?* (1937)

548   To be able to field well is to enjoy it.

> *Ibid.*

549   I have always maintained that although every player cannot be an all-rounder in the fullest sense of the term, there is no reason at all why all cricketers should not be able to hold their own in the field.

> **Leslie Ames**
> *Close of Play* (1953)

550   Stupendous scores he never made,
But perished even with despatch:
No bowling genius he displayed,
But once, in a forgotten match,
He made a catch.

> **Alfred Cochrane**
> *The Catch* in *Collected Verses* (1903)

551   Had I but youth, keen-sighted I would lour
To track the flying ball, or fleet foot scour
The field all day to save the quick-snatched run
And feel, how good they were, when sets the sun,
Those hours of Life!

> **D L A Jephson**
> *Had I But Youth* in *A Few Overs* (1913)

552   He leaps once more, with eager spring,
To catch the brief-glimpsed, flying ball
And quickens to its sudden sting:

> **John Arlott**
> *The Old Cricketer*

553   The quivering poise! the dart!
       The wristy, magical, and stern
       Completeness of that punishing Return.

> **Norman Gale**
> *Back Numbers!*

554   Fielding is a double-edged weapon. Smart work, especially the
       snapping up of those half-chance catches, has a detrimental
       effect on the batsmen, but at the same time it puts the bowler's
       tail up.

> **Leslie Ames**
> *Close of Play* (1953)

555   The sun in the heavens was beaming;
       The breeze bore an odour of hay,
       My flannels were spotless and gleaming,
       My heart was unclouded and gay;
       The ladies, all gaily apparelled,
       Sat round looking on at the match,
       In the tree-tops the dicky-birds carolled,
       All was peace till I bungled the catch.

> **P G Wodehouse**
> *Missed!*

556   'Sorry,' said Norris, throwing the ball back.
          'That's all right,' replied the bowler, comforting himself with
       the vision of a game in which Tarrant and J Douglas fielded in
       the slips to his bowling, while in the background Norris
       appeared, in a cauldron of boiling oil.

> **P G Wodehouse**
> *A Prefect's Uncle* (1903)

557   A missed catch, like a missed putt, can leave a lifetime legacy
       of sudden shivers in the night.

> **R C Robertson-Glasgow**
> *Lord's Cricket Ground* (1946) reprinted in *The Observer on
> Cricket* (1987)

558   The crowd's dejected, the scorer scores,
       And I'm expected to save the fours!

> **Herbert Farjeon**
> *Long-on Blues* in *Cricket Bag* (1946)

559   Fielding in the so-called 'silly' positions, after all, is not merely an act of courage which deserves applause when it is truly that and not a half-hearted pretence. It is also an intimidation of the batsman, an emotional pressure which can only be justified if the fieldsmen are prepared to yield their own security in return, and as much of a distraction as the presence of a spectator alongside a grandmaster's chess-board. The use of an artificial aid to increase the already heavy odds in favour of the bowling side and against the solitary bat is to tip the fine balance between what is fair play and what it not.

Geoffrey Moorhouse
The Best-Loved Game (1979)

560   Everyone ought to have his fixed position in the field and stick to it.

Sir John Cecil Masterman
Fate Cannot Harm Me (1935)

561   Mid-on is one of the easiest places in the field; for there is no twist on the ball, and the fieldsman has plenty of time to see it coming.

W G Grace
Cricket (1897)

562   Mid-on is perhaps the best place to put a duffer, if you are unfortunate enough to have one on your side. He will do less harm there than anywhere else.

K S Ranjitsinhji
The Jubilee Book of Cricket (1891)

563   A captain of an XI feels himself very often bound by an unwritten tradition to put the notoriously worst field in his XI short-leg.

Hon R H Lyttleton
The Badminton Library — Cricket (1904)

564   As I once heard a sarcastic Scotchman say up at Selkirk, 'Macdonald is a good fielder, nothing can pass his feet.'

A E Knight
The Complete Cricketer (1906)

565   Every cricketer knows what it's like to go out to field in the evening, when the hot tea brings out the sweat on one's brow, to be followed, soon after, by a cool fresh feeling.

M D Lyon
A Village Match and After (1929)

566   A real wicket-keeper is an artist.

F A H Henley
The Boy's Book of Cricket (1933)

567   The wicket-keeper must never think of getting hurt.

Viv Richards
Cricket Masterclass (1988)

568   Quietness and efficiency beat all the gallery work in the world.

H M Herman
How's That? (1937)

569   The first business of a wicket-keeper is to make the opposing batsmen feel at home.

Stacy Aumonier
The Match in *Miss Bracegirdle and Other Stories* (1923)

570   He had that curious, sympathetic mothering quality which every good wicket-keeper should have.

Ibid.

571   It is impossible to estimate too highly the qualities that make up a good wicket-keeper. It demands the quickest of eye, the staunchest of nerve, the steadiest of purpose, the most unflinching of resolution.

'Quid' (R A Fitzgerald)
Jerks in from Short Leg (1866)

572   The central figure on the field must always be the man behind the stumps. Not only does he have the opportunity to make more catches than anyone else, but he delivers the *coup de grâce* in the majority of run outs, and he is also responsible for the stumpings. He can transform the whole appearance of the fielding side, camouflaging the poorer returns and adding colour to the proceedings.

Trevor Bailey
The Greatest of My Time (1968)

573   Of all the skills of cricket, wicket-keeping seems to have lost most in recent years.

Keith Andrew
The Handbook of Cricket (1989)

574   Great wicket-keepers are born and not made.

Ibid.

575   The standard declined sadly and quickly. Soon the game was full of long stops.

E M Wellings
Vintage Cricketers (1983)

576   Slow bowlers lost much from not having their wicket-keeper breathing down the batsman's neck and inhibiting his moves down the pitch.

Ibid.

577   A 'keeper is a specialist and if he can bat, that's a bonus, but shouldn't be essential.

E J Smith
'Tiger' Smith (1981)

578   I hold the view that a man should be played if he is an outstanding 'keeper, even if he is no use at all with the bat; but he must really be outstanding for that, and not just a mediocrity.

Learie Constantine
The Young Cricketer's Companion (1964)

579   There used to be an old cricketing maxim − which has never been discredited even if it is sometimes ignored nowadays − that, in picking a cricket team, you should always pick the wicket-keeper first.

John Arlott
Glamorgan CCC Year Book (1951)

580   The position of the wicket-keeper in his standing should be that of a man preparing to spar, so that he may in an instant move any way he pleases.

John Nyren
The Young Cricketer's Tutor (1833)

581   He can so often lift the team when the game is going against them and even afterwards in the dressing-room, he can play his part.

Keith Andrew
The Skills of Cricket (1984)

582   Wicket-keeping is an art, the skilful wicket-keeper an artist. It is as great a distinction to be a wicket-keeper in cricket as it is to be a Hardy in fiction.

'Blazer'
Some Cover Shots (1924)

583   Personally, I should like to see the wicket-keeper more handsomely rewarded than he is, and I would infringe upon the delightful social communism of our fees to the extent of awarding him an extra sovereign in every match.

A E Knight
The Complete Cricketer (1906)

LEADERSHIP
AND
AUTHORITY

Captaincy seems to involve half-hearing conversations which you'd rather not hear at all.

584   Tennessee Williams remains in America, which probably accounts for the fact that no dramatist has yet utilised the terrible frustrations of county captains as a vehicle for modern tragedy.

Douglas Insole
Cricket from the Middle (1960)

585   An ethereal chess player controlling ten pieces on a vast board and directing his natural intelligence and native cunning towards the confusion and eventual defeat of his opponent.

Ibid.

586   A thick-skinned representative of the upper class, carried and sustained in thought and action by his professionals, and looking upon his position as a sort of social attainment.

Ibid.

587   An honest-to-goodness unimaginative son of the soil, a yeoman who, true to British tradition, has accepted the burden of captaincy with a philosophical shrug of the shoulders and nominal expenses for entertainment.

Ibid.

588   Captaincy seems to involve half-hearing conversations which you'd rather not hear at all.

Peter Roebuck
It Never Rains (1984)

589   It is a strange fact connected with cricket that a good captain is but seldom met with.

A G Steel
The Badminton Library − Cricket (1904)

590   A captain's job, nevertheless, is bound up with the aim of removing batsmen by any fair means at his disposal, and there is certainly some psychology involved in this.

Keith Fletcher
Captain's Innings (1983)

591   While I may not be an advocate of talking to batsmen, I am very much in favour of ignoring those who want to talk.

Ibid.

592   Some captains believe in having an over or two themselves
       when leather-hunting becomes unpleasantly perpetual, but the
       practice is not to be recommended. It causes friction among
       team-mates and stiffness between the shoulder-blades.

                                                    Bernard Hollowood
              Captaincy − Next Year, Punch reprinted in *The Boundary
                                                            Book* (1962)

593   As captain you can never be one of the boys.

                                                         Tony Lewis
                                                 Playing Days (1985)

594   Captaincy is of such importance that to impart knowledge and
       advice concerning it at the very start of a cricket career is of
       supreme assistance to the individual as well as to the sides
       which he may be called upon to lead.

                                        Sir Henry Levenson-Gower
                                          Off and on the Field (1953)

595   A good captain tries to identify himself so completely with his
       side, as a whole and in all its parts, that he fields with every
       fieldsman and bowls every ball with his bowlers. He is, in
       truth, the soul of his side.

                                                K S Ranjitsinhji
                                 The Jubilee Book of Cricket (1897)

596   He is the Commander-in-Chief, in exclusive charge of the
       thinking, the strategy, the tactics; and more depends on him,
       his competency, his judgement, his temper, than on anyone
       else.

                                    'An Old Hand' (Ernest Prothero)
                                        A Book About Cricket (1924)

597   It is scarcely too much to say that almost as many games are
       lost, at all events in the lower-class cricket, through bad
       generalship as through inferior play.

                                                                  Ibid.

598   The ideal captain must possess a sound knowledge of the game,
       a cool judgement, tact, and, above everything else, enthusiasm
       − for enthusiasm is a quality which enriches life and gives it

zest, and the man who is enthusiastic about his XI and their doings will, unless his influence and authority are sapped by disloyalty and want of co-operation, soon inspire the same feelings of zeal for the common cause in his followers.

Sir Pelham Warner
The Book of Cricket (1911)

599   A Napoleon among cricket captains can do nothing if the rank and file are disloyal.

Ibid.

600   Cricket has become so scientific that the captain of today has to work hard.

Ibid.

601   The ideal captain is he whose personality can win the confidence and enthusiasm of his team, and whose knowledge of cricket and gift for seizing opportunity (where the average player often sees nothing) enable him to force victory or avoid defeat.

R S Young
Cricket on the Green (1947)

602   The sure sign of greatness is an ability to stand alone, to accept as inevitable that people are saying things behind your back which they would not dream of saying to your face.

Sir Neville Cardus
Good Days (1934)

603   The great captain is the captain who imposes his will on the game: some captains achieve this by dissecting the strengths and weaknesses of their opponents, others by sleight of hand, some simply by dint of commanding a powerful side; once in a blue moon a captain imposes his influence not just upon his opponents, but on a generation of cricketers by sheer force of personality.

James P Coldham
F S Jackson (1989)

604   The mental strain becomes greater for the untutored captain as
he begins to realise what he has to do and what is required
from him if he is to maintain his own reputation.

Brigadier M A Green
Sporting Campaigner (1956)

605   Then I panicked and, instead of trusting my side, I switched
myself into fielding positions where I imagined the catches were
likely to go. So I wasn't controlling the game anymore – just
being pushed along by the current of events.

J L Carr
A Season in Sinji (1967)

606   I don't attach much significance to the art of captaincy. I think
it's a bit of a mystique.

E J Smith
'Tiger' Smith (1981)

607   You're a great skipper if the side's doing well and a b.f. if it's
struggling.

Ibid.

608   These days a captain has to concentrate on making his players
believe that they have the ability to succeed.

Bob Willis
The Captain's Diary (1983)

609   A captain has to be seen to be keen and attentive at all times.
Any lapse transmits itself immediately to the players and the
result will be seen on the field.

Ibid.

610   Winning must be the ultimate of any captain, but not winning
at all costs.

Keith Andrew
The Skills of Cricket (1984)

611   A new element has crept into the duties of Test captains in
recent times, namely the need to dictate to players the balance
between doing their job and making money.

Bob Willis
The Captain's Diary (1984)

612 Captaincy is, of course, an individual thing. There are as many styles as there are captains. I admire some captains who never lose their tempers or blame their own players unfairly.

J M Brearley
Phoenix from the Ashes (1982)

613 He must be warm and open with players; but he must be prepared to keep some distance, to avoid showing undue personal preferences off the field.

Ibid.

614 He must be capable of firm autocratic decisions in a crisis; and of consulting his team wherever possible. He should intermingle optimism with realism.

Ibid.

615 An organism must have a central principle to make it efficient, and a captain ought to be this central principle to his side.

K S Ranjitsinhji
The Jubilee Book of Cricket (1897)

616 The captain creates the moral atmosphere of his side. If he is slack and indifferent, so are the other ten; if he is keen and enthusiastic, so are they. Unconsciously, the side as a whole assumes the captain's attitude towards cricket and towards a particular match.

Ibid.

617 I was never an advocate of advice from the ring and thought the captains should be left to themselves.

Lord Harris
A Few Short Runs (1921)

618 *Roger:* I'm the captain. It's me who controls whether we win or lose and I want to win, Mim, no point else. There's this very fine balance. It's all psychology. Which means tact and diplomacy.

Richard Harris
Outside Edge (1979)

619   Ideally, captaincy is a job which requires keen observation and a mind open to all possibilities, the capacity to choose between them, selecting the one which offers the best chances under the circumstances and then sticking to it until the conditions have changed, or it has been shown clearly that the notion will not do.

H E Dollery
Professional Captain (1952)

620   It is almost an axiom for the follower of cricket that no losing team ever had a good captain.

Ibid.

621   A professional captain should, I think, be careful that he is not involved in any 'incident'.

Ibid.

622   Pray God, no professional shall ever captain England. I love and admire them all but we have always had an amateur skipper and when the day comes when we shall have no more amateurs captaining England it will be a thousand pities.

Lord Hawke
Reply to Vote of Thanks, Yorkshire CCC AGM (1925)

623   Freedom of action is one of the good things which were lost when it was decided to do away with the amateur.

Trevor Bailey
Wickets, Catches and the Odd Run (1986)

624   I possessed a good knowledge of the game, but lacked calm judgement, while any ability I may have possessed in inspiring confidence in others was reduced because I personally had never required motivation.

Ibid.

625   I was probably too excitable at the time, because I was liable to become too emotionally involved.

Ibid.

626   The chief qualifications for a good captain are a sound knowledge of the game, a calm judgement and the ability to inspire others with confidence.

A G Steel
The Badminton Library — Cricket (1904)

627   One word sums up a successful cricket captain: versatile. He
needs the patience of a saint, the diplomacy of an ambassador,
the compassion of a social worker and the skin of a rhino.

Ray Illingworth
Captaincy (1980)

628   I firmly believe, however, that the extrovert will always have an
advantage over the introvert.

Ibid.

629   As a county captain, one seems to spend an inordinate amount
of time filling in forms of which no one takes the slightest
notice.

Ray Illingworth
Yorkshire and Back (1980)

630   Successful cricket teams are invariably well led, though it is
equally true that successful captains invariably have good
teams.

Christopher Martin-Jenkins
Cricket – A Way of Life (1984)

631   A cricket field is a lonely place for captains, especially when
two batsmen are in full flight, the bowlers are wilting and
catches have been dropped.

Ibid.

632   Decisiveness has always been an essential quality for captains in
a sport which demands much more from its leaders than any
other.

Ibid.

633   A captain cannot make a bad side into a good one, but a great
side can make an indifferent captain into a moderate one.

D R Jardine
Evening News (1933) reprinted in *An Ashes Anthology* (1989)

634   Cricket teams have often suffered from captains who have
arrived, done queer things, departed and been forgotten.

R C Robertson-Glasgow
Cricket Prints (1943)

635 It was not my custom to interfere with the private lives of the players, but I did like to keep them together off the field — as well as on — when away from home; apart from that small thing it is my belief that the captain's duties start in the dressing-room.

W S Surridge
In the Field in *The Boundary Book* (1962)

636 It is, I consider, the duty of a captain to consult the wishes of his team now and then, particularly when he is in command of such a heterogeneous collection of professions as I was.

A A Milne
The Day's Play (1910)

637 It is easier for a football manager to 'play God', to read the riot act to players, because he does not have to perform himself. Sales managers don't sell, foremen don't hump bricks. All cricket captains bat and field, and some bowl. We receive repeated intimations of our own fallibility.

J M Brearley
The Art of Captaincy (1985)

638 If you were to ask a representative of almost any profession — policemen, nurses, politicians, prostitutes, tailors, greengrocers, stockbrokers, bookmakers, etc — what were the essential qualities of their calling, they would almost certainly say honesty, integrity and a sense of humour. In a good village cricket captain these qualities would be utterly redundant.

Robert Holles
The Guide to Real Village Cricket (1983)

639 One of the major arts of captaincy is knowing when to change the bowling. All too often the average skipper is deficient in this important tactic.

Ibid.

640 Cricket has become so scientific that a captain of today has to work hard. Gone are the days when a captain could change the bowling by the clock or set the field in the same position for every batsman.

Sir Pelham Warner
Long Innings (1951)

641   Every manoeuvre must be tried in a desperate state of the game; but, above all things, be slow and steady, being also especially careful that your field do not become confused. Endeavour by every means in your power − such as, by changing the bowling, by little alterations in the field, or by any excuse you can invent, to delay the time, that the strikers may become cold and inactive. And when you get a turn in your favour, you may push on the game a little faster; but even then be not too flushed with success, but let your play be still cool, cautious, and steady.

John Nyren
The Young Cricketer's Tutor (1833)

642   I believe that in first-class cricket it is important for all captains to think more than some do about the crowd which has paid to watch them.

Sir Leonard Hutton
Just My Story (1956)

643   Cricket depends more almost than any game on the quality of leadership, and the difficulty today of happening on the right man where several probably are of similar seniority and background is one of its most pressing problems.

E W Swanton
Sort of a Cricket Person (1972)

644   Captaincy by committee on or off the field is lamentable.

A E Knight
The Complete Cricketer (1906)

645   I have always felt bitter about the treatment of professionals.

E M Wellings
Vintage Cricketers (1983)

646   The county cricketer of those days enjoyed less security and less physical comfort than his counterpart today, and to win the title, with the cash and kudos that went with it, meant relatively more to the players, not less, than in 1975.

E W Swanton (1975)
Reprinted in *As I Said at the Time* (1983)

647   Clearly the idea that the players were private servants of the county clubs was widely held.

> **Ric Sissons**
> *The Players* (1988)

648   Being selected for the county first XI and subsequent match performance determined whether a player lived well or struggled to survive.

> *Ibid.*

649   Throughout my career I encountered nobody on the county scene whom I actively disliked, and only three in international cricket, which really does say much for the game. I can think of no other group of people to which it could also apply.

> **Trevor Bailey**
> *Wickets, Catches and the Odd Run* (1986)

650   With the sun shining at Weston there was no shortage of amateurs who wanted to play. So the pros lost their places – and their match money.

> **Bill Andrews**
> *The Hand That Bowled Bradman* (1973)

651   And all the while your place would be in jeopardy because of the amateurs. No matter how talented or promising the pro, if an amateur were available, he'd play instead.

> **E J Smith**
> *'Tiger' Smith* (1981)

652   It has been truly said that a country gets the government it deserves. So does a cricket club, for it is governed by its committee, and the membership has the power and responsibility of electing any kind of committee it pleases.

> **R S Young**
> *Cricket on the Green* (1949)

653   Here, then, is the heart of the club; if it beats strongly it will put vigour into every activity of its life.

> *Ibid.*

654   The rank and file of a large general committee, meeting
       infrequently, are often reluctant to rebel against
       recommendations from their executive. This is particularly the
       case where a proposal comes before them which has not been
       widely ventilated in advance.

Gerald Pawle
R E S Wyatt (1985)

655   The amateur tradition in cricket had the same defects off the
       field as on.

Derek Birley
The Willow Wand (1979)

656   Polite and discreet dissent was as far as the professionals were
       prepared to go for many years.

Ibid.

657   Alcohol and the psychological blow, when retirement came, of
       descending into obscurity after having been a respected and
       well-known figure, were the undoing of many.

Christopher Martin-Jenkins
Cricket – A Way of Life (1984)

658   It is the greatest mistake in the world to give so much time to a
       game that when your playing days are coming to an end you
       having nothing to occupy you and no particular talent or ability
       for anything but games playing.

A W Carr
Cricket with the Lid Off (1935)

659   The trouble about playing first-class cricket regularly, year after
       year, is that it is impossible to follow any other occupation.

Ibid.

660   Selectors on accepting their office practically sign a self-denying
       ordinance, for they become the Aunt Sallies of everybody,
       because each individual thinks he can choose a better side off-
       hand than the combined selectors do after sitting for hours over
       the problem.

Sir Home Gordon
Background of Cricket (1939)

661 To the cricket public at large the task of the selectors was often regarded as something of a sinecure, providing a welcome pretext for the pleasant journeys round England to vet players of promise and meetings from time to time in the comfort of a West End club or luxury hotel in the provinces to compare notes.

Gerald Pawle
R E S Wyatt (1985)

662 Test selectors are rarely in the limelight, although the popular press often takes them to task for their inexcusable lack of foresight in ignoring some popular figure, or picking a player temporarily out of form.

Ibid.

663 The selection committee, like the Navy, is a 'silent service'.

Walter Hammond
Cricket's Secret History (1952)

664 Many a romantic leap to cricketing fame begins because of a quiet word spoken at a club or hotel to one of its members.

Ibid.

665 One criticism levelled at the selectors from many cricket pavilions has been that they are, in general, of an age when active contact with cricket's problems is behind them.

Ibid.

666 It is less what the present holders of TCCB office might do that causes concern as their successors in future generations.

E W Swanton
'Gubby' Allen (1985)

667 Although I was appointed captain of England in four of the five Tests that year I never really had a free hand. I was constantly being advised to do this or that.

A W Carr
Cricket with the Lid Off (1935)

668 In retrospect, it would appear that England's teams were selected without much trouble from an almost shoreless sea of great names, but it did not always appear so at the time.

James D Coldham
Lord Harris (1983)

669   I am old-fashioned enough to believe in the need for discipline in a cricket team, as in less serious pursuits.

H W Lee
Forty Years of English Cricket (1948)

670   Cricket sorely needs one reform – the hanging of a microphone over the middle of the pitch with loud speakers connected all round the ground; here would be an unfailing remedy for poor gates. Why shouldn't we hear our cricket as well as see it; share in these little asides that so frequently leave us guessing.

Bruce Harris
Jardine Justified (1933)

671   The post of secretary is of supreme importance. His duties comprise almost every activity, and any weakness or inefficiency on his part will expose itself sooner or later in some slackness in the life of the club.

R S Young
Cricket on the Green (1947)

672   When I get to my reserved parking spot (one of the few privileges of the county secretary) there is a member awaiting my arrival. He may be anxious to enquire after my health, or to pass some urgent message to me. But, more likely, he will want to complain.

Peter Edwards (1981)
Reprinted in *A Walk to the Wicket* (1984)

673   The county cricket secretary has to be a versatile person. He should be able to organise and administer, and he must ensure that the players are given as much consideration as possible. Also, his committee and the public must be nursed.

Brigadier M A Green
Sporting Campaigner (1956)

674   Umpiring is as difficult as batting or bowling.

Learie Constantine
The Young Cricketer's Companion (1964)

675   In earliest days umpires were inclined to be ignorant and social stresses often made impartiality difficult for them.

E W Swanton
Introduction to *The Men in White Coats* (1987)

676 The umpire at cricket is like the geyser in the bathroom; we cannot do without it, yet we notice it only when it is out of order.

Sir Neville Cardus
Good Days (1934)

677 That he was 'in' the batsman never doubted
Delighted he'd escaped the dreaded 'blob' –
When suddenly 'How's that?' was loudly shouted;
The umpire answered, 'Out! I *wins five bob!*'

W N Cobbold
A Village Cricket Match

678 It is an absolute impossibility to find an umpire who will not make mistakes at times.

A G Steel
The Badminton Library – Cricket (1904)

679 Umpires are almost as old as cricket but they have not had an easy ride.

Teresa McLean
The Men in White Coats (1987)

680 Umpires were just as likely to cause as to settle trouble.

Ibid.

681 Part policemen, part traffic-warden, they were doomed to unpopularity and went through half a century of trouble and grief.

Ibid.

682 In no department of the game has so little progress been made as in that which is summed up in the little word 'umpire'.

'Quid' (R A Fitzgerald)
Jerks in from Short Leg (1866)

683 The amateur captains, following tradition, were set above the umpires in the English system and in county cricket were in effect their employers.

Derek Birley
The Willow Wand (1979)

684   The humbler ranks of cricket left their umpires more room for personal and local interpretation of the laws, seasoned with local custom. Any robust village umpire would deplore servitude to the laws.

Teresa McLean
The Men in White Coats (1987)

685   It is probable, if the truth were known, that more county matches have been won by umpires than either batsmen or bowlers.

E V Lucas
One Day and Another (1909)

686   Given the tensions of having to make hairline decisions which could have a crucial bearing on matches involving a great deal of money and prestige, not to mention the livelihoods of individual players, it is hardly surprising that occasionally an umpire's judgement should fail him.

Christopher Martin-Jenkins
Cricket Characters (1987)

687   I learned more in my first year as an umpire than in all the previous 26 years of playing the game.

E J Smith
'Tiger' Smith (1981)

688   Concerted team appealing meant that a number of first-class umpires developed thick skins which stood them in good stead when it came to pronouncing unpopular decisions.

Teresa McLean
The Men in White Coats (1987)

689   Umpires are very peculiar individuals; once let it enter their heads that a bowler is trying to 'jockey' a decision out of them, up go their backs, and they suddenly become a mechanical toy that glibly answers every appeal with the two words 'Not out', and those only.

A G Steel
The Badminton Library – Cricket (1904)

690   *Bennett:* And cricket. If there's a junior umpiring, you appeal
loudly when you know the man's not out. You put
shoe polish on the ball.

Julian Mitchell
Another Country (1982)

691   *Major:* My God! It's got him on the chin.
Dickie: He's out! The umpire's got his hand up.
Twigg: You are our captain, Major. You must protest against
this − this shameful decision! The ball hit him on the
chin and he's given out leg before wicket.
Major: Oh, for God's sake shut up! He's been given out and
that's the end of it.

R C Sherriff
Badger's Green (1930)

692   *Miles:* LBW. That was a deliberate biased, petty and vindictive
piece of umpiring.

Alan Ayckbourn
A Cricket Match, Intimate Exchanges (1982)

693   If anyone were to ask us the question 'what class of useful men
receive most abuse and least thanks for their service?' we
should, without hesitation, reply, 'Cricket umpires'.

A G Steel
The Badminton Library − Cricket (1904)

694   Umpires train themselves to brood as little as possible, but
every umpire remembers his big mistakes.

Teresa McLean
The Men in White Coats (1987)

695   Tougher laws would only worsen the legal congestion of
modern cricket.

Ibid.

696   The umpire is the law of cricket personified, image of the noble
constitution of the best of games.

Sir Neville Cardus
Good Days (1934)

697   The umpire standing at Clay's end was Dai Davies, and it was
       quite fitting that these two stalwarts of the pre-war era should
       combine, in an amusing way, when the last man, Charlie Knott
       was dismissed. He was hit on the pads right in front of the
       wicket. Clay and the rest of the fielders made a rousing appeal,
       to which Davies said: 'That's out and we've won the
       Championship!'

Andrew Hignell
The History of Glamorgan CCC (1988)

698   English umpires, generally speaking, are better than Australians.

Sir Donald Bradman
Farewell to Cricket (1950)

699   The standard of umpiring throughout the world remained
       depressingly weak against this barrage of intimidation and any
       efforts at meting out justice were invariably met by histrionic
       self-righteousness.

Bob Willis and Patrick Murphy
Starting with Grace (1986)

700   The interpretation of unfair short-pitched fast bowling is
       inexact and umpires are too lax in their attitudes to the law.

Ibid.

701   For the game's decline ruling bodies must accept much blame.

E M Wellings
Vintage Cricketers (1983)

702   We worship democracy with its built-in compromise, but it
       must be admitted that cricket was much more settled when
       autocratic rulers, who were not given to compromise, abounded
       in the counties.

Ibid.

703   Umpires, particularly if they be obese and getting on in years,
       are somehow apt to be figures of fun.

William Pollock
Talking About Cricket (1941)

704   The umpire never need fear that sense of failure which comes at times to all cricketers: given good sight, good hearing, and the power of concentration, he should not make mistakes.

'**A Country Vicar**' (R L Hodgson)
The Happy Cricketer (1947)

705   Like politicians, their decisions rarely satisfy both parties.

Vic Marks
TCCB Guide to Better Cricket (1987)

706   Most umpires find LBW one of the easiest decisions, maybe because they cannot be proved conclusively right or wrong by action replay.

Ibid.

707   I must avoid that umpire, too.
One ball, I'm pretty sure,
That hits my bat before my leg
And he'll give me leg-before.

A M Robertson
The Cricket Match

708   Umpires sometimes take it upon themselves to impose good batsmanship upon their charges much as moral re-armers hope to impose decency on society.

Peter Roebuck
It Never Rains . . . (1984)

709   It is amazing to think that there should have been two such complete idiots standing so close to one another at a given moment.

C P Foley
Autumn Foliage (1935)

710   An umpire should be a man − they are, for the most part, old women; and he should have a thorough practical initiation into the mysteries of the game.

'**Quid**' (R A Fitzgerald)
Jerks in from Short Leg (1866)

711   They *must* make their hay while their sun shines. Age will soon
bowl them out; younger aspirants tread closely on their heels;
and all they have to look forward to, when the eye has lost its
keenness, the arm its muscle, and the system its nerve, is the
precarious existence of an umpire.

Ibid.

WICKETS
AND
WEAPONS

Strange fascination of a wooden bat!
Weird magic hidden in a leathern ball!

712   *Henry:* This thing here, which looks like a wooden club, is
        actually several pieces of particular wood cunningly put
        together in a certain way so that the whole thing is
        sprung, like a dance-floor. It's for hitting cricket balls
        with. If you get it right, the cricket ball will travel 200
        yards in four seconds, and all you've done is give it a
        knock like knocking the top off a bottle of stout, and it
        makes a noise like a trout taking a fly.

Tom Stoppard
The Real Thing (1982)

713   You may have paid your Income Tax
       And bought the wife a hat;
       Adjusted each domestic bill;
       Reduced anxiety to nil.
       Quite likely, too, you've made your will;
       But – have you oiled your bat?

F A J Godfrey
The Vital Question in *The Bradfield Chronicle*

714   Give me a willow wand and I
       With hide and cork and twine
       From century to century
       Will gambol round my shrine!

Rudyard Kipling
Cricket Humour in *Verses on Games* (1898)

715   Willow the King is a monarch grand;
       Three in a row his courtiers stand;
       Every day, when the sun shines bright,
       The doors of his palace are painted white,
       And all the company bow their backs
       To the King with his collar of cobbler's wax.

E E Bowen
Harrow School Song No 7 (1876)

716   Strange fascination of a wooden bat!
       Weird magic hidden in a leathern ball!

D L A Jephson
A Few Overs (1913)

717   Wherever men are English and the flag's unfurled,
You will there find cricket
And the willow and the wicket,
And there's not a game to lick it
In the whole wide world!

R St J Ainslie
Cricket Song (1896)

718   I'm a cricket bat, a cricket bat
Is what I'm proud to be.
My father was Alf Gover
And my mum a willow tree.

Cardew Robinson
The Cricket Bat in *The Boundary Book − Second Innings*
(1986)

719   His bat hangs in the dark pavilion lone,
Unheeded through each dreary winter day,
But in the summer one may chance to stay
A moment when the eager throng has flown,
And seeing it, may think of him who's gone;
And half recalling the dim past, may say:
' 'Twas with that bat that here I saw him play −
How well! − a hundred times.'

E P V Christian
Hic Iacet in *At the Sign of the Wicket* (1894)

720   Who would think that a little bit of leather, and two pieces of
wood, had such a delightful and delighting power!

Mary Russell Mitford
Our Village (1824 − 32)

721   The most remarkable instance of a hybrid animal is the cricket
bat.

J A Hammerton, editor
Mr Punch's Book of Sports (1906)

722   The British 'Sphere of Influence' − the cricket ball.

Ibid.

723   How we love to clutch it with a sort of romantic exultation and toss it to one another! For it is upon *it* that the story of the day will turn.

Stacy Aumonier
The Match in *Miss Bracegirdle and Other Stories* (1923)

724   It is the scarlet symbol of our well-ordered adventure, as yet untouched and virginal, and yet strangely pregnant of unaccomplished actions.

Ibid.

725   Don't swear at the ball, in fact, don't swear at all,
Do not rave at the state of the wicket.

Harry and Leo Trevor
Cricket in *Country House Ditties* (1898)

726   When old familiar sounds I know
Float up – the heavy roller's sound
Clanking across the county ground –
The busy whirr no spring forgets
Of cricket balls in cricket nets.

Herbert Farjeon
The Call of May – *W G Loquitor* in *Cricket Bag* (1946)

727   An instant, poised in air,
A rosy light delayed;
Dropt, and a willow blade
Flashed like a golden share,
Flashed – and a throbbing star
Waned to a spark, afar!

George Francis Wilson
A Sixer in *Cricket Poems* (1905)

728   Since cricket was invented when science was in its cradle, and plastics were unknown, our actual cricket balls are most unworkmanlike objects, and so by an absolute fluke open the door for a myriad bowling ingenuities.

Christopher Sly
How To Bowl Them Out (1948)

729   A Bat, a Ball, two wickets and a Field –
What *words* are these that can such magic yield!

George Francis Wilson
A Century of Fours, LIII in *Cricket Poems* (1905)

730 We use a rose-bush for a wicket,
But at least it makes for brighter cricket!

A A Thomson
Almost Cricket in *Out of Town* (1935)

731 My only sweetheart is a bag –
A faithful girl of dark brown leather,
Who's travelled many a mile with me
In half a hundred sorts of weather.

Norman Gale
The Forerunners

732 A cricket ball is a shining miracle of leather, cork and twine,
but when dispatched by a bat swung by a Bonner or a Dexter it
becomes a missile of enormous power and speed.

Gerald Brodribb
Hit For Six (1960)

733 The allure of a cricket ball flying through space is too simple
for words, inexplicable but equally irrefutable, making the great
gulf between the level-tempered pleasure of the expert and the
involuntary and unrestrained joy of the mere human being.

Hon T C F Prittie
Mainly Middlesex (1947)

734 'Ay, there's a deal o' human natur' in a treble-seam, sir; it
don't like getting knocked about any more than we do.'

E W Hornung
A Bowler's Innings in *Old Offenders and a Few Scores* (1923)

735 When Lord Frederic Beauclerk first saw leggings he never
imagined they would be allowed in a match – 'so unfair to the
bowler'.

Rev James Pycroft
Oxford Memories (1886)

736   Little boxes in the sports shop
      Little boxes are for cricketers
      Little boxes made of plastic
      Little boxes, all the same.
      There's a white one and a pink one
      And one made of aluminium
      For the tender bits of cricketers
      And it still hurts quite a lot.

                                        Fred Wedlock
                                             Boxes

737   The batsman had an abdominal protector between his legs, but
      strapped *outside* his trousers.
          ''E's got 'is bollock box showin'!' howled Sinker, doubled up.
      The colonel reeled and held Mott's shoulder for support.

                                        Dennis Castle
                                  Run out the Raj (1975)

738   He is the only clerk beside Jalim Singh to possess such a cricket
      appendage . . . naturally he is proud to reveal it.

                                              Ibid.

739   'The box is not then,' said Mookerjee, 'worn like a Scottish
      sporran . . . ?'

                                              Ibid.

740   Ever since his project of going to London was abandoned, Ned
      had audibly consoled himself with meditations on cricket.

                                        Charles Morgan
                                 Portrait in a Mirror (1929)

741   A tearing of brown paper and a snapping string revealed
      concentric circles, green and pink, with a green button in their
      midst!

                                              Ibid.

742   In the course of the morning he tried on brown cricket shoes.
      He inspected eight shirts and eight pairs of trousers, showing
      his wife how successfully moths had, during the winter, been
      kept from them.

                                              Ibid.

743   The ball soared. The sun gilded it. The swallows observed it.

Ibid.

744   The ball reached its zenith, vanished in a glittering haze,
      emerged, descended, became a cannon-shot.

Ibid.

745   When leg-pads were first introduced they were worn *under* the
      trousers, as though the hardy cricketer was ashamed of his
      cowardice in wearing them.

Sir Spencer Ponsonby-Fane
Preface to *Lord's and the MCC* (1914)

746   *Toby:* You see, it's a widely held belief among these primitive
      cricketers that providing you can hang the right
      combination of numbers on these nails here, you can
      keep the enemy out there and afraid to come in and take
      over your hut.

Alan Ayckbourn
A Cricket Match, Intimate Exchanges (1982)

747   O yes, I love that bit of greensward there!
      For on it I forget my worldly care
      When two opposing parties, with a will,
      Join to display and test each other's skill.

William Bange
Fair Grove in *The Happy Village and Other Poems* (1848)

748   A cricket ground is no place to separate the good from the bad.
      It's us and them.

Caryl Phillips
Playing Away (1989)

749   In every school there is a sacred place
      More holy than the chapel. Ours was yours:
      I mean, of course, the first-eleven pitch.
      Here in the welcome break from morning work,
      The heavier boys, of milk and biscuits full,

Sat on the roller while we others pushed
Its weighty cargo slowly up and down.
We searched the grass for weeds, caressed the turf,
Lay on our stomachs squinting down its length
To see that all was absolutely smooth.

Sir John Betjeman
Cricket Master

750   Somewhere it has been written that the cultured man of money
can best use it by keeping a string quartet and commissioning a
first-class yacht. To this should be added the creation of a
pretty well-appointed cricket ground.

Tom Watson
Ibis Cricket, 1870 – 1949 (1950)

751   Amidst thy bowlers the tyrant's hand is seen,
The rude pavilions sadden all thy green;
One selfish pastime grasps the whole domain,
And half a faction swallows up the plain;
Adown thy glades, all sanctified to cricket,
The hollow-sounding bat now guards the wicket:

Lewis Carroll
The Deserted Parks (1867)

752   County cricket had traditionally been watched by three men and
a dog, but now, it was said, even the dogs had had enough.

Gerry Cotter
The Ashes Captains (1989)

753   Country-house cricket reminds one of days spent in eating
apples under an old tree, reading the *Earthly Paradise* of
William Morris.

A E Knight
The Complete Cricketer (1906)

754   It seems to me not only futile, but absolutely mad, to expect
lads to enjoy their cricket on a pitch from which balls are
flying about.

G A Faulkner
Cricket: Can It Be Taught? (1926)

755   Hard-wicket cricket is like chess − there is no element of chance in it, and only those who perfect themselves survive.

W J Edrich
Cricket Heritage (1948)

756   The day was warm and the wicket still so beautiful that the bowlers might well have watered it with tears.

Sir Neville Cardus
Good Days (1934)

757   One of his less successful experiences, as such, was when he spent one exhausting and unprofitable morning against Hobbs and Sandham at The Oval. On his way up the pavilion steps at lunchtime he paused to make a brief confidential report: 'It's like bowling to God on concrete.'

Ben Travers of R C Robertson-Glasgow
A-sitting on a Gate (1978)

758   The wicket is still being blamed. It has been libelled, slandered and blasphemed, accused in turn of being a fickle and vicious Jezebel and a slumbering, lifeless old dog.

David Foot
Cricket's Unholy Trinity (1985)

759   My spirits are low and my scores are not high,
But day after day, we've soaked turf and grey sky,
And I shan't have a chance till the wickets get dry,
Oh willow, wet-willow, wet willow!!!

J A Hammerton, editor
Mr Punch's Book of Sports (1906)

760   For every plumb wicket there is a more responsive one round the corner.

John Arlott
George Cox Benefit Booklet (1951) reprinted in *Arlott on Cricket* (1984)

761   More than one village side in north Hampshire was reputed to
spend the winter coaxing plantains or bents to grow about the
length spot of their main fast bowler.

John Arlott
The Haig Village Cricket Annual (1977)

762   I understand that the square is sprayed with a green preparation
in the month of April, but when we were there we found that
the sun had bleached it completely, and the light from this
white area was too strong for comfort.

Sir Henry Levenson-Gower
Off and on the Field (1953)

763   To prepare a good, fair wicket which will be fast in fine
weather: therein should lie the groundsman's art. And he must
be led, gently but forcibly, to an appreciation of the fact.

E W Swanton (1938)
Reprinted in *As I Said at the Time* (1983)

764   *Toby:* His father spent 20 years of his life making that one of
the best strips in the county. Hepplewick's destroyed it in
three days. It now has all the fine texture of the inside of
a rowing boat.

Alan Ayckbourn
A Cricket Match, Intimate Exchanges (1982)

765   *Toby:* Do you know, he marked out the first team cricket pitch
and made it a yard short. A whole yard. Bloody ball
whistling round their ears. Nearly killed the openers.

Alan Ayckbourn
A Gardener in Love, Intimate Exchanges (1982)

766   Long ago, nothing was covered, which meant that after rain the
spin bowler had a feast: not only was the wet pitch his to
exploit, but there was no competition from the faster bowlers,
since they couldn't stand up on the slippery turf.

David Frith
The Slow Men (1984)

767   That is not to say that the old infatuee does not nurse his
grievances. First and foremost, to his way of thinking, the
administration of the game has, of recent years, been based on
a cardinal fallacy, namely that the greatest attraction cricket has
to offer is easy run-getting under conditions favouring the
same. This has not only resulted in the discouragement of the
spin bowler; it goes deeper than that. It means that the younger
generation never, or very seldom, has the chance of seeing the
most enthralling spectacle cricket has to offer, the absorbing,
anguishing fascination of watching great batsmanship on a
ruined wicket.

Ben Travers
The Infatuee in *The Cricketer's Bedside Book* (1966)

768   Such words as 'dangerous', when applied to wickets, imply a
normal man not of unique eyesight nor acrobatic celerity. They
have no meaning to the genius who cuts from his eyebrows.

A E Knight
The Complete Cricketer (1906)

769   Fertilisers have made outfields, which once used to become
deserts in dry weather, into permanent green pastures, thus
keeping the shine on the ball and making life sweeter for seam
and swing bowlers, and much less so for the spinners.

Christopher Martin-Jenkins
Cricket − A Way of Life (1984)

770   The pitch for the last Test at Kanpur was completely dead and
the 22 players merely went through the motions for the
statutory five days.

Peter Wynne-Thomas
The Complete History of Cricket Tours (1989)

771   All the matches were played on jute matting rather than coir,
which meant that life was easier for the batsmen.

Ibid.

772   The wicket reminded me of a middle-aged gentleman's head of
hair, when the middle-aged gentleman, to conceal the baldness
of his crown, applies a pair of wet brushes to some favourite
long locks and brushes them across the top of his head.

Frederic Gale
Bell's Life, 4 July, 1868 reprinted in *Lord's, 1787−1945* (1946)

773   It was clear that, after an apathetic youth and a hearty middle-age, the wicket was finishing its life in a mood of arthritic crotchetyness.

Denzil Batchelor
The Match I Remember (1950)

774   In the eighties, so rough were the wickets, even at headquarters, that winning the toss almost decided the result.

Sir Home Gordon
Background to Cricket (1939)

775   On a treacherous wicket all the batsman can do is to watch the ball with all his might and let the bat follow the eye.

K S Ranjitsinhji
The Jubilee Book of Cricket (1897)

776   It is needless to dwell here on the orgy of over-prepared wickets.

Sir Home Gordon
Background to Cricket (1939)

777   The groundsmen are the only uncontrolled dominant factor. Their influence is as much felt as that of the permanent civil servants or members of the Cabinet.

Ibid.

778   The rough land at the pithead or behind the factory was enough pitch, and the game flourished in the soot of the new tall chimneys.

John Arlott
Cricket (1953)

779   I asked Jim Laker whether he felt we should bat or insert our opponents. He went out to have a look and was missing for a very long time. I asked Jim where he had been and he said that he had been looking for the pitch and was still not sure whether he had found it.

Trevor Bailey
Wickets, Catches and the Odd Run (1986)

780   The wicket that day was a piece of galvanised iron propped up with a stick and two stones. Whatever drawbacks it may have had in appearance, it nevertheless had its advantages. In such games, there was never any doubt when a batsman was bowled.

Undine Giuseppe
Sir Frank Worrell (1969)

PEOPLE
AND
PLACES

But international cricket matches are not only cricket matches. They tend as well to excite and promote a kindly feeling between the nations which take part in them.

781   Cricket grounds are like seaside resorts. They come alive in the
       summer with the sunshine and the deck chairs and the bunting
       and the bands, but like seaside resorts I find them oddly
       appealing out of season when they are empty and windswept.

Tim Heald
The Character of Cricket (1986)

782   Lord's − I'd never played there, but what cricketer who ever
       breathed wouldn't jump at the chance?

George Macdonald Fraser
Flashman's Lady (1977)

783   If I close my eyes I can see Lord's as it was then, and I know
       that when the memories of bed and battle have lost their
       colours and faded to misty grey, that at least will be as bright
       as ever.

Ibid.

784   It caught my youthful imagination, and from that day I have
       loved every stick and stone of Lord's, and as the years pass I
       love it more and more. Even now, after so many years, I feel
       something of a thrill as I walk down St John's Wood Road,
       and my heart, maybe, beats a shade faster as I enter the
       ground.

Sir Pelham Warner
Long Innings (1951)

785   History haunts Lord's. The past gives it a special atmosphere.
       It is the home of cricket − the place which has seen the growth
       and development of England's national game. No other ground
       can claim that heritage.

'A Country Vicar' (R L Hodgson)
Cricket Memories (1930)

786   I always feel as though I am stepping into history.

J M Kilburn
Overthrows (1975)

787   Lord's has something no other cricket ground quite possesses.
       There is an enveloping atmosphere of tradition and peace about
       the place.

J H Fingleton
The Ashes Crown the Year (1954)

788   It is said that the hardest-headed Australian has a quasi-
       religious respect for Lord's, and feels an extra urge to succeed
       there.

John Arlott
An Eye for Cricket (1979)

789   It is the best of all games, and I thank my stars that my early
       footsteps took me to Lord's, for, with all respect to the other
       great grounds, to me it is the best place in the world to play.

Denis Compton
Foreword to *Denis Compton: A Cricket Sketch* (1948)

790   Lord's – it's a magical world to me, the 'open sesame' to a
       lifetime of happiness.

Margaret Hughes
All on a Summer's Day (1953)

791   Lord's cricket, cricket straight out of Debrett.

Sir Neville Cardus
The Summer Game (1929)

792   Lord's! What tender recollections
       Does the famous name suggest!

Harry Graham
Lord's in *Adam's Apples* (1930)

793   Lord's is the Mecca of all cricketers and a pilgrimage thereto
       when they are in London provides a hallowed memory that
       must sustain the faithful in many a barren outpost.

E W Swanton
Denis Compton: A Cricket Sketch (1948)

794   Marylebone is the *Omphalos,* the *Delos* of cricket.

Andrew Lang
The Badminton Library – Cricket (1904)

795   Lord's is the Valhalla of cricketers; countless days, famous for
       great deeds, have come to a resting place at Lord's.

Sir Neville Cardus
The Summer Game (1929)

796   Lord's must be a bit like Heaven. There are many mansions in it. It caters for all tastes, classes, colours, ages, points of view, degrees of skill, levels of knowledge.

T C Dodds
Hit Hard and Enjoy It (1976)

797   Lord's is a world apart. It is a community, an establishment, a living monument, an atmosphere.

Ibid.

798   For your good cricketer the ends of the earth have come to a resting-point at Lord's, and wherever he may be at the fall of a summer's day his face should turn religiously towards Lord's.

Sir Neville Cardus
Days in the Sun (1924)

799   'Lord's' – that festival which the War had driven from the field – raised its light and dark blue flags for the second time, displaying almost every feature of a glorious past.

John Galsworthy
To Let in *The Forsyte Saga* (1922)

800   It was like a huge green salver bounded by a white rail. Behind the white rail the people were crowding onto the benches or onto the tiers of the tall white stands.

Ernest Raymond
To the Wood No More (1954)

801   He directed Susannah's eyes to the cropped and shining turf and said that it was the most sacred grass in the world and had been so for 100 years; he turned her eyes towards the crimson and ochre pavilion and assured her that, as the headquarters of cricket all over the world, it was to this most noble religion as the Vatican to the Universal Church.

Ibid.

802   Lord's lay deserted. A great airy structure of excitement, like the invisible and evanescent palace it was, had collapsed into silence, and there was nothing left but the green veldt and the white railings and the empty white stands.

Ibid.

803   There never was a better way of watching cricket than at Lord's.

Eric Parker
Playing Fields (1922)

804   In the evening light Lord's is a place of infinite peace and quiet friendly charm.

Hon T C F Prittie
Mainly Middlesex (1947)

805   Is there a more beautiful view in *England,* I wonder, than the view you get from one of the stands in *Lord's* on a fine day? There is the green and white of the field − as restful as a daisy field in *Chaucer.* But there is also at Lord's a noble and multiple idleness that takes the imagination, not to *Chaucer,* but to the *South Seas.*

Robert Lynd
The Sporting Life and Other Trifles (1922)

806   I can never walk about Lord's without some such reflections as may be supposed in Rip Van Winkle after his sleep of 20 years: the present and the past come in such vivid contrast before my mind.

Rev James Pycroft
Oxford Memories (1886)

807   Yes, that ring at Lord's shows me every gradation in the scale of life − the once active now stiff and heavy, the youthful grey, the leaders of great XIs passing unrecognised and alone.

Ibid.

808   They cannot rise superior to the background of office and Stock Exchange growing year by year cheaper and shoddier. But Lord's, on the day of the Eton and Harrow match, touches their souls with a magic of its own and they wear their traditions with grace and confidence.

Dudley Carew
England Over (1927)

809   Little did I know that I was in for a surprise
A thunderbolt which shook me to the core
For there in the pavilion and before my very eyes
A man without a coat walked through the door
There he stood without a coat, no coat in Lord's Pavilion
He couldn't have been English, he was probably Brazilian.

Peter Christie
Lord's Pavilion

810   I once recommended an Australian visitor to go to Lord's and immediately he referred to it as the place where you take your hat off as you go in! No gesture could be more appropriate, for Lord's does command respect and in return it has to offer the most delightful prospect cricketers can know.

J M Kilburn
In Search of Cricket (1937)

811   We did not speak of course; we had not been introduced. Suddenly two workmen entered the Long Room in green aprons and carrying a bag. They took down the bust of W G Grace, put it into the bag, and departed with it. The noble lord at my side watched their every movement; then he turned to me. 'Did you see, sir?' he asked. I told him I had seen. 'That means war,' he said.

Sir Neville Cardus
Autobiography (1947)

812   There are many human beings, a trifle vague as to its origins and functions, who believe that it is firmly associated with our peerage rather than plain Mr Lord.

John Marshall
Lord's (1969)

813   From its inception, the Marylebone Club has been known for its sportsmanlike spirit, and to this day there is no ground whereon the game is more strictly played, none where the sporting element is more predominant, none whose habitués are more truly lovers of the game, or more free from partisan spirit.

A E Knight
The Complete Cricketer (1906)

814   Lord's is the only cricket ground where I had the experience of being able to have a hot plunge-bath after a hard day in the field. With a steward in attendance, the service was typical of that of an ocean liner, where bathroom attendants are always on hand.

Daniel Reese
Was It All Cricket? (1948)

815   Outside my own country I have played Test cricket in Australia, New Zealand, India, Pakistan, the West Indies and South Africa. Nowhere, not on any ground, have I experienced the thrill, the inward thump that occurs before the first ball is bowled on the first morning of a Test at Lord's between England and Australia.

Ted Dexter and Clifford Makins
Testkill (1976)

816   But as he passed down the steps of the pavilion, where men were talking gloomily and the atmosphere had a sense of panic, and emerged from the gate onto the turf, he became aware of only one thing − that his side was in straits, and that side was England.

Beatrice Fry and C B Fry
A Mother's Son (1907)

817   All England was absorbed in one question at that moment. Politics, business, even taxation had passed from people's minds. The one engrossing subject was the fifth Test match.

Sir Arthur Conan Doyle
The Story of Spedegue's Dropper in *The Maracot Deep and Other Stories* (1929)

818   Cricket was to have a world headquarters, for it had come of age − a sturdy watchman of code and character, of cant and nonsense, of manners and empire.

Christopher Lee
From the Sea End (1989)

819   No human institution is perfect, but it would, in my opinion, be impossible to find nicer men than those who constitute the government of Lord's.

Sir Pelham Warner
Lord's 1787−1945 (1946)

820   This is, of course, something much more considerable than a place where cricket of the highest calibre is played and watched. It is nothing less than an international institution as well, because of its history and because of what it represents.

> **Geoffrey Moorhouse**
> *Lord's* (1983)

821   Traditionalists should perhaps take comfort from the fact that this ground has in the past seen some alien manifestations, admitted purely for entertainment, which have had no startling effect on cricket itself, the game having continued to potter on its own evolutionary way, its patterns changing gradually so that nothing jarred too much.

> *Ibid.*

822   It has usually kept pace with the times (ah, but the times are becoming disordered now) and often it has led the way in matters which demonstrably helped the cricket-watcher without disturbing the tradition of cricket itself.

> *Ibid.*

823   Within Lord's lurked fear of the changing order, suspicion of professionalism in cricket, immutable allegiance to the amateur and the old hierarchy.

> **Tony Lewis**
> *Double Century* (1987)

824   By the time he [Jack Bailey] took over from Billy Griffith, the job had changed. Certainly he had become the manager of a large estate in north-west London, but he had little authority in cricket matters.

> *Ibid.*

825   Especially in matters of discipline, MCC is still portrayed as establishment, reactionary, everlastingly public school and Oxbridge, and a power-centre for those who live in London and the home counties.

> *Ibid.*

826   . . . enunciated the grace in slightly unparsonic tones, which
       implied that he was not only Rector of Rotherden but also a
       full member of MCC.

                                              Siegfried Sassoon
                              Memoirs of a Fox Hunting Man (1928)

827   One fact seems sure;
       That, while the Church approves, Lord's will endure.

                                              Siegfried Sassoon
                       The Blues at Lord's in *Satirical Poems* (1926)

828   Cricket, lovely cricket,
       At Lord's where I saw it;
       Cricket, lovely cricket,
       At Lord's where I saw it;
       Yardley tried his best
       But Goddard won the Test.
       They gave the crowd plenty fun;
       Second Test and West Indies won.
       With those two little pals of mine
       Ramadhin and Valentine.

                                                  Lord Beginner
                                             Victory Calypso (1950)

829   It's remarkable how great a grip cricket's got over so many
       parts of the Commonwealth, and not merely on people of
       European stock. I can't help thinking that there's some
       connection between a liking for democratic ideals and the game
       of cricket.

                                                    R E S Wyatt
                                        Three Straight Sticks (1951)

830   But international cricket matches are not only cricket matches.
       They tend as well to excite and promote a kindly feeling
       between the nations which take part in them.

                                                 Bishop Weldon
                         Introduction to *How We Recovered the Ashes* (1904)

831   Test cricket is not a light-hearted business, especially that
       between England and Australia.

                                              Sir Donald Bradman
                                          Farewell to Cricket (1950)

832 Unconsciously, and perhaps without any suspicion on their part that such is the case, the Australians have seriously and perceptibly aggravated the symptoms of a commercial spirit in cricket.

James Lillywhite
Cricket Annual (1983)

833 Australians will not tolerate class distinction in sport.

J H Fingleton
Cricket Crisis (1946)

834 In any case, the only sane view of the amateur or professional question is the Australian one – 'Call us what you something well like but we want half the gate.'

J C Clay
Glamorgan CCC Year Book (1938)

835 I admire the Australians' approach to the game; they have the utmost ability for producing that little extra, or instilling into the opposition an inferiority complex that can have, and has had, a crushing effect. Australians have no inhibitions.

Sir Leonard Hutton
Just My Story (1956)

836 The Australians came down like a wolf on the fold,
The Marylebone Club for a trifle were bowled,
Our Grace before dinner was very soon done,
And Grace after dinner did not get a run.

Punch (1878)

837 It was pointed out that a great cricket match like England and Australia was one of the severest tests to which human nerves could be put.

Beatrice Fry and C B Fry
A Mother's Son (1907)

838 The taste of blood stimulated the Australians; they are terrible when they feel a grip on their prey, almost carnivorous.

Sir Neville Cardus
Good Days (1934)

839   There can be no doubt of the central significance of cricket in creating an Australian identity.

> **Derek Birley**
> *The Willow Wand* (1979)

840   I know plenty of professionals whom I would delight to have as guests in my own home, but I am afraid I cannot say the same thing about most of the Australians whom I have met.

> **A W Carr**
> *Cricket with the Lid Off* (1935)

841   Here in England we do not know the bitterness which these games engender, because when we are beaten we take it calmly and, after a couple of groans, forget it. In Australia, however, another spirit prevails. There, Test matches are not carried out as games, but with all the ferocity of war.

> **Lord Castlerosse**
> *Sunday Express* quoted in *Cricket with the Lid Off* (1935)

842   When the Australians come to England people here tend to lose their sense of proportion about the game.

> **Margaret Hughes**
> *All on a Summer's Day* (1953)

843
In Affectionate Remembrance
of
ENGLISH CRICKET
which died at The Oval
on
29th August, 1882,
Deeply lamented by a large circle of sorrowing
friends and acquaintances.
RIP
NB – The body will be cremated and the
ashes taken to Australia.

> *Sporting Times* (September, 1882)

844   Gone for ever are the days when we and the Australians thought that we were the only people who could really play cricket!

> **Sir Pelham Warner**
> *Long Innings* (1951)

845   Cricket is a stalwart Goliath striding across the British Empire.
MCC is his devoted wife, only anxious to further his best
interests. Cricket and MCC will never be divorced. Therefore
they are a very old-fashioned couple.

Sir Home Gordon
Background of Cricket (1939)

846   What do they know of cricket who only cricket know? West
Indians crowding to Tests bring with them the whole past
history and future hopes of the islands.

C L R James
Beyond a Boundary (1963)

847   Cricket was – and remains – the only expression of unity in
the West Indies.

Gerald Howat
Cricket's Second Golden Age (1989)

848   The West Indies were unable to put a federation together and
at times have difficulty in giving life and meaning to their
regional economic institutions. At those times the typical West
Indian becomes tiresomely insular. But when the cricket team is
playing the whole area surges together into a great regional
hubbub of excitement and involvement.

Michael Manley
A History of West Indies Cricket (1988)

849   Greatness is finally revealed not so much in success as in the
response to failure.

Ibid.

850   The erratic quality of West Indian cricket is surely true to racial
type. At one moment these players are eager, confident, and
quite masterful; then as circumstances go against them you can
see them losing heart.

Sir Neville Cardus
Cricket (1930)

851   West Indian cricket has arrived at maturity because of two
factors: the rise in the financial position of the coloured middle
class and the high fees paid to players by the English leagues.

C L R James
Beyond a Boundary (1963)

852   As clearly as if it was written across the sky, their players said:
Here, on the cricket field if nowhere else, all men in the island
are equal, and we are the best men in the island. They had
sting without the venom.

Ibid.

853   West Indies' batsmanship, like that of the Australians, is
always, for our good, mocking the utilitarian and the
humdrum.

E W Swanton (1950)
Reprinted in *As I Said at the Time* (1983)

854   I had been brought up to believe that colour was immaterial:
what mattered and counted was the character and cricketing
ability of the player concerned. I soon discovered that this
outlook was far too naive for the West Indies, where degrees of
colour were considered so vital.

Trevor Bailey
Wickets, Catches and the Odd Run (1986)

855   The various tensions inherent in West Indian society have
shown themselves in cricket.

Derek Birley
The Willow Wand (1979)

856   The first West Indian cricketers caught the imagination of the
cricketing publics of England and Australia because they
brought to the game a free-moving, free-stroking, lithe
athleticism which was all their own.

Michael Manley
A History of West Indies Cricket (1988)

857   Not having death as its objective, cricket provides room for
humour, even when the contest is most keenly joined. Here
then was the most perfect sport for the West Indian personality.

Ibid.

858   Perhaps one day the people of the Caribbean will do more than
admire their cricket team; they might even seek to emulate its
success by discovering for themselves the unity which is its
secret.

Ibid.

859 The beginnings of cricket in the Pacific were not invariably attended by the spirit of brotherhood that this noble sport was once believed to inspire.

Sir Arthur Grimble
A Pattern of Islands (1952)

860 But I like best of all the dictum of an old man of the Sun clan, who once said to me: 'We old men take joy in watching the kirikiti of our grandsons, because it is fighting between factions which makes the fighters love each other.

Ibid.

861 It is urged, in general, that for Europeans cricket is not a game best suited to the conditions of modern India. It is, to begin with, too long a game. You want, in India, a game which is both violent and short.

Cecil Headlam
Ten Thousand Miles Through India and Burma (1903)

862 I fear it is only the violent enthusiast who can, generally speaking, enjoy cricket in India.

Philip Trevor
The Lighter Side of Cricket (1901)

863 India has an infinite capacity to absorb punishment. Everything blows over in the end.

Edward Docker
History of Indian Cricket (1976)

864 It has been noticed before in Indian cricket that there is a tendency for those who might be expected to give a lead at certain vital times to slip away into a kind of nether world where they cannot be held accountable. They render themselves *incommunicado.*

Ibid.

865 Cricket is such a potent force in the country that a cricket Test provides an irresistible marketing occasion, particularly a Calcutta Test.

Mihir Bose
A Maidan View (1986)

866 It goes against the grain of our country, against our tradition to play sports the way they do in the west.

Ashwini Kumar
Quoted in *A Maidan View* (1986)

867 It is in the matter of patience that I think the Indian will never be equal to the Englishman.

Lord Harris
A Few Short Runs (1921)

868 If everything else in India but cricket were to be destroyed, we would get no sense of the country just from the practice of cricket. We would have some sense of the spectacle of Indian cricket, and some idea of cricket fever that could grip India during Test matches, but nothing more.

Mihir Bose
A Maidan View (1986)

869 The real, astonishing thing about Indian cricket is not its popularity but the nature of that popularity. It is not cricket so much, but Test cricket that is popular.

Ibid.

870 For Indian cricket is more than a game; it is an essential part of modern industrial India. Ruled by an elite anxious to convince the world that it heads the tenth largest industrial power, one capable of producing atom bombs and exporting food grains and machinery, cricket is an essential status symbol.

Ibid.

871 In the social set-up of modern urban India, cricket is one sure way of obtaining acceptance.

Ibid.

872 The Pakistani looked as though he could reproduce one of the eternal innings with which the subcontinent has sprinkled the record books.

A C H Smith
Extra Cover (1981)

873   Pakistan is the only country in the world where cricket is played between commercial organisations and not between regions, zones, cities or states. The result, I'm afraid, is abysmal.

Imran Khan
Imran (1983)

874   Pakistan, as a country based on two cricket-playing cities, has made a remarkable amount out of little.

Scyld Berry
A Cricket Odyssey (1988)

875   For those who are able to play it, cricket offers a fantasy of possibilities – a fantasy that has begun to acquire a new solidity with the granting of Test status. Cricket is not played in Sri Lanka because of any post-imperial nostalgia.

Shiva Naipaul
Sri Lanka (1983) reprinted in *The Observer on Cricket* (1987)

876   'Spiritual' may sound over-sentimental to a modern generation, but I stand by it, as everyone else will who has witnessed the moral teaching-force of the game in malarial jungle, or sandy desolation, or the uttermost islands of the sea.

Sir Arthur Grimble
A Pattern of Islands (1952)

877   But the players from abroad often give the impression of wanting to learn more and enjoy the game more than their English counterparts.

Alan Ross
West Indian Summer (1988)

878   Everywhere they went, Hawke's team brought a breath of English air with them; that was the magic of the first tours, now quite lost with the advent of television and the jet.

James P Coldham
F S Jackson (1989)

879   In England an unpredictable climate would appear to have made both officials and players more ready to accept a drawn game than is the case, say, in Australia.

Allen Synge
Cricket: The Men and the Matches that Changed the Game
(1988)

880   Lord's and The Oval truly mean
Zenith of hard-won fame,
But it was just a village green
Mothered and made the game.

G D Martineau
The Village Pitch in *The Way of the South Wind* (1925)

881   There was high feasting held on Broad-Halfpenny during the
solemnity of one of our grand matches. Oh! it was a heart-
stirring sight to witness the multitude forming a complete and
dense circle round the noble green. Half the county would be
present, and all their hearts with us − Little Hambledon, pitted
against all England was a proud thought for the Hampshire
men. Defeat was glory in such a struggle − victory, indeed,
made us only 'a little lower than angels'.

John Nyren
The Young Cricketer's Tutor (1833)

882   They were choice fellows, staunch and thorough-going. No
thought of treachery ever seemed to have entered their heads.
The modern politics of trickery and 'crossing' were (so far as
my own experience and judgement of their actions extended) as
yet 'a sealed book' to the Hambledonians; what they did, they
did for love and honour of victory; and when one (who shall be
nameless) sold the birthright of his good name for a mess of
potage, he paid dearly for his bargain.

Ibid.

883   Their cricket then seemed a mixture of the convivial, epic and
idyllic.

John Arlott (1974)
Introduction to *The Young Cricketer's Tutor* (1833)

884   Bleak Broad-Halfpenny is now ploughed land; the slopes of
Windmill Down glow yellow with corn, its summit given over to
weed and copse.

A E Knight
The Complete Cricketer (1906)

885   Troy has fallen and Thebes is a ruin. The pride of Athens is
decayed and Rome is crumbling to the dust. The philosophy of
Bacon is wearing out and the victories of Marlborough have

been overshadowed by greater laurels. All is vanity but cricket; all is sinking into oblivion but you. Greatest of all XIs, fare ye well!

Rev John Mitford
Gentleman's Magazine (1833)

886   To my dying day, I shall remember gratefully these afternoons in Kent, afternoons full of the air and peaceful sunshine of England.

Sir Neville Cardus
The Summer Game (1929)

887   Canterbury in its festival finery is the nearest thing to a pre-war tableau from one of those summers when the sun always shone and the ball scorched just wide of cover point's right hand to the ropes.

David Foot
The Guardian reprinted in *Waiting for Cheltenham* (1989)

888   The notable pride verging on insularity associated with Kent was even then strengthening.

David Frith
The Golden Age of Cricket 1890 – 1914 (1978)

889   There are few scenes in cricket to compare with the Cheltenham Festival on a sunny day. It embodies the very best traditions of the game.

Grahame Parker
Gloucestershire Road (1983)

890   In some ways Cheltenham is a glorious anachronism and one would be forgiven for wondering how it has survived into the world of late-20th century county cricket.

George Plumptre
Homes of Cricket (1988)

891   Even now the idea of Eastbourne being reported to Lord's seems akin to the questioning of a Mother Superior's chastity.

David Lacey (1982)
Reprinted in *The Guardian Book of Cricket* (1986)

892   Spectators who did not fall asleep before tea at the Saffrons yesterday were undoubtedly kept awake by the town hall clock which, for much of the time, was striking more frequently than the Sussex batsmen.

> **Doug Ibbotson**
> *Daily Telegraph* (1988) reprinted in *Waiting for Cheltenham* (1989)

893   Unless the play becomes completely stagnant, however, most cricket provides pleasure at the Saffrons.

> **N W D Yardley and J M Kilburn**
> *Homes of Sport − Cricket* (1952)

894   Hove is a paradoxical ground. To the casual visitor it is nothing to look at, with blocks of flats at both ends and an appalling heterogeneous clutter along one side which is the pavilion and attendant quarters. And yet people love it.

> **George Plumptre**
> *Homes of Cricket* (1988)

895   Whatever the strict details of geography may insist Sussex cricket is essentially cricket-by-the-sea. Spiritually this means cricket of holiday atmosphere.

> **N W D Yardley and J M Kilburn**
> *Homes of Sport − Cricket* (1952)

896   When you play cricket on a ground that is steeped in history and you spend over a decade there, of course it becomes a favourite place for you, but Hove was more than that for me. I always felt that it gave people value for money.

> **Ted Dexter**
> *A Walk to the Wicket* (1984)

897   The club reminds me of a close friend of mine who was invariably kind, hospitable and very generous. He should have been able to live in style for the whole of his days and indeed might have become 'filthy, stinking, rich', but unfortunately he lacked business acumen. It seems to me that this same basic weakness has hampered Sussex.

> **Trevor Bailey**
> *Wickets, Catches and the Odd Run* (1986)

898   Slowly, Essex have assumed the characteristics of their captain
– a cussed effectiveness and determination to prevail.

Peter Roebuck
Men of Essex (1984) reprinted in *The Guardian Book of Cricket*
(1986)

899   A major reason why Essex cricket was so much fun was having
eight different centres. It was rather like being on tour.

Trevor Bailey
County Champions (1982)

900   Although they have played the game seriously and keenly, there
has always been an abundance of laughter and humour. This is
something to be proud of, because cricket which is not enjoyed
is not worth playing.

Ibid.

901   If Chelmsford will never be a picturesque ground it is certainly
one which caters for the modern game, with an air of confident
prosperity.

George Plumptre
Homes of Cricket (1988)

902   Even on the most dismal of days, when unrelenting rain has
ensured that there will be no play well before the umpires are
due to walk out, Worcester does much to live up to its
reputation. There is no question that the cathedral is the most
impressive backdrop to any county ground and, even if it is not
England's finest, it still provides the most celebrated of cricket
pictures.

Ibid.

903   Certainly there can be few more picturesque grounds,
surmounted as it is by the cathedral on the banks of the River
Severn to the east, and to the west the distant Malvern Hills.

Rev Hugh Pickles
County Champions (1982)

904   The charm is not in the ground, it is in the setting. Many times
I have seen people stand at the secretary's office window, and
gaze across the green grass to the greying stones of the
cathedral mellowed a hazy pink by the setting sun, and say,
'What a lovely ground this is.'

Brigadier M A Green
Sporting Campaigner (1956)

905   There was no play because of rain. He came out of the box and
saw low smoke scudding over the ground from a high modern
electric works on the road side and said, 'Heavens, this must be
Huddersfield!'

Ibid.

906   I don't like Worcester. They say it's a pretty ground but I find
the atmosphere unsympathetic.

Peter Roebuck
It Never Rains . . . (1984)

907   Worcestershire is the queen of all our counties; with a
personality of her own and a fascination it is almost impossible
to resist. Who is there among the followers of cricket who have
visited that glorious ground by the banks of the Severn and
failed to be completely captivated by its charm.

Roy Genders
Worcestershire (1952)

908   The history of Somerset county cricket has for ever been tinged
with poetry: romantic notions and intense feelings and
metaphors that mischievously leap from horror to hilarity.

David Foot
Sunshine, Sixes and Cider (1986)

909   It is the most companionable and pervasive of county grounds.

John Arlott
Somerset CCC Year Book (1982)

910   There was something about Somerset cricket which transcended
such a trifling matter as defeat.

Tim Heald
County Champions (1982)

911 The tented fields of the south were all very lovely in their way, but they had not the same tense atmosphere of the northern grounds which were devoted to cricket and to cricket only.

Dudley Carew
The Son of Grief (1936)

912 There is a myth that when Yorkshire cricket prospers, peace breaks out in the county of the broad acres; but history shows that Yorkshire cricket has to be at peace with itself for it to prosper.

James P Coldham
F S Jackson (1989)

913 Cricket in Yorkshire is not as it is elsewhere. It never has been. The club has always been a battleground between warring factions. Civil war is never far below the surface of Yorkshire cricket.

Ibid.

914 Yorkshiremen are not quick to understand, and even less prompt to forgive, what they rightly or wrongly see as defection.

John Hampshire
Family Argument (1983)

915 The Yorkshireman's intolerance of an enemy's prowess is simply the measure of the Yorkshireman's pride in his county's genius for cricket.

Sir Neville Cardus
Days in the Sun (1924)

916 The Yorkshire hardness, attributed and cultivated, is a defensive quality expressed in the form of aggressiveness. It is resistance to challenge, unwillingness to bend the knee or doff the cap.

J M Kilburn
Overthrows (1975)

917 It is, significantly, almost impossible to find people in Yorkshire taking part in any sport or pastime unless there is something tangible at the end of the road.

John Callaghan
Yorkshire's Pride (1984)

918   It is, of course, easy to mistake this straightforward approach as conceit or arrogance, but invariably a Yorkshireman's opinion is based on logic and false modesty never brought success on or off the field.

Ibid.

919   Yorkshire has been the backbone of English cricket, because its inhabitants enjoy a special affinity with bat and ball – a relationship which has stood the test of time – and the summer sport will always have first claim on the county's affections.

Ibid.

920   Standing against the background of cricket, Yorkshire can see themselves important among the undistinguished and pre-eminent among the eminent.

J M Kilburn
A History of Yorkshire Cricket (1970)

921   Yorkshire cricket is particular. It dominates the characters rather than the characters dominating the county.

Peter Thomas
Yorkshire Cricketers 1839 – 1939 (1973)

922   No county ever commanded a deeper loyalty from its players, or from its officials, or its supporters.

J M Kilburn
History of Yorkshire County Cricket 1924 – 1949 (1950)

923   Yorkshire cricket is a private enterprise with a public responsibility.

Ibid.

924   The ways of selection committees are sufficiently difficult and mysterious, but a solid phalanx of five Yorkshiremen at least ensures a gratifying sufficiency of skilled determination.

D R Jardine
England v Australia, The Oval (1938) reprinted in *The Observer on Cricket* (1987)

925   This is the age of cruisers in the sky,
Of speed gone mad, of funerals in a hurry.
See to it then, that none of us shall die
Of tedium, Yorkshire, Lancashire and Surrey!

Norman Gale
A Point of View

926   They say the weather in Manchester is not as bad as it is made
out, but I must confess that I have always considered a raincoat
an essential piece of equipment for Mancunian cricket watchers.

Trevor Bailey
Wickets, Catches and the Odd Run (1986)

927   The ground I like best is Old Trafford, though the vicissitudes
of the Manchester climate have rendered several pilgrimages
null and void so far as play is concerned.

Sir Home Gordon
Background of Cricket (1939)

928   To thousands of Londoners who live north of the river there is
only one transpontive resort, and that is The Oval.

E V Lucas
London Revisited (1926)

929   Being nearer the fashionable areas, and having the Eton and
Harrow match and the Oxford and Cambridge match, those
favoured opportunities for the modiste, Lord's has not only a
cricket public but a butterfly public. And this means not only
awnings and comfort but a more careful standard of male attire
too. The Oval crowd is far liker a football crowd. It is almost
wholly composed of men, and men who must earn their living,
and their keenness is not only far more articulate than any at
Lord's, but greater too.

Ibid.

930   At The Oval, men seem to have rushed away with some zest
from their City offices. At Lord's there is a *dilettante* look, as
of men whose work, if ever, has yet to come.

Rev James Pycroft
Oxford Memories (1886)

931   Though wayward Time be changeful as Man's will,
       We have the game, we have The Oval still,
       And still the Gas-Works mark the Gas-Works End
       And still our sun shines and the rains descend.

John Masefield
Eighty-five to Win in *The Bluebells and Other Verse* (1961)

932   The Oval is green,
       Flats, gnats,
       And white-clothed figures move with grace,
       The bat and the ball!
       These above all,
       And the thrill, and the air of this place!

Leslie Frewin
*On Seeing Sir Learie Constantine Return (Temporarily) from
Diplomacy to Cricket* (1963)

933   But whatever change has taken place in cricket − or in me − I
       swear there is no change in the jolly Oval crowd. It is, as it has
       always been, the liveliest, most intense, most good-humoured
       mob that ever shouted itself hoarse at cricket. It is as different
       from the Lord's crowd as a country fair is from Church
       Congress. At Lord's we take our cricket as solemnly as if we
       were at a prayer-meeting.

A G Gardiner
Many Furrows (1924)

934   A fine day at The Oval makes us all akin, and a pleasant sight
       it is to see the vast assembly, every man with his eyes riveted on
       the wicket, every man able to appreciate the most delicate
       strokes in the game, and anxious to applaud friend or
       adversary.

Andrew Lang
Introduction to *Kings of Cricket* (1893)

935   Rightly has it been called 'The People's Ground', this pool of
       green in the desert of south-east London brick and asphalt.
       Here is no atmosphere of leisured privilege, no Establishment,
       no aping of Lord's. For this is a ground confident of its own
       individuality, of its own setting, of its own honourable history.

Aylwin Sampson
Grounds of Appeal (1981)

936   No other ground has so captured the affection of its neighbours.

Ibid.

937   There is an inescapable feeling of tradition about Trent Bridge which those who care for cricket cannot escape.

John Arlott
Nottinghamshire CCC Annual (1970)

938   My heart is always at Trent Bridge and the mind is often flooded with memories of those splendid characters who paraded their talents for our lasting wonder and delight.

Michael Jayston
County Champions (1982)

939   Looking back on those days at Trent Bridge, I realise now that most of the time defeat or victory was unimportant.

Ibid.

940   You get the feel of cricket the moment you pass through the friendly portals of Trent Bridge.

E W Swanton (1981)
Reprinted in *As I Said at the Time* (1983)

941   Though modern development has led to encroachment, enough of the old scene remains to suggest a smooth field beside a river-bank.

Ibid.

942   It is a friendly ground, possessing that endearing mix of old and new.

Aylwin Sampson
Grounds of Appeal (1981)

943   While the names of all other counties conjure up images of dales and downs and country pubs and softly-rustling fields of wheat, the name of Middlesex produces in the mind's eye only an endless vista of Tescos.

Barry Norman
County Champions (1982)

944   Nobody could possibly feel any loyalty or sentimental attachment to Middlesex the geographical area, were it not for the fact that it does have Lord's and Lord's houses the Middlesex cricket team.

Ibid.

945   Players of other clubs, as they look at Warwickshire, are often envious, and they are primarily envious of the good-natured spirit which seems to pervade our club.

A C Smith
The Story of Warwickshire Cricket (1974)

946   Of all English cricket grounds Edgbaston is the only one which gives the immediate feeling of being a stadium, an amphitheatre.

George Plumptre
Homes of Cricket (1988)

947   While facilities are its forte, shortage of character is its main weakness. Perhaps it is a reflection on the city of Birmingham of which Edgbaston is one of the more prosperous suburbs.

Ibid.

948   There are not many people you can find to extol the virtues of the county ground at Wantage Road, Northampton, or even, for that matter, of the history of Northamptonshire CCC.

Ibid.

949   For the majority of their lives, both ground and county club have struggled for recognition and praise.

Ibid.

950   It is doubtful if even the most partisan supporter of Northamptonshire would assert that the county ground at Wantage Road was beautiful.

Aylwin Sampson
Grounds of Appeal (1981)

951   It is a setting of dull brick terraces of houses, a workaday ground with a no nonsense air about it.

Ibid.

952 It has become customary to arrange a game on the school ground at Wellingborough. This is a pleasant experience for both Northamptonshire and their visitors, making a complete contrast to the workaday setting in which county cricket is usually played and reminding the players that the game is a recreation as well as a business.

N W D Yardley and J M Kilburn
Homes of Sport − Cricket (1952)

953 There is no doubt that Derbyshire has been one of the least fashionable of cricketing counties; maybe the grounds have put visitors off.

Ted Moult
County Champions (1982)

954 The County Ground is undoubtedly the most bleak in England, unpopular with the Aussies and as recently stated in the *Guardian* 'not entirely unconvincing as an opening set for *Macbeth*'.

Ibid.

955 Cricket in its garden setting of Queen's Park, Chesterfield, remains sharp in the memory.

John Arlott
Mike Hendrick's Testimonial Brochure (1980)

956 It remains one of the most companionable − and most beautiful − cricket grounds in the world.

Ibid.

957 The Welsh crowd, who have supported Glamorgan in large numbers since the War, are enthusiastic and voluble. They are rapidly acquiring a sound cricket knowledge and are capable of a fair appraisement of both sides.

Wilfred Wooller
Cricket in the Counties (1950)

958 Glamorgan were humorous and happy, a fine side at a Saturday night party, a fighting outfit on the field in a tight spot.

Tony Lewis
Playing Days (1985)

959   To have appeared, even on one occasion only, for Surrey or
       Hampshire or whoever, by whatever curious mistake of fortune
       at however remote a time, invests a man with a *cachet* that
       must make him for the rest of his life, however dishonourable
       or unrewarding, the envy of those of lesser attainment or
       fortune.

                                                      Ronald Mason
                                        Sing All a Green Willow (1967)

960   Cricketers are found almost everywhere that the English
       language is spoken; as well as in Yorkshire and Lancashire.
       They are not of course found in America − which explains a
       lot!

                                                    Cardew Robinson
                            What is a Cricketer? in *The Boundary Book* (1962)

961   Why am I standing in this comic pose,
       Hemmed in by men that I should like to maim?
       I might be lying in a punt with Rose −
       I can't imagine why I play this game.

                                                    Sir A P Herbert
                                Ninth Wicket in *A Punch Anthology* (1932)

962   The sun came out after tea and I went and sat on the roller. I
       was more in touch with the players there, and not just a distant
       spectator.

                                                       Nico Craven
                                           Tea for Twenty-two (1983)

963   Sometime, when I'm older
       perchance my mind will range
       over days when I was a cricketer
       unaware of time's colder ways.

                                                         John Snow
                      Sometime, when I'm older in *Moments and Thoughts* (1973)

964   In spite of playing so much cricket I was never quite good
       enough to get a blue.

                                                     Brian Johnston
                                         It's Been a Lot of Fun (1974)

965   The lower school naturally looked on with interest at this rivalry between the two head forms, the result of which, as might have been expected, was the reverse of beneficial for the discipline of the school generally.

Talbot Baines Reed
The Fifth Form at St Dominic's (1887)

966   For a moment he stood aghast, contemplating the ruin of his wicket; then, with a gesture of despair, turned and ran for the pavilion.

Edward Bucknell
Linden Lea (1925)

967   He had never been popular even with the crowd, who had little patience with a man who, with a century to his credit, continued to play the bowling with the caution of a man striving to break his duck after a series of batting failures.

Graham White
Batsman's Holiday in *Cricket on Saturday* (1947)

968   He has never succeeded in applying the right stroke to the right ball, and now, in the autumn of his career, it is doubtful if he ever will.

Graham White
Simpson and Some Others in *Cricket on Saturday* (1947)

969   A genial and charming game makes a natural appeal to many genial and charming people.

Graham White
Cricket and Cant in *Cricket on Saturday* (1947)

970   I was never much of a cricketer, though I enjoyed it at prep school. That was a lovely ground: thatched pavilion and the Quantocks in the background.

Tim Heald
The Character of Cricket (1986)

971   Winning mattered too much, laughing on the field of play would have been a beatable offence if anyone had even contemplated it.

Ibid.

972 I opened the innings and was bowled first ball. The humiliation was too much and I hung up my boots for good.

Ibid.

973 As I traipsed about the Kingdom from cricket match to cricket match I became increasingly aware that there are few better places to be on a summer's day; that the natives are friendly and the beer well kept.

Ibid.

974 I had not reached the stage when I could admire a cricketer simply for his skill, if he was on the wrong side.

Alan Gibson
Growing Up with Cricket (1985)

975 Altogether the second XI was the one for me. For one thing the players were almost entirely our own, the same men as I saw spraying apple-trees or gaining inn parlour doors or fixing taps; among whom even the clerk from the railway station, which was a little out of the way from the village street, was something of a guest.

Edmund Blunden
Cricket Country (1944)

976 Some boys of course did not enjoy cricket, and we wondered at them, and thought them unsocial.

Ibid.

977 That they wore moustaches and lived and loved like passionate humanity did not seem to matter compared with the arithmetical progression of their averages.

Compton Mackenzie
Sinister Street (1913)

978 So deeply and happily had the cricket absorbed him that it was not until midnight that he remembered he must sooner or later go back to France.

John Masters
The Ravi Lancers (1972)

THE MASTERS

There remains a handful of men who through sheer genius and physical prowess have cast a longer shadow across the game than any number of legislators.

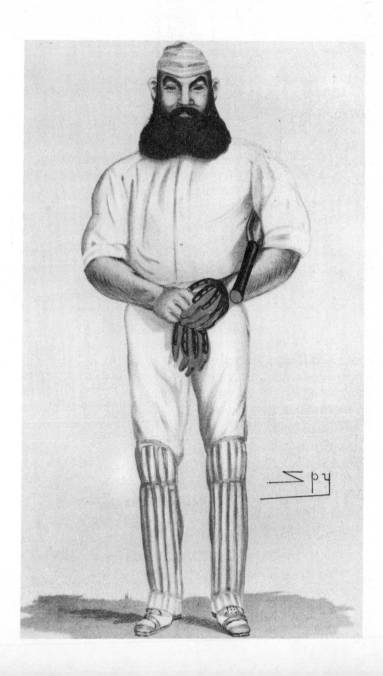

979   Heroes in fact die with one's youth. They are pinned like butterflies to the setting board of early memories − the time when skies were always blue, the sun shone, and the air was filled with the sounds and scents of grass being cut.

Alan Ross
Cricket Heroes (1959)

980   There remains a handful of men who through sheer genius and physical prowess have cast a longer shadow across the game than any number of legislators.

Allen Synge
Cricket: The Men and the Matches that Changed the Game
(1988)

Abdul Qadir
981   Abdul Qadir's great contribution to cricket may be to force the world's selectors to review their policy of massive investment in pace and defensive off-spin.

Ibid.

982   He has kept the art of back-of-the-hand spin alive against the odds and one can only pray that he has inspired a generation of imitators.

Christopher Martin-Jenkins
Cricket Characters (1987)

983   Abdul Qadir thus bore the responsibility of holding a life in his hands, for true leg-spin, delivered from a compact, even cocky, approach and with all the mystique of a dozen different wrist-angles allied to strength of finger and pinpoint length, really belonged to another age.

David Frith
The Slow Men (1984)

984   Wrist spin contains mysticism which appeals to the little magician from Pakistan.

Trevor Bailey
The Spinners' Web (1988)

985   He has come to regard spin bowling as almost a religion, which he worships and to which he has devoted much of his life.

Ibid.

986   Watching him bowl has been one of the great pleasures of my life.

> **Khadim Hussain Baloch**
> *Imran's Summer of Fulfilment* (1988)

Abel, R
987   Who that ever saw it could forget that curious little figure, surmounted by a somewhat faded and shrunken chocolate cap, the slow half-waddling gait that marked its progress to the wicket, and then the mastery of technique that could reduce all but the very greatest bowlers to frustration.

> **H S Altham**
> *A History of Cricket, Volume One* (1926)

988   You do not try to teach a boy to bat like Abel as you teach him to bat like Hayward. Robert Abel was an unconscious artist, and he still remains an enigma.

> **Philip Trevor**
> *Cricket and Cricketers* (1921)

989   He was the 'little wonder' of his time; and we still wonder at our recollections of him.

> *Ibid.*

990   Of Abel, after his second season, it was said that he had been of 'little use except in the field'. But for the wise continuance of the experiment of playing him regularly the most consistent batsman of late years would have been lost to the county.

> **E B V Christian**
> *Surrey Cricket* (1902)

Allen, G O
991   Perfectionists are not always easy people to live with, and Gubby has always been a perfectionist, whether in the Committee Room at Lord's, or on the golf course, re-writing the MCC Coaching Book, tending his car or his roses, ordering his dinner, or even describing in close anatomical detail his latest strain or his last hip operation.

> **E W Swanton**
> *'Gubby' Allen* (1985)

992   It is inevitable that so strong a personality, having held so
       many positions of authority from boyhood to old age, will have
       aroused dislike in some, perhaps a reluctant tolerance in others.

Ibid.

993   Allen was a very fine cricketer, better at playing than at
       administration.

E M Wellings
A History of County Cricket: Middlesex (1972)

994   Allen had one of the most perfect actions imaginable. He was
       not a big man, but that beautifully geared run-up and delivery
       enabled him to bowl in the express class.

Ibid.

Ames, L E G
995   He was a grand master of two crafts, and was once, I seem to
       recall, called an 'idle devil' because he didn't take up bowling!

Ted Dexter
From Bradman to Boycott (1981)

996   There have been more spectacular keepers, but few more
       reliable.

R L Arrowsmith
A History of County Cricket: Kent (1971)

997   A beautiful field anywhere, he must be ranked with the world's
       great all-rounders.

Ibid.

998   Batsman-wicket-keeper or wicket-keeper-batsman, there has
       never been another like him in the annals of cricket.

G D Martineau
The Valiant Stumper (1957)

999   His success as an administrator was based on respect. He
       received it from all sides — committee members, players,
       members, fans. He was respected because he knew the game so
       well, because he analysed in a simple, direct manner and
       because he had the greatest assets of any leader — strict
       impartiality.

Dudley Moore
The History of Kent CCC (1988)

Armstrong, W

1000   In his ascendancy he was respected, if not always beloved, at Headquarters, being a determined and somewhat dictatorial man.

Diana Rait Kerr and I A R Peebles
Lord's 1946 – 1970 (1971)

1001   He wanted his own way and he got it, seeming to care less than most for the diplomatic niceties. Above his great shoulders watchful eyes glinted out of a square-set uncompromising face, which to casual eyes looked cruel.

Ronald Mason
Warwick Armstrong's Australians (1971)

1002   Armstrong's circus provided rare entertainment, its ring master provoked much abuse.

Kenneth Gregory
In Celebration of Cricket (1978)

1003   He achieved a memorable record, and his name and fame are still bogeys to frighten babies with.

Ronald Mason
Sing All a Green Willow (1967)

1004   It is excellent to have a giant's strength, but it is tyrannous to use it like a giant; we have it on Shakespeare's authority, and we must charitably argue in Armstrong's favour that he had not recently read *Measure for Measure.*

Ibid.

1005   The respect he commanded from his players because of his long service, the manner in which he fought to improve his players' conditions, and his success over humdrum administrators have combined to make Armstrong a brilliant captain.

Jack Pollard
Australian Cricket (1982)

Bailey, T E

1006   Trevor always showed infinite capacity for rising to an occasion and he was never perturbed by spectators who might sometimes not appreciate his worth when he took a long time over his runs.

Sir Leonard Hutton
Just My Story (1956)

1007   His courage was tremendous, his concentration intense, and the Australians good-humouredly admitted that he had been an infuriating opponent to bowl at.

Rex Alston
Over to Rex Alston (1953)

1008   Bailey awoke from an apparent coma to strike a boundary.

P G Wodehouse
Dulwich College Magazine

1009   Watching Bailey, Test match in and Test match out, one had begun to wonder whether, as a batsman, he is ever out of form.

Keith Miller and R S Whitington
Gods or Flanelled Fools? (1954)

1010   Bailey, of course, watches the ball in a way that, had they emulated it, would have made many more talented strokemakers than him into champions.

Ibid.

1011   That yeoman of the singles.

Ibid.

Barnes, S F

1012   On the field Barnes radiated belligerency. Like all the best bowling craftsmen he hated batsmen and believed that every ball delivered should be their last.

Bernard Hollowood
Cricket on the Brain (1970)

1013   Barnes scythed through batsmen because he believed in the divine right of Barnes.

Ibid.

1014   Art, resolution, stamina, he commanded them all. Well might a man who saw him in his prime have found himself saying, 'Here was a Caesar, when comes such another?'

H S Altham
Barclays World of Cricket (1980)

1015   In my humble opinion he is, on all wickets, the finest bowler England has ever possessed.

Sir Pelham Warner
The Book of Cricket (1911)

1016   Many astute judges of the game have gone on record as saying that, on all wickets, Barnes was the greatest bowler the game has ever known.

Leslie Duckworth
S F Barnes – Master Bowler (1967)

1017   After that it was a case of the boa constrictor and the rabbits, the only matter of interest being how long he would take to dispose of them.

C L R James
Nelson v Rawtenstall (1932) reprinted in *The Guardian Book of Cricket* (1986)

Barnett, C J
1018   He is a rebel against stale custom. He is like the office boy who kicks the wastepaper-basket against the head clerk's shins, gives notice a second before he receives it, and runs out to slide on the pavement.

R C Robertson-Glasgow
Cricket Prints (1943)

1019   His batting, like his outlook on life, is strong, free, yet controlled. There is a gusto about it.

Ibid.

1020   He was no ordinary opening batsman watching the balls go by.

Grahame Parker
Gloucestershire Road (1981)

1021   To the very end with his no nonsense batting he continued to thrill crowds everywhere.

Ibid.

Barrington, K F
1022   He was the players' man both spiritual and temporal.

Frank Keating
Ken Barrington (1981) reprinted in *The Guardian Book of Cricket* (1986)

1023   He was more than a run-accumulator who set records: he was a character, a genial, engaging man whose personality endeared him to cricketers and cricket-lovers all over the world.

Brian Scovell
Ken Barrington (1982)

1024   He was a great fighter. No one fought harder than he did when he was batting.

W S Surridge
Ken Barrington (1982)

1025   Ken was not only a great cricketer but an honest-to-goodness, upright man who always acted honourably in his all too short life.

Alec Bedser
Twin Ambitions (1986)

Bates, W E
1026   He brought with him a toughness gained from the hard school of Yorkshire leagues, a quality which many of the impetuous Welsh amateurs lacked.

Andrew Hignell
The History of Glamorgan CCC (1988)

1027   He was known as 'The Marquis' because of his sartorial elegance and he was once described as being 'not the greatest cricketer Yorkshire ever produced, but easily the most elegantly dressed!'

Ibid.

Beauclerk, Lord Frederick

1028 Even among all the hagiography that exists about cricketers, an unqualified eulogy of Beauclerk has never been seen, and that is significant. But he was a fine cricketer.

Rowland Bowen
Cricket, A History of its Growth and Development (1970)

Bedi, B S

1029 Bishen Bedi was much more than just another great bowler. He was above all an artist, who brought to his chosen craft an expertise and a beauty which was timeless, indeed he would have fitted perfectly into the 'Golden Age' when the best left armers were, first and foremost, slow bowlers, not merely spinners.

Trevor Bailey
The Spinners' Web (1988)

1030 In the sixties and seventies Bishen served as a constant reminder of how beautiful cricket at the very highest level can be.

Ibid.

1031 Bedi cherished the art of slow bowling. So much so that he refused to sell out for the one-day county game.

David Frith
The Slow Men (1984)

1032 None has been more admired for the purity and beauty of his bowling action.

Pat Murphy
The Spinner's Turn (1982)

1033 He will be remembered for the beauty of his bowling, his Corinthian attitude to the game and for the days when spectators would rush to that prosaic ground at Northampton if the home side was in the field.

Ibid.

1034 When Bishen Bedi bowled, every day seemed bathed in sunshine.

Ibid.

Bedser, A V

1035   All through his career, in days of triumph or frustration,
Bedser was manifestly a bowler of quality. He never neglected
the basics which proclaim that a straight good-length bowler is
a good bowler.

J M Kilburn
Overthrows (1975)

1036   Bedser was a thinking bowler, who knew how he achieved his
effects.

E M Wellings
Vintage Cricketers (1983)

1037   A genial giant with a striking similarity to Maurice Tate in the
snappy movement of the ball off the pitch.

David Frith
The Fast Men (1975)

1038   'Big Al' was unquestionably the greatest bowler of his type
since the War. I would classify him with Maurice Tate and only
just behind Sydney Barnes.

Trevor Bailey
Wickets, Catches and the Odd Run (1986)

Beldham, W 'Silver Billy'

1039   It was a study for Phidias to see Beldham rise to strike; the
grandeur of the attitude, the settled composure of the look, the
piercing lightning of the eye, the rapid glance of the bat, were
electrical. Men's hearts throbbed within them, their cheeks
turned pale and red. Michael Angelo should have painted him.

Rev John Mitford
The Gentleman's Magazine (1833)

Benaud, R

1040   He played his cricket with a boundless enthusiasm that could
not fail to rub off on his players.

Gerry Cotter
The Ashes Captains (1989)

1041   Benaud has always had the will to challenge the bowler. In fact,
he has both as batsman and captain, waged unceasing war
against stodge.

A G Moyes
Benaud (1962)

1042   There haven't been better captains.

> **Phil Edmonds**
> *100 Greatest Bowlers* (1989)

1043   The nearest thing we are ever going to get to the perfect cricket captain. He matched boyish enthusiasm with ceaseless concentration, calculated attack and non-stop encouragement.

> **Ray Illingworth**
> *Captaincy* (1980)

1044   His instinctively aggressive approach to cricket and his skill in the neglected chores of public relations revitalised Test cricket wherever his team played.

> **Jack Pollard**
> *Australian Cricket* (1982)

Berry, L G
1045   He is one who gives an enabling strength to those prepared to fail around him rather than an arresting figure to those who compile the averages.

> **R C Robertson-Glasgow**
> *More Cricket Prints* (1948)

Blacknam, J M
1046   An original Australian hero comparable with Phar Lap, Les Darcy and Boy Charlton.

> **Jack Pollard**
> *Australian Cricket* (1982)

1047   He stood up to the stumps and eliminated the need for a long-stop with his safe hands.

> *Ibid.*

1048   During the whole of his first-class career he was peerless as a wicket-keeper. One could not help admiring him as he stood behind the stumps at a critical period of a game. With eyes keen as a hawk, and regardless of knocks, he would take the fastest bowling with marvellous dexterity, and woe betide the batsman who even so much as lifted the heel of his back foot as he played forward and missed the ball.

> **George Giffen**
> *With Bat and Ball* (1898)

Blythe, C
1049   The very look on his face, the long, sensitive fingers, the
       dancing approach, the long last stride, the elastic back sweep of
       the arm before delivery, with the right hand thrown up in
       perfect balance against it, and the final flick of the left hand as
       it came over − all these spoke of a highly sensitive and nervous
       instrument, beautifully co-ordinated, directed by a subtle mind,
       and inspired by a natural love for its art.

H S Altham
A History of Cricket, Volume One (1926)

1050   A great student of bowling theory, he was the most artistic of
       bowlers and made full use of his gifts.

R L Arrowsmith
A History of County Cricket: Kent (1971)

Border, A R
1051   You can see by his walk to the wicket, like a terrier out for a
       walk in a neighbourhood bristling with bigger dogs, that he is
       ready for a fight and not afraid of his ability to look after
       himself.

Christopher Martin-Jenkins
Cricket Characters (1987)

1052   Leadership has not come naturally to him. It has made him a
       sterner, more anxious character than the brilliant, carefree
       player of his early days.

Ibid.

1053   He plays still with a basic simplicity − even purity − of stroke
       and method.

John Arlott
100 Greatest Batsmen (1986)

Bosanquet, B J T
1054   Bosanquet came from a very unusual family, and it is when we
       examine his environment, linked with the forces of heredity,
       that it becomes a little less surprising to us that somewhere
       inside the complacent soul of this tall, elegant bachelor, there
       was a heretic trying to get out.

Benny Green
A History of Cricket (1988)

1055 . . . was no more the inventor of the googly than Wilbur and Orville Wright, around the same time, were the inventors of propelled flying machines. Others had dabbled, though in the case of the googly ball the instances were undoubtedly accidental. What Bosanquet and the Wright brothers had in common was that they are acknowledged as the first to succeed 'in the field'.

David Frith
The Slow Men (1984)

1056 The mystique surrounding the revolutionary ball was hardly lessened by its being given a name. Indeed, the name of its first regular exploiter (pronounced Bo-san-kay) hinted at something foreign: and therefore not to be trusted!

Ibid.

Botham, I T
1057 He lifted the game from a state of conventional excitement to one of unbelievable suspense and drama and finally into the realms of romantic fiction.

Henry Blofeld
Taunton (1974) reprinted in *The Guardian Book of Cricket* (1986)

1058 Ian Botham has many spectacular achievements to his name, but it's possible that his most outstanding contribution was to ensure the continued popularity of 'official' Tests.

Allen Synge
Cricket: The Men and the Matches that Changed the Game (1988)

1059 On his good days, and there are many, he bats like every boy and man in the land dreams of doing.

Keith Andrew
The Handbook of Cricket (1989)

1060 The sheer strength of the man is remarkable. Here he was, in the evening, opening the bowling again as if he'd been strolling around the Quantock hedgerows with his twelve-bore all day.

David Foot (1985)
Reprinted in *The Guardian Book of Cricket* (1986)

1061   The members rose in doting tribute to his brutal brilliance.

Ibid.

1062   Botham, when batting or bowling, even when fielding in the slips, is capable of spreading an excitement that makes fans of people who would normally subscribe to the crude prejudice than cricket is only slightly less boring than watching celery grow or car bumpers rust.

Hugh McIlvanney
The Magic Touch (1982) reprinted in *The Observer on Cricket* (1987)

1063   On the cricket fields, we would not forget him if we could (and could not forget if we would), as morning after morning the summer's sun rose for him and he went forth and trod fresh grass − and the expectant, eager cry was sent about the land. *Botham's In!*

Frank Keating
High, Wide and Handsome (1986)

1064   Left to himself, he looked to be in danger of destroying his talent, his image and ultimately himself.

Graeme Wright
Botham (1985)

1065   His instincts are not tamed, his zest for life has not mellowed. His whole-heartedness leads to triumphs and troubles, to success and scrapes, for it is not balanced by a shrewd appreciation of public relations nor by a tolerance of rudeness or criticism.

Peter Roebuck
Slices of Cricket (1982)

Boycott, G
1066   He has unquestionably given the most single-minded attention to the subject of batting, if not the art of batting, in the history of the game.

Keith Andrew
The Handbook of Cricket (1989)

1067   He believes himself to be misunderstood by the media and
        therefore misunderstood by the public at large, and it makes
        him unhappy. He is not, he insists, the remorselessly dedicated
        monster he is made out to be. He loves cricket, that's all; that's
        why he tries so hard.

Barry Norman
Geoffrey Boycott (1973) reprinted in *The Observer on Cricket*
(1987)

1068   Boycott's idea of bliss might be to bat all night (so long as it
        was not for Mr Packer), having batted all day.

John Woodcock
Barclays World of Cricket (1980)

1069   This Boycott is the committed cricketer, a lonely perfectionist
        moved to the heart at coming to such a high peak of
        performance before his own people.

John Arlott
Headingley (1977) reprinted in *The Guardian Book of Cricket*
(1986)

1070   He thought little of fellow cricketers who failed to live up to
        the high standards he set himself, and it is said that some
        promising batsmen, overawed by his presence in the XI, failed
        to do themselves justice.

Anthony Woodhouse
The History of Yorkshire CCC (1989)

1071   Some would say that the presence of such a figure was very
        much to the county's detriment, but others felt it was the one
        redeeming feature in a lack-lustre side. The truth lies
        somewhere in between.

Ibid.

1072   What has been forgotten amid the complicated controversies
        Boycott has got into, is his ability to play near-perfect against
        all kinds of bowling and on all kinds of wickets.

Sunil Gavaskar
Idols (1984)

1073   He built a fortress around himself, in life as at the wicket.

Christopher Martin-Jenkins
Cricket Characters (1987)

1074   Because he believed that everyone was out to get him –
        personally – he was at his very best when things were tough.

Ibid.

1075   Geoffrey Boycott was a lonely perfectionist, unloved but
        grudgingly admired by those who knew him; adored by
        thousands who did not.

Ibid.

1076   For Boycott, though a remorselessly good and utterly
        professional batsman, had become over the years a captain and
        a player about whom there were two opinions even in
        Yorkshire, and only one in most other places – that he was
        more than a little self-centred.

Derek Birley
The Willow Wand (1979)

1077   Boycott is very much a loner so far as his colleagues are
        concerned and his tunnel vision in the quest for runs has led
        him to trample across the path of lesser men on a number of
        occasions, believing that his presence at the wicket was of
        greater usefulness. That he was usually correct did not save him
        from stricture.

John Callaghan
Boycott (1982)

1078   If he has been scathing to the less able, he had plenty of cause,
        for Yorkshire cricket has lacked application to a frightening
        degree. Above all, he remained faithful to his ideals.

Ibid.

Bradman, D G
1079   Bradman was one of the most curious mixtures of good and
        bad batting I have ever seen.

P G H Fender
The Turn of the Wheel (1929)

1080   Promise there is in Bradman in plenty, though watching him
        does not inspire one with any confidence that he desires to take
        the only course which will lead him to a fulfilment of that
        promise.

Ibid.

1081 He seems to live for the exuberance of the moment.

Ibid.

1082 No bigger than a cloud the size of a man's hand when he first appeared, he was destined to plague and dominate our bowlers for nearly a quarter of a century, and to write his name in very big letters in the chronicles of the game.

Sir Pelham Warner
Long Innings (1951)

1083 What were the secrets of his triumphal march through England? First, immense natural skill. Secondly, an idealism which urged him to learn everything he possibly could, and to profit by the lessons learned. Thirdly, tremendous concentration of mind. Fourthly, physical strength. Fifthly, extreme fitness; and lastly, a cool, calm temperament.

Sir Pelham Warner
Introduction to *Don Bradman's Book* (1930)

1084 He was blessed with a wonderful eye, steel-like wrists, and small and beautifully neat feet, which a Genée or a Pavlova might have envied.

Ibid.

1085 Bradman triumphed mentally over the opposition because he really did regard his wicket as impregnable.

Bernard Hollowood
Cricket on the Brain (1970)

1086 The bat was more of a sabre than a pendulum. But if perfect balance, co-ordination and certainty of execution be accepted as the principal ingredients of batsmanship, we who watched the Don in his early manhood will not hope or expect ever to see its art displayed in a higher form.

E W Swanton
Sort of a Cricket Person (1972)

1087 But as I have written in another place, 'In the many pictures that I have stored in my mind from the "burnt-out Junes" of 40 years, there is none more dramatic or compelling than that of Bradman's small, serenely-moving figure in its big-peaked green cap coming out of the pavilion shadows into the sunshine, with the concentration, ardour and apprehension of surrounding thousands centred upon him, and the destiny of a Test match in his hands.'

H S Altham
The Cricketer Spring Annual (1941) reprinted in *In Celebration of Cricket* (1978)

1088 If genius is the art of doing the simple things properly Bradman was a classic example. While lesser players tend to create complications, or theorise themselves towards a state of mental exhaustion, Bradman knew precisely what he intended to do, and went his way with the minimum of fuss.

Alec Bedser
Cricket Choice (1981)

1089 Millions, who had not a notion of an off-break or a square-cut knew him only as the International Bogeyman of cricket.

Margaret Hughes
All on a Summer's Day (1953)

1090 He gave to the man-in-the-street the greatest possible value for his admission money and he brought to cricket the most pronounced publicity the game had ever known.

Jack Fingleton
Brightly Fades the Don (1949)

1091 Apart from [one instance] I never heard him praise a player unduly, or motivate his team with discussions of tactics. Perhaps his main resource as a leader was the example he set his men in concentration and the relentlessness of his attack.

Jack Fingleton
Batting From Memory (1981)

1092 Few, if any, had so disciplined themselves to physical excellence, or fielded and thrown with such agility and accuracy. The critics were not educated to such perfection, and it was fashionable to decry the supreme artist as an automaton. But Bradman, the breaker of records, was but reflecting the spirit, even the demands, of a record-hunting age.

R C Robertson-Glasgow
Bradman (1946) reprinted in *The Observer on Cricket* (1987)

1093 He dominated and he dazzled. He defied belief yet inflicted no outrage on cricketing logic or dignity.

J M Kilburn
Thanks to Cricket (1972)

1094 Don used to be the third in the trio that was Sydney's pride — 'Our bridge, our harbour and our Bradman'.

Kenneth Farnes
Tours and Tests (1940)

Brearley, J M
1095 I cannot remember an innings of his, but I can certainly remember his presence on the field.

Keith Andrew
The Handbook of Cricket (1989)

1096 It must be admitted that he is somewhat flattered by his record, which was achieved almost entirely against teams who had been denuded by World Series Cricket.

Trevor Bailey
Wickets, Catches and the Odd Run (1986)

1097 The statistics suggest he is one of the greatest England captains. The luckiest would be more the truth.

Ray Illingworth
Captaincy (1980)

1098 Do not be fooled by the educated facade. He is a shrewd, ruthless leader.

Ibid.

1099   Much of Mike Brearley's quality as a captain stems from his ability to stand back from cricket and observe cricketers as people.

John Arlott
The Guardian Book of Sport 1981/2 (1982)

1100   It is difficult, though, to believe that Test cricket has ever known a better captain, strategically, tactically, above all, in psychological perception and consequent handling of men.

Ibid.

Cameron, H B
1101   Whether he was batting or behind the stumps he showed unfailing determination and almost invariably retrieved the position when an innings was tottering.

Louis Duffus
Giants of South African Cricket (1971)

1102   He was a man of high principles, resolute, hardy and full of character, a staunch friend, one given to boyish playfulness, but in every sense a man's man.

Ibid.

Cardus, N
1103   His gift was a capacity to invest cricket and cricketers with a heroic stature: he interpreted the feelings of the literate cricket enthusiast and, in doing so, changed the entire shape of writing about the game.

John Arlott
An Eye for Cricket (1979)

1104   Cardus was scarcely a man of the people, and as he grew older even his staunchest admirers began to think that, as Warner said of Lord Hawke, he was sometimes inclined to dwell too much in the past.

Derek Birley
The Willow Wand (1979)

1105   He is conscious on the one hand of the elements of display and ritual and style; yet on the other he is aware of the fierce demands of the contest. He looks on them amorally.

Ibid.

Carr, A W
1106 His forbidding and intractable facade was in fact softened by some noble human qualities. But his judgement was suspect.

> **David Foot**
> *Cricket's Unholy Trinity* (1985)

1107 He might have been on the losing side of the bodyline argument, but he showed greater loyalty and integrity than certain of those who brought about its demise.

> **Christopher Douglas**
> *Douglas Jardine* (1984)

Cartwright, T W
1108 When I come to picture him in the twilight of my life, it is the run-up and delivery action I shall remember as much as anything that subsequently happened down at the receiving end.

> **Peter Walker**
> *Cricket Conversations* (1978)

Chapman, A P F
1109 There have been others who played the game harder – not from a personal angle, but who, having got their opponents down, saw to it that they were given no chance of rising again. But I will say this about him, he was one of those majestic personalities who are conspicuous by their absence from present-day cricket.

> **Leslie Ames**
> *Close of Play* (1953)

1110 He was one of the last of the cavalier captains, whose misfortune was to overlap with the roundheads who turned Test cricket into a war of attrition.

> **Gerry Cotter**
> *The Ashes Captains* (1989)

1111 His cavalier approach meant that he was not a great tactical analyst, but he was a very perceptive judge of a cricket match; his bowling changes and field placings were successful far too often for a critic to say he was just lucky.

> *Ibid.*

1112 His team loved him, and blossomed under his old-fashioned idea that the game was meant to be enjoyed.

Ibid.

1113 The golden boy of his epoch.

David Kynaston
Archie's Last Stand (1984)

1114 Tall, charming, and handsome, the world lay before him.

Ibid.

1115 He was by the end the skeleton in the cupboard of English cricket history, perhaps because he was everyone's guilty conscience.

Ibid.

Chappell, G S
1116 A quite superb batsman and catcher, he has borne his many honours modestly.

John Arlott
100 Greatest Batsmen (1986)

1117 He set his face against the permissive, sledging, sloppy-dressing and general bad manners of that era, to such a stern extent that he was dubbed 'the major general': and he strove to maintain high standards.

John Arlott
Arlott on Cricket (1984)

Chappell, I M
1118 A cricketer of effect rather than the graces.

John Arlott
An Eye for Cricket (1979)

1119 No player has had more influence on Australian cricket over the past 20 years but it is doubtful if he has used his unique position in the best interests of himself or of the game.

Jack Pollard
Australian Cricket (1982)

1120 He has been an exciting player to watch in all he did but one cannot discard his long, consistent history of unfortunate behaviour which suggests that his judgement often went astray.

Ibid.

Close, D B
1121 An unselfish man whose infectious enthusiasm is a vastly underestimated influence.

Ray Illingworth
Captaincy (1980)

1122 Only Richie Benaud was a better captain.

Ibid.

1123 Close had the dash, the flair. He would introduce fielding changes which seemed to possess no cricket logic at all and yet produced a wicket.

John Hampshire
Family Argument (1983)

Collins, H L
1124 Collins withdrew deeper and deeper into the hard shell of his dour and invincible spirit. Cromwell would have welcomed him as one of his lieutenants; he knows how to watch and how to fight.

Dudley Carew (1926)
Quoted in *The Ashes Captains* (1989)

1125 He gambled with his own fortunes but protected Australia's cricket prestige with a Scrooge-like intensity.

Jack Pollard
Australian Cricket (1982)

Compton, D C S
1126 Never was such a hero as Denis Compton in those first post-war years: never has Lord's rung to such affectionate applause.

E W Swanton
A History of Cricket, Volume Two (1962)

1127   Whereas the methodical runner is like a traveller who consults weather, routes and timetables Denis was more akin to the lover of nature who, seeing a glimpse of sunshine, snatches up his hat and sets out just for the joy of life.

I A R Peebles
Denis Compton (1971)

1128   Compton was so joyously haphazard that John Warr remarked that his call was merely an opening bid.

Diana Rait Kerr and I A R Peebles
Lord's 1946 – 1970 (1971)

1129   Middlesex have not since produced players with the same magnetism, and Lord's has been the poorer.

Ibid.

1130   Part of his charm lay in his own fallibility, sometimes shown in a total lack of concentration that would have been an annoying trait in anyone else.

Keith Andrew
The Handbook of Cricket (1989)

1131   I cannot think of any reigning batsman who brings to his craft the *fun* which Denis Compton did, either in his own crease or, as occasionally happened, when he turned up unexpectedly in his partner's or, more frequently, when he got stranded between the two.

I A R Peebles
The Unorthodox Brigade (1977) reprinted in *The Guardian Book of Cricket* (1986)

1132   The song of his bat is as natural as summer's warmth. But he is like those natural wits whose sayings are waited for by professional joke-gatherers. The statisticians prowl and prowl around.

R C Robertson-Glasgow
Denis Compton (1948) reprinted in *The Observer on Cricket* (1987)

1133 Many other players have batted excitingly or skilfully or bravely
– and Compton's batting has had all three of these qualities –
but he is rare in the gaiety which seems to emanate from his
play so that all but the most partisan of spectators have felt a
liking for him completely divorced from statistics, scores,
failure or success.

John Arlott
Cricket (1953)

1134 Compton belonged in the Golden Age. He had the same
adventurous spirit as the top batsmen of that time.

E M Wellings
Vintage Cricketers (1983)

1135 His face beamed down from hoardings, from the pages of
magazines and newspapers, from the backs of buses, until he
was known and, in a curious way, celebrated even by the non-
cricketing public.

Benny Green
A History of Cricket (1988)

1136 The two cricketers I would bequeath to schoolboys yet unborn,
Compton and Miller. The sun was afraid not to shine when
they strolled onto a cricket field.

Kenneth Gregory
In Celebration of Cricket (1978)

Constantine, L N
1137 No other cricketers seem to catch the imagination in the same
way as the West Indians. Their image as the world's most
exciting cricketers was built up when they were introduced to
Test cricket more than 50 years ago by the unpredictable genius
of one extraordinary man, Learie Constantine.

Henry Blofeld
One Test After Another (1985)

1138 No batsman had hit the ball so flamboyantly and so thrillingly
before Constantine, no one had bowled with energy which was
so frenetic as to add yards to his pace, and perhaps no one had
played cricket at this level who was so engagingly cheerful.

Ibid.

1139   The electricity that he imparted consisted as much of surprise as delight in what Constantine was doing.

Michael Manley
A History of West Indies Cricket (1988)

1140   Contrary to all belief, popular and learned, Constantine the magician is the product of tradition and training.

C L R James
Beyond a Boundary (1963)

1141   No one could appear to play more gaily, more spontaneously, more attractively, than Constantine. In reality he was a cricketer of concentrated passion.

Ibid.

1142   Constantine, the heir-apparent, the happy warrior, the darling of the crowd, prize pupil of the captain of the West Indies, had revolted against the revolting contrast between his first-class status as a cricketer and his third-class status as a man.

Ibid.

1143   He wanted to field all the time, everywhere, and there were many moments when he appeared to be doing just that.

J M Kilburn
Overthrows (1975)

1144   For Constantine made himself for all predictable time into the great representative symbol of West Indian cricket, partly by the accident of history and partly by the sheer stunning impact of skill and personality.

Ronald Mason
Sing All a Green Willow (1967)

1145   The crowd loves the spectacular, sixes and tumbling catches and stumps cartwheeling; Constantine provided the lot, very often in the space of an hour or so; and he provided it with what I think must have been the element that, away and above the explosive spectacle, endeared him to the millions: his infectious delight in his own consuming energy.

Ibid.

1146   He offered the cricket of lyric and freedom; the joy of those
       whose forefathers had shed the bondage of slavery.

Gerald Howat
Cricket's Second Golden Age (1989)

Cowdrey, M C
1147   What is a far greater tribute, in an age when, if one may
       believe journalists and the endless stream of worthless books
       published under the names of prominent players, cricket at the
       top level is a mass of petty jealousies and enmities, is that one
       never hears Colin mentioned personally without the greatest
       affection and respect.

R L Arrowsmith
A History of County Cricket: Kent (1971)

1148   The name of Cowdrey is synonymous with friendliness, charm,
       good manners, modesty and other related virtues you can think
       of, all underpinned by his religious beliefs.

Gerry Cotter
The Ashes Captains (1989)

1149   He knew the game thoroughly, but was not the sort to take a
       daring gamble.

Ibid.

1150   Cowdrey, even in youth, was liable to long spells of
       introspection, of self-doubt.

Alan Gibson
The Cricket Captains of England (1979)

1151   Cowdrey was long one of the world's greatest bats, yet had he
       given full play to his natural abilities he could have been even
       greater.

R L Arrowsmith
Barclays World of Cricket (1980)

1152   His ability to provide encouragement when things were not
       going particularly well was quite uncanny.

Derek Underwood
Introduction to *The History of Kent CCC* (1988)

Denness, M H
1153   . . . had the misfortune to be appointed England captain too
early in his career.

Ray Illingworth
Captaincy (1980)

Denton, D
1154   A sober-minded cricketer, a keen Methodist and a man who
brought up his family in a strictly Christian code, he was proud
of his ability as a cricketer and there was no doubt that the way
he played his cricket appealed to the spectators who flocked to
watch him and his colleagues.

Anthony Woodhouse
The History of Yorkshire CCC (1989)

1155   His catches were legion and they have become legend.

Peter Thomas
Yorkshire Cricketers 1839 – 1939 (1973)

Dexter, E R
1156   He was a controversial character and an exciting batsman, the
ideal mixture. In full flow it was not too much to claim that he
was worth at least double the admission price.

Trevor Bailey
The Greatest of My Time (1968)

1157   He is a temperamental cricketer, and temperamental cricketers
depend on the stars being right for them.

Alan Ross
Australia '63 (1964)

1158   Tall, handsome and aristocratic in appearance he was often
referred to as 'Lord Edward', and in his moody moments
before the years mellowed him, he could behave in a cold and
aloof manner.

Gerry Cotter
The Ashes Captains (1989)

1159   Dexter never quite made the most of his exceptional talents
both at cricket and golf.

E M Wellings
Vintage Cricketers (1983)

1160   Dexter's captaincy alternately maddened, mystified, or drew horse-laughs from his critics, yet he set a superb example in the field, and, which was important in such a series, looked, as the West Indians did, to be loving cricket.

John Clarke
Cricket with a Swing (1963)

1161   . . . displayed the cavalier aggression; a total commitment to attack and calculated risks; and an insatiable appetite for runs which had the spectator perched on the edge of his seat and enchanted beyond words.

Alan Hill
The Family Fortune (1978)

1162   While others had cause to repent their haste he cleverly paced the game like an adroit chessmaster.

Ibid.

D'Oliveira, B L
1163   His behaviour in what might have been difficult situations has always been impeccably dignified and courteous.

John Arlott
The Guardian (1968) reprinted in *Arlott on Cricket* (1984)

1164   It is often said that the best fighters are hungry fighters. If so, then Basil D'Oliveira's appetite for recognition in the cricketing world outside Cape Town gave England her most steadfast champion of the post-war period.

Peter Walker
Cricket Conversations (1978)

Douglas, J W H T
1165   Douglas was a man of character. He possessed courage and determination in a marked degree, and was always the essence of fitness.

Sir Pelham Warner
Long Innings (1951)

1166   He had a magnificent physique, it is true, but little natural gift for either sport.

Charles Bray
Essex County Cricket (1950)

1167   The harder the job and the tougher the opposition, the more tenacious he became and the more his bulldog spirit showed itself.

Ibid.

1168   He was a strict disciplinarian. He lived for cricket and he thought all others should have the same enthusiasm, the same keenness and the same guts that he had.

Ibid.

1169   To meet him away from Essex in other cricket was to find a thoroughly sporting companion. As skipper of that county he was not only bad but brutal, almost incredible in his ruthlessness.

Sir Home Gordon
Background of Cricket (1939)

1170   His dogged enthusiasm for cricket was unsurpassable, but he had a grim way of getting enjoyment out of it.

Ibid.

1171   For it is only the truth that Douglas, as an England captain, time and again strained our patience and philosophy to breaking-point.

Sir Neville Cardus
Days in the Sun (1924)

1172   Tact may not always be his characteristic, and as a captain he is not resourceful or very observant, but as a hero of the cricket field there have been few who have done more valuable hard work.

Lord Hawke
Recollections and Reminiscences (1924)

1173   He was not a great captain, but he was most assuredly a great man and, if he was not an attacking batsman, a persistently attacking bowler.

Dudley Carew
To the Wicket (1946)

Duckworth, G

1174 God Almighty decided some 64 years ago that Lancashire
needed a wicket-keeper. I don't think He had England in mind;
I think He was primarily concerned with Lancashire.

Sir Leonard Hutton
George Duckworth (1966) reprinted in *The Observer on Cricket*
(1987)

1175 No Lancashire player has been so abundantly Lancashire, no
stumper has been more nimble and certainly none more vocal.

John Marshall
Old Trafford (1971)

1176 Duckworth's appeals became a feature of cricket at Old
Trafford and all other cricket grounds upon which he appeared.
It was not so much an appeal as an assertion.

Ibid.

1177 A batsman was always well aware of Duckworth's presence, for
he was rarely still and he expended a tremendous amount of
energy in the course of an innings.

Gerald Hodcroft
My Own Red Roses (1984)

1178 Throughout his career he never lost his tremendous zest for the
game or his ebullient boyishness.

Rex Pogson
Lancashire (1952)

Duleepsinhji, K S

1179 Duleepsinhji, with a capacity for practice and hard work that
used to amaze his team-mates, burdened by a sense of duty
stemming from the knowledge that he owed everything to the
uncle who had supervised his cricket career since the age of
eight, was a potential world-beater, if only he could have been
left to himself.

Edward Docker
History of Indian Cricket (1976)

1180 Duleep, all charm and elegance at the wicket.

Alan Ross
Blindfold Games (1986)

East, R E

1181 East has a look in his eye, the glint of the fellow in *Apocalypse Now* who lost the smell of napalm in the morning. It is the haunted look of a man to whom something outrageous has just happened or is about to happen.

Peter Roebuck

Men of Essex (1984) reprinted in *The Guardian Book of Cricket* (1986)

1182 Ray East is one of the few players in the modern game who can make a crowd laugh.

Patrick Murphy
The Spinner's Turn (1982)

1183 East, one of the funniest men ever to tread a first-class field, almost certainly did himself a disservice by not leaving his clowning in the dressing-room.

David Frith
The Slow Men (1984)

Edmonds, P H

1184 His personality was not blending easily with those around him.

Ibid.

1185 He sometimes gives the impression of aloofness and detachment on the field of play. That would be unfair to a man who possesses a keen desire to win but sees no reason why he should take refuge in the clenched fist and tight-lipped image which many cricketers love to affect.

Patrick Murphy
The Spinner's Turn (1982)

1186 One can imagine him flourishing in the Edwardian era — tossing the ball up to invite the slog, launching into his booming straight drives with optimistic vigour and dazzling self-indulgency in the field. He would probably have captained England.

Ibid.

1187 . . . is a singular man. His cricket career has been extraordinary, characterised by selectorial caprice, unsympathetic handling, and the growth of an unmerited reputation for being a monster of egotism.

Simon Barnes
Phil Edmonds: A Singular Man (1986)

1188 He seems to lack a number of the familiar traits and opinions you would expect to find in an Englishman.

Ibid.

1189 For Edmonds, bowling is an emotional matter, into which he must pour his strength, his will, his anger and his concentration if he is to make things happen in a worthwhile way.

Ibid.

1190 Cricket needs its eccentrics, needs such singular men as Edmonds if it is to remain sane. The game will be infinitely poorer if Edmonds is, indeed, the last great amateur.

Ibid.

Edrich, J H
1191 The plaudits fell short when it came to the superlatives. They almost seemed to be grudging, to dismiss him as a plodder who might come in useful in hard times but for whom some more exciting substitute might be found.

Ralph Barker
The Cricketing Family Edrich (1976)

1192 He was probably the least selfish great player I ever knew.

Pat Pocock
Percy (1987)

1193 I also never knew a great player who thought less about the technicalities of the game, which was one of the factors which was to make him such a poor captain.

Ibid.

Edrich, W J

1194   Bill was a popular cricketer not so much for his successes as for his repeated triumphs over prejudice and adversity. His pugnacity and aggression, allied to the serene temperament and natural manners which characterise all the Edriches, were there for all to see.

Ralph Barker
The Cricketing Family Edrich (1976)

1195   Relishing a scrap, he never gave up in any game until the last entry was made in the scorebook.

John Warr
Barclays World of Cricket (1980)

1196   He came perkily down the pavilion steps with the confident aggression of the small man.

Barry Norman
County Champions (1982)

1197   Edrich's batting was always a thing of guts and belligerence; watching him facing a fast bowler was like watching some unexpectedly tough little kid walking up to the school bully and kicking him smartly in the shins.

Ibid.

Emburey, J E

1198   Success sits easily on his unflappable shoulders; he has known many disappointments in the game and sees no reason to get over-worried about temporary lapses in form.

Patrick Murphy
The Spinner's Turn (1982)

1199   . . . a quiet, calm, sensible individual, shrewd and undramatic.

Trevor Bailey
The Spinners' Web (1988)

1200   He has a somewhat clinical approach to his chosen profession, is prepared to listen and consider advice, and excels in a crisis because he does not panic.

Ibid.

1201 He has one record which he would possibly like to forget and that is he is possibly the only bowler to have played in a Test series as an automatic choice without taking a wicket.

Fred Trueman
The Spinners' Web (1988)

1202 Tall, sedate, with a remodelled nose through injury and a leisurely Jack Benny walk, chest out in somewhat matronly fashion . . .

David Frith
The Slow Men (1984)

1203 Emburey's main function has been to keep the game tight while England's pace bowlers have rested and recovered their breath.

Phil Edmonds
100 Greatest Bowlers (1989)

Emmett, T
1204 He was popular because of his enthusiasm for play; he was memorable because of his sharp wit, uninhibited comment and unfailing readiness to make good-humoured capital from his own discomfiture.

J M Kilburn
A History of Yorkshire Cricket (1970)

1205 He was the smile on the face of cricket, a smile that has hardly faded even now in these days of less mirthful men in more immaculate flannels.

Peter Thomas
Yorkshire Cricketers 1839–1939 (1973)

1206 Tom Emmett was the greatest 'character' that ever stepped onto the field, a merry wag who could never lose his heart or his temper.

Lord Hawke
Recollections and Reminiscences (1924)

1207 There was no brighter spirit in the field, and there was none more willing. He worked heart and soul in every department of the game, and was always ready to do a spell of bowling to oblige anyone.

W G Grace
Cricket (1891)

1208   . . . a left arm capable of bowling a cricket ball at speed with spin from leg, and a tongue which uttered a lifetime of sardonic quotes.

David Frith
The Fast Men (1975)

Evans, T G
1209   I never saw another who could react as quickly as Evans.

E M Wellings
Vintage Cricketers (1983)

1210   He is by far the most energetic keeper I have ever seen. He seems prepared not only to do his own particular job of work but also to relieve the in-fieldsmen of some of theirs.

W J O'Reilly
Cricket Conquest (1949)

1211   Godfrey Evans was, quite simply, the finest wicket-keeper I have seen. At his very best he was capable of making catches and stumpings which no other man would have considered chances.

Trevor Bailey
The Greatest of My Time (1968)

1212   His unlimited enthusiasm and vitality meant that whenever he was in the middle there always was a sparkle to the game.

Dudley Moore
The History of Kent CCC (1988)

1213   No wicket-keeper has ever been so constantly in the picture. None has been so spectacular.

R L Arrowsmith
A History of County Cricket: Kent (1971)

1214   There has perhaps never been a greater than Godfrey on his day, and his days were many and his off-days few.

Ibid.

1215   He believed that the game should be gay and spirited.

Alan Knott
Stumper's View (1972)

1216   He was a man of tremendous zest and bounce.

Ibid.

1217 Whether it was the first over of the day or the last, the effort would still be the same. He seemed capable of keeping going for as long as required.

Ibid.

1218 Godfrey Evans has said that if people did not think he was showing off, he would have kept without pads.

Ibid.

Faulkner, G A
1219 Despite the abundance of talent the game has produced in the 50 years since last he played, Faulkner has strong claim to be numbered among the six greatest all-rounders the game has yet seen.

I A R Peebles
Spinner's Yarn (1977)

1220 He was inclined to be touchy and defensive and, in the four years that I knew him, he had no close friends.

Ibid.

1221 Faulkner never tried to project any form of 'image' (he even kept his flannel trousers up with string). I believe his directness and dynamism would have been accepted because of his great ability and understanding of youth.

Tom Reddick
Giants of South African Cricket (1971)

1222 He believed a challenge should always be presented.

Ibid.

1223 He loved the cricketer that gave his all for the game.

Ibid.

Fender, P G H
1224 He hated the dull finish, the formal declaration, the expected stroke, the workaday over. He rescued treasures of cricket from dust and oblivion, snatched off the covering, and showed them to an astonished and delighted public.

R C Robertson-Glasgow
More Cricket Prints (1948)

1225   The greatest captain of his time.

J L Carr
Carr's Dictionary of Extra-ordinary English Cricketers (1977)

1226   He should be content with the service and personality he
contributed to the game – P G H Fender, renowned in initials
and unforgettable in appearance by a generation of enthusiasts,
and established in the annals of cricket as the greatest captain
in the history of one of the greatest counties.

Ronald Mason
Sing All a Green Willow (1967)

1227   Loyally as he always served other captains, particularly Surrey
captains under whom he played when at last he was superseded,
he was at his best and most valuable when in control. Reduced
to subordinate rank, he looked lost and fettered, a great prince
in prison lying.

Ibid.

1228   He very closely resembled one particular film star, a very great
favourite of my own whom I never see without recalling the
happy likeness – I mean Groucho Marx.

Ibid.

1229   It was more true of P G H Fender than of most cricketers that
figures were an inadequate reflection of his qualities.

E W Swanton (1981)
Reprinted in *As I Said at the Time* (1983)

1230   There was, perhaps, no more arresting figure on the English
cricket scene between the wars, nor one whose personality got
across more clearly to the crowd. He was an unashamed
showman, believing that people deserved a bit of excitement for
their money.

Ibid.

Fletcher, K W R
1231   His air of enigmatic simplicity is as cultivated as his garden. It
is designed to create an impression of mystical wisdom.

Peter Roebuck
Men of Essex (1984) reprinted in *The Guardian Book of Cricket*
(1986)

1232   There is no swagger when he goes out to bat, and at times he appears almost apologetic; while his captaincy is completely without histrionics.

> **Trevor Bailey**
> *County Champions* (1982)

1233   He is both liked and respected by his fellow professionals for his ability, honesty and for the way he has always played his cricket.

> *Ibid.*

Foster, F R
1234   My bowling was simply a gift from God.

> **F R Foster**
> *Cricketing Memories* (1930)

1235   . . . imparted a bold and adventurous spirit to the style of play; he inspired courage and stirred hope. He created backbone.

> *The Birmingham Post* (1911)
> Quoted in *The Story of Warwickshire Cricket* (1974)

1236   He was a fanatic for brighter cricket and he'd always accept a challenge.

> **E J Smith**
> *'Tiger' Smith* (1981)

1237   Foster was a great gambler, inordinately so in later life.

> **Leslie Duckworth**
> *The Story of Warwickshire Cricket* (1974)

Foster, R E
1238   He is one of those cricketers who have all the faculties required for a batsman, and also, what does not necessarily follow, a graceful and elegant manner of using them.

> **C B Fry**
> *The Book of Cricket* (1899)

1239   As a stylist, he approached MacLaren, with great variety of stroke, and he excelled at the off-drive and the late-cut.

> **Sir Pelham Warner**
> *Long Innings* (1951)

Freeman, A P

1240   Freeman's outstanding characteristics were his sustained effort
and humility. Everyone loved him. He may not have wanted to
be one of the game's characters but he was. All knew that
determined hitch of the trousers and the Napoleonic fold of the
arms, revealing the satisfaction from doing a job well.

Dudley Moore
The History of Kent CCC (1988)

1241   He was beyond all comparison the greatest wicket-taker county
cricket has ever known.

R L Arrowsmith
A History of County Cricket: Kent (1971)

1242   In one respect he differed markedly from the modern bowler:
he would bustle back his five yards as if he could hardly wait
to get at his victim − a good psychological point.

Ibid.

1243   There was something grotesque in the way the little gnome of a
man came rocking up to the stumps, and flicked one ball after
another, all so nearly the same, and yet so vitally different,
until the victim would either commit some act of indiscretion
or, more probably, fall to his own timidity.

E W Swanton
A History of Cricket, Volume Two (1962)

1244   Considering the small size of his hands and fingers, the amount
of spin he could put onto the ball was astonishing. That,
coupled with the colossal burden of work that he bore, made
his control of length equally notable.

C S Marriott
The Complete Leg-Break Bowler (1968)

1245   Tich, however, had in abundance that most precious quality of
the first-rate spin bowler: the guts and capacity to stand
unshaken under heavy punishment, no matter what blows
adverse fortune struck.

Ibid.

1246   He made up for his short stature with a wonderful gift of
deceptive flight.

Ibid.

1247 Everything about him was small – apart from his annual
wicket tallies – and with his dwarflike digits, the index finger
came in for more work than is customary.

David Frith
The Slow Men (1984)

1248 No bowler was ever more indifferent to punishment or more
convinced he could force the attacking batsman to pay the
penalty: and he detested being taken off.

Sir Home Gordon
Background of Cricket (1939)

1249 No one saw the smoothness of Freeman's hair ever ruffled by
any gale wind.

Ibid.

Fry, C B
1250 He was one of the last of his kind – and certainly the finest
specimen of it – the amateurs, the smiling gentlemen of games,
intensely devoted to the skill and the struggle but always with a
certain gaiety, romantic at heart but classical in style.

J B Priestley
The English (1973)

1251 Fry could properly be called a polymath, but he was above all a
classic.

Alan Gibson
The Cricket Captains of England (1979)

1252 He is a nice, good-looking young fellow, who can sing a song
and can illustrate a notebook with caricatures of his Dons.

Vanity Fair
Men of the Day No 584 (1894)

1253 His marvellous physique made him impervious to fatigue, his
self-control never slackened.

H S Altham
A History of Cricket, Volume One (1926)

1254   From Percy Chapman I heard of his first sight of Fry at a
country house game. Percy was taken along as a spectator and
Fry was a player. The pavilion enclosure was surrounded by a
very low white fence. Fry appeared carrying a tea tray for the
ladies. He hurdled the low white fence, cut it too fine and nose
dived, tea tray and all. 'My first sight of the great athlete,'
Percy commented.

E M Wellings
Vintage Cricketers (1983)

1255   . . . would have done better as sole selector of the England XI
for many years than any selection committee has achieved.

E H D Sewell
Well Hit! Sir (1947)

1256   As a young man, stripped, he had the finest figure I have ever
seen, such as a sculptor might have chosen for model of a
Greek god.

Sir Home Gordon
Background of Cricket (1939)

1257   Nobody could talk to him without pleasure or without growing
wiser.

Ibid.

1258   He had the inbred arrogance of someone who knows that
nature has allotted him an undue share of her gifts, yet he
could be shy and insecure, his domineering manner being only
by way of compensation.

Clive Ellis
C B Fry (1984)

1259   An immortal figure, representing all that is admirable and
valuable about amateur sport, in an age where money has
consumed sport, his qualities are the finest testimony to the
Olympic ideal.

Ibid.

Garner, J

1260   Dreamy-eyed, seemingly slow-motion in movement because of
the exceptional length of his jutting arms and legs and torso, he
is a freak among fast bowlers.

David Frith
The Fast Men (1982)

1261   Garner might be termed, in a cricket sense, a freak. He looks
more like a basketball player than a fast bowler.

Fred Trueman
From Larwood to Lillee (1983)

1262   Everyone in the first-class game now acknowledged that he was
the most difficult fast bowler to score runs off. Yet it wasn't
just his pace: it was the bounce he obtained, his devastating use
of the yorker, the problems of picking up the flight of the ball
quickly as he released it from that prodigious height. His arm
always looked as high as the pavilion clock.

David Foot
Sunshine, Cider and Sixes (1986)

1263   After a particularly successful day he will stroll round the main
streets of Taunton with the whites of his eyes and gleaming
teeth visible for miles around, thoroughly pleased with the
glances of the astonished children and terrified babies.

Peter Roebuck
Slices of Cricket (1982)

Gatting, M W

1264   It is always reassuring to see Mike's stocky, squarish frame
make its way out to the crease.

Frances Edmonds
Another Bloody Tour (1986)

1265   . . . is vaguely reminiscent of a shire horse. Strong, sturdy,
reliable, unflappable.

Ibid.

1266   His chunky, even porky, build encourages his admirers to think
of him as being of the British Bulldog breed.

Christopher Martin-Jenkins
Cricket Characters (1987)

Gavaskar, S M

1267 He repulsed them by means of a stout heart, a profound
     determination to succeed for himself and his country, and a
     batting technique of purest orthodoxy.

Ibid.

1268 Generally he has been a dignified man as well as a dignitary.

Ibid.

1269 Defining his peculiar talent is not easy. His personality is too
     self-effacing for his batting to be too dramatic.

Peter Roebuck
Slices of Cricket (1982)

1270 Here is a man with the drive to make things happen, and the
     character to engage the co-operation of his team-mates.

Ted Dexter
From Bradman to Boycott (1981)

1271 Although he never conquered Europe or invaded Russia,
     Gavaskar has persistently wrought havoc at the crease. And if
     there is a single part of his batting style which accounts for
     consistent success against the strongest attacks in the world, it is
     the 'straightness' of his bat.

Ibid.

1272 Perhaps it is best to say that, if all living things in India are
     incarnations, Gavaskar is technical orthodoxy made flesh.

Scyld Berry (1983)
Reprinted in *The Observer on Cricket* (1987)

Gibbs, L R

1273 He was a popular club-man, his expertise at forecasting horse-
     racing results being almost on a par with his knowledge of
     cricket strategy.

Christopher Martin-Jenkins
The Complete Who's Who of Test Cricketers (1987)

1274   Bulbous but dreamy eyes, close-cropped hair and loosest of gaits gave Gibbs the appearance of a New Orleans trombonist; but his patience as a spin bowler was immense, his accuracy torturesome.

David Frith
The Slow Men (1984)

1275   Of all the spinners I faced on good wickets, I found Lance to be the most frustrating as, unless I took a calculated risk, I could never see where any runs, apart from the unintentional edge, were to be had.

Trevor Bailey
The Spinners' Web (1988)

1276   He was in the best sense a true professional, and I can think of very few players I would prefer to have in my side, because he was completely dependable.

Ibid.

Giffen, G
1277   He was not a good captain, as he never knew when to take himself off, and always seemed to think that the best possible change of attack was for him to give up bowling at one end and go on at the other.

W G Grace
W G – Cricket Reminiscences and Personal Recollections
(1899)

1278   He was called Australia's W G Grace and remains one of the few Australian players to have a grandstand named after him.

Jack Pollard
Australian Cricket (1982)

Goddard, T L
1279   Whatever the cause of his continual frustrations it seemed part of the destiny of his cricket that throughout his long career he had to struggle by ceaseless hard work to reach the goals that won him so much distinction.

Louis Duffus
Giants of South African Cricket (1971)

1280   In all he did he was the artisan *par excellence*. The
distinguishing attributes of 'Goddard the Grafter' were
application, dedication and perseverance.

Ibid.

Goddard, T W J

1281   He was a tall man with a craggy, genial face, and vast hands
which never looked better than when clasping a pint: the horny
hands of toil.

Alan Gibson
Growing Up with Cricket (1985)

1282   Tom was a ripe character, full of chaff, and what one might
call a genial grumbler, the real old sweat.

E W Swanton
Gloucestershire Centenary Booklet (1970)

Gooch, G A

1283   . . . needs only a bushy beard to give him, from a distance, the
appearance of a youthful W G Grace.

Christopher Martin-Jenkins
The Complete Who's Who of Test Cricketers (1987)

1284   There are few sights in modern cricket to equal the one of
Gooch in full sail.

Christopher Martin-Jenkins
Cricket Characters (1987)

Gower, D I

1285   . . . immense and natural dignity through thick and thin.

Ibid.

1286   There was, indeed, a real gallantry about the young Gower's
play. Alone among his contemporaries he was instantly
memorable.

Ibid.

1287   He is every inch the perfect English gent in success and failure
alike.

Frances Edmonds
Another Bloody Tour (1986)

1288   . . . enthused everyone by his sense of timing and his apparently carefree attitude to the batting art. With his blond, curly hair and juvenile appearance Gower seemed to step out of the now defunct pages of *The Boys' Own Paper*.

E W Swanton (1978)
Reprinted in *As I Said at the Time* (1983)

1289   He remains a laid-back charming goldilocks with a touch of genius at the crease, no histrionic tactics or tantrums in the field, an ambassadorial approach to the world.

Frank Keating
The Guardian Book of Cricket (1986)

1290   In his disappointment, Gower handed over the reins with a chivalrous straightforwardness, which is more than can be said for the machinations of the mandarins of Lord's.

Ibid.

Grace, E M
1291   The stir that E M made was all the greater because of the scandalous manner in which he outraged every law of batting that had hitherto been held sacred.

Bernard Darwin
W G Grace (1934)

1292   The fame of E M's doings spread everywhere and his style of batting was freely criticised.

W G Grace
Cricket (1891)

Grace, W G
1293   Grace's praise demands my song,
Grace the swift and Grace the strong,
Fairest flower of cricket's stem,
Gloucester's shield and England's gem.

E B V Christian
Ode to W G

1294   Through W G Grace, cricket, the most complete expression of popular life in pre-industrial England, was incorporated into the life of the nation.

C L R James
Beyond a Boundary (1963)

1295   A famous Liberal historian can write the social history of
        England in the 19th century, and two famous Socialists can
        write what they declared to be the history of the common
        people of England, and between them never once mention the
        man who was the best-known Englishman of his time. I can no
        longer accept the system of values which could not find in these
        books a place for W G Grace.

                                                                    Ibid.

1296   He was far better known by sight than any man in England.

                                                        Bernard Darwin
                                                        W G Grace (1934)

1297   Grace, then, is the Beethoven of cricket, bridging the old game
        and the modern just as Beethoven bridged the classical and the
        romantic in music.

                                                        Gerry Cotter
                                                The Ashes Captains (1989)

1298   Had Grace been born in Ancient Greece the *Iliad* would have
        been a different book. Had he lived in the Middle Ages he
        would have been a Crusader and now would have been lying
        with his legs crossed in some ancient abbey, having founded a
        great family. As he was born when the world was older, he was
        the best known of all Englishmen and the king of that English
        game least spoilt by any form of vice.

                                                    Bishop of Hereford
                            The Memorial Biography of Dr W G Grace (1919)

1299   Simple zest was what W G brought to cricket. Not all
        subsequent captains of England have done the same. But those
        who have, win or lose, are the ones we like best.

                                                        Alan Gibson
                                        The Cricket Captains of England (1979)

1300   All his life he was facing the next ball.

                                                        A A Thomson
                                                The Great Cricketer (1957)

1301   He revolutionised cricket. He turned it from an accomplishment
        into a science.

                                                        K S Ranjitsinhji
                                        The Jubilee Book of Cricket (1897)

1302 He turned the old one-stringed instrument into a many-chorded lyre.

Ibid.

1303 What W G did was to unite in his mighty self all the good points of all the good players, and to make utility the criterion of style.

Ibid.

1304 He is distinctly individual and original in his style of play: he is all himself: yet his style is a study in correctness and orthodoxy.

C B Fry and G W Beldam
Great Batsmen (1905)

1305 Almost as truly as it was said of Napoleon, did W G 'cast a doubt upon all past glory, and render all future renown impossible'.

H S Altham
A History of Cricket, Volume One (1926)

1306 He did more to popularise cricket than any man who ever lived: his genial personality, his Jovian form, his inexhaustible vitality and stamina and enthusiasm, all combined with his prodigious prowess to make him the focus for an empire's devotion to the game.

Ibid.

1307 As a cricketer I do not hesitate to say that not only was he the greatest that ever lived, but also the greatest that can ever be, because no future batsmen will ever have to play on the bad wickets on which he made his mark and proved himself so immeasurably superior to all his contemporaries.

Lord Hawke
Recollections and Reminiscences (1924)

1308 Cricket with W G was never a game to be played in deathly silence.

Bernard Darwin
W G Grace (1934)

1309 To W G, cricket, being a game, was a vehicle for a practical, rough-and-tumble humour.

Ibid.

1310 He never did what he thought a dishonourable thing, but he had a different standard of honour from our own. I believe that in W G was found something of a survival of this old tradition.

Ibid.

1311 W G Grace was an autocrat and liked having his own way.

Tom Watson
Ibis Cricket 1870 – 1949 (1950)

1312 'The Champion', 'The Big 'Un', whose portrait in a pre-existence may be seen engraved upon Assyrian tablets in the British Museum.

J L Carr
Carr's Dictionary of Extra-ordinary English Cricketers (1977)

1313 He seems to have been one of those men in whom the characteristics of life as lived by many generations seemed to meet for the last, in a complete and perfectly blended whole.

C L R James
Beyond a Boundary (1963)

1314 His humours, his combativeness, his unashamed wish to have his own way on the field of play, his manoeuvres to encompass this, his delight when he did, his complaints when he didn't, are the rubs and knots of an oak that was sound through and through.

Ibid.

1315 Dr W G Grace
Had hair all over his face.
Lord! how the people cheered
When a ball got lost in his beard!

E C Bentley
W G in Baseless Biography (1939)

1316   In my opinion, the two great secrets of his success have been his great self-denial and his constant practice.

> **Richard Daft**
> *Kings of Cricket* (1893)

1317   None of the English cricketers could waltz like W G.

> **C B Fry**
> *Life Worth Living* (1939)

1318   Arguably, cricket and Grace died together.

> **Eric Midwinter**
> *W G Grace* (1981)

Graveney, T W
1319   Tom was a great batsman and always a friendly fellow.

> **Alan Gibson**
> *Growing Up with Cricket* (1985)

1320   It is, and always has been, in Tom's nature to show his strokes, of which he has the fullest range, and to dictate to the bowler where he can.

> **E W Swanton** (1969)
> Reprinted in *As I Said at the Time* (1983)

Greenidge, C G
1321   Greenidge has grafted on to his natural West Indian flair the fruits of a wide experience and become a magnificent and mature batsman with an immaculate technique who always seeks to take immediate control at the start of an innings yet will seldom give his wicket away.

> **Christopher Martin-Jenkins**
> *The Complete Who's Who of Test Cricketers* (1987)

1322   . . . the best ever opener from the Caribbean.

> **Michael Manley**
> *A History of West Indies Cricket* (1988)

Gregory, J M
1323   He employs his face also to add to the dismay his approach is calculated to inspire.

> **A C MacLaren**
> *Cricket, Old and New* (1924)

1324   There was a gusto in all he did on a cricket field that made him the biggest crowd pleaser in cricket in the years immediately after the First World War.

Jack Pollard
Australian Cricket (1982)

Gregory, S E
1325   His running between wickets frequently disorganised fielding sides and occasionally brought his own dismissal.

Ibid.

1326   He was an inspiration to his colleagues in the field and a joy to the spectators, clever in anticipation, quick to move and fielding the hardest hits cleanly and returning the ball with deadly accuracy.

Ibid.

Greig, A W
1327   The most controversial figure in world cricket.

Ibid.

1328   He was a colourful player who blossomed on big occasions.

Ibid.

1329   One of the most imposing and influential captains in English cricket. The true gauge of his charismatic personality was the great spirit he instilled into a side that tasted failure before success.

Ray Illingworth
Captaincy (1980)

1330   The extrovert image, fuelled by quick-fire quotes, overshadowed technical deficiencies.

Ibid.

1331   He was a batsman of high courage who used his physical advantages to the full.

E W Swanton
Barclays World of Cricket (1986)

1332   There is scarcely an episode in English cricket history more poignant or depressing than the rise and fall of Tony Greig.

Ibid.

Grimmett, C V

1333 Thomas Carlyle once declared that genius was an infinite capacity for taking pains. No cricketer I knew could better illustrate the truth underlying the dictum than Clarence Victor Grimmett.

> **Jack Fingleton**
> *Fingleton on Cricket* (1972)

1334 Clarrie was responsible, self-disciplined, considerate and studious. This man thought a full toss was the worst form of cricket vandalism and the long hop a legacy from prehistoric days when barbarians rolled boulders towards the enemy.

> **Arthur Mailey**
> *10 for 66 and All That* (1958)

1335 One of the gentlest of bowlers ever to lift a ball, he walked gently, picked up a cup of tea gently, arranged his tie with whispering fingers.

> *Ibid.*

1336 He is compounded of tea, leather, patience, and subtlety.

> **R C Robertson-Glasgow**
> *Cricket Prints* (1943)

1337 With his small, stringy frame and his weary, surprised smile, as if the slaves of the leg-breaks shouldn't expect to hear or transmit anything funny, he might have been what is known as a pathetic figure. The constancy with which he took the best wickets in England stopped that idea.

> *Ibid.*

1338 For those who love the art of bowling it was, as Professor Moriarty said to Sherlock Holmes, 'an intellectual treat', to watch him in action.

> **I A R Peebles**
> *Barclays World of Cricket* (1980)

1339 For Clarrie Grimmett leg-break and googly bowling was the main reason for living. Taking a cricket ball away from Clarrie during a match was like taking a bone from a dog.

> **R S Whitington**
> *Time of the Tiger* (1970)

Grout, A W
1340 A marvellous example in the field in a very enthusiastic side.

Bob Taylor
Wicket-Keeping (1979)

1341 A high-roller among wicket-keepers, who chanced his skill and his health against a few years of enjoyment from international cricket.

Jack Pollard
Australian Cricket (1982)

Gunn, G
1342 He had originally been destined to be a musician, and he brought to cricket the art and imagination, not to say gentle eccentricity, of the musical profession.

I A R Peebles
Lord's 1946 – 70 (1971)

1343 He is the only batsman I have seen who carried his fancies to the wicket and indulged them there.

E V Lucas
100 Years of Trent Bridge (1938)

Hadlee, R J
1344 While effortlessly simple in its final appearance, his rhythmical method took him years to perfect.

Phil Edmonds
100 Greatest Bowlers (1989)

1345 . . . as near mechanical perfection as it is possible for a human to be.

Ibid.

1346 One may say of Hadlee as one may say of few other cricketers of any era that any team he plays for becomes a quite different proposition, formidable by virtue of his brilliant bowling and potentially destructive batting.

Christopher Martin-Jenkins
Cricket Characters (1987)

Hall, W W
1347 Wes Hall's personality was such that no one, not even the batsmen whom he bombarded, could take exception to him.

David Frith
The Fast Men (1975)

Hammond, W R

1348 He walked to the wicket, this son of an army major, as if he already knew his worth. The step carried the suggestion of a swagger; the appearance was immaculate, down to the silk handkerchief which peeped out of the trouser pocket.

David Foot
Cricket's Unholy Trinity (1985)

1349 For Hammond was majesty and power; Hammond was grace and beauty and courage. One glorious cover-drive from him and I would be content.

Margaret Hughes
All on a Summer's Day (1953)

1350 From the moment he walked from the pavilion to begin his innings, he looked the master. Such a giant of the game seemed always to dwarf the rest of the team, and the moment he faced up to bowling that had held difficulties for the other batsmen, that bowling appeared to lose its venom.

Sir Leonard Hutton
Just My Story (1956)

1351 His batting was the result of complete purity of style allied to an exceptionally strong and beautifully-proportioned physique. He could have excelled at any game, and his choice was cricket's good fortune.

E W Swanton
A History of Cricket, Volume Two (1962)

1352 There was power, yet accompanied by grace. One did not immediately become conscious of the force of the shot until it hit the rails. Just as a single stroke can outlast in memory the many in an innings of mammoth proportions, so that one stroke, the cover-drive, refused to be erased from my memory. Grace and power had become intermingled.

A D Nourse
Cricket in the Blood (1950)

1353 There was no obvious dancing footwork with Hammond in command. It was as though he knew beforehand what the bowler's intentions were and would forestall his hopes almost as he delivered the ball.

Ibid.

1354   He was a cricketer without limitation and of epic performances.

Grahame Parker
Gloucestershire Road (1983)

1355   Good looking and with a physical presence, he was every part the classic sporting hero.

Ibid.

1356   It is very difficult to assess his precise motivation; perhaps at its root lurked an element of inferiority.

Ibid.

1357   Hammond gave to cricket, and cricket gave to Hammond, everything – except the things he wanted most.

Alan Gibson
The Cricket Captains of England (1979)

1358   It was not easy to get to know Hammond. He was not a ready mixer and he could be disconcertingly abrupt.

E M Wellings
Vintage Cricketers (1983)

1359   He could be moody, he could withdraw into himself, and he did not make friends quickly.

Ibid.

1360   He expressed himself within the framework of the game as he found it and enlarged its scope by the magnificence of manner. His portrayal of cricket was the thing of beauty that is joy for ever and abundance lay about him from seed time to harvest. Grandeur was his cloak and gratitude for it must be his memorial.

J M Kilburn
Cricket – The Great Ones (1967)

Hanif Mohammad

1361   He liked to cruise relentlessly on in a steady rhythm.

Colin Cowdrey
Barclays World of Cricket (1986)

1362 When strength and confidence were added to his concentration
and technique, Hanif became a complete batsman. His journeys
across the sub-continent were royal progresses.

Scyld Berry
A Cricket Odyssey (1988)

Harris, David
1363 Harris may be considered the first bowler who knew the power
of a good-length ball.

W G Grace
Cricket (1891)

1364 David Harris used sometimes to walk to the ground on
crutches, but bowled splendidly, we are told, when he got
warm.

Hon R H Lyttleton
The Badminton Library − Cricket (1904)

Harris, Lord
1365 As for Lord Harris, the one quality of good captaincy which he
did not possess was that of close sympathy with the side under
his command.

P C Standing
Cricket of Today and Yesterday (1904)

1366 No cricketer is quicker to congratulate a comrade on a fine
performance.

W G Grace
Cricket (1891)

1367 Perhaps Harris was a bit of a dictator, but he was eminently
just and fair.

Sir Pelham Warner
Long Innings (1951)

1368 Certainly he was autocratic, but he mellowed as he matured and
his fairness meant that he was much respected.

Gerry Cotter
The Ashes Captains (1989)

1369 There is something of the fourth Lord Harris in each of us who
loves cricket.

James D Coldham
Lord Harris (1983)

Harvey, R N
1370   Neil Harvey always had sunlight gleaming across his cricket.

David Frith
Cricket Heroes (1985)

Hassett, A L
1371   A cricketer of immense cunning who drilled his small frame to perform exhilarating feats of daring or steamrolling defence.

Jack Pollard
Australian Cricket (1982)

1372   He was a marvellous blend of impish prankster, skilled batsman, clever tactician, and sparkling speaker.

Ibid.

1373   In the art of making friends for Australian cricket, there has never been anybody like him.

Ibid.

Hawke, Lord
1374   Hawke broke the mould of English cricket and substantially remade the summer game in the modern image.

James P Coldham
F S Jackson (1989)

1375   Cricket was a mighty power for good in the world and throughout his life he did his utmost to ensure that no man used it otherwise.

Ibid.

1376   He led the way in making large and necessary improvements in the lot of the professional cricketer.

Alan Gibson
The Cricket Captains of England (1979)

1377   His contribution to the game was great, especially in raising the standard of professional conduct and comfort, together with provision after retirement, but he sometimes dwelled too much in the past, and was not sufficiently receptive of new ideas when conditions were changing.

Sir Pelham Warner
Lord's 1787–1945 (1946)

1378 Autocrat he may have been, but a benevolent autocrat
nevertheless.

> **John Marshall**
> *Headingley* (1970)

1379 He is a splendid captain, inspiring his men by the example he
gives them of pluck and resource.

> **W G Grace**
> *W G – Cricketing Reminiscences and Personal Recollections*
> (1899)

1380 As a cricketer, he was not up to England standard. In strict
terms of cricketing merit, he was not worth his place in the
great Yorkshire sides which he captained at the beginning of the
20th century.

> **Alan Gibson**
> *The Cricket Captains of England* (1979)

1381 Hawke was not the ogre he sometimes seemed, but for too long
he had been judge and jury in the court of Yorkshire cricket.

> **James P Coldham**
> *F S Jackson* (1989)

1382 It is one of the ironies of our first-class game that the seventh
Lord Hawke, who in his way tried hard to give the
professionals of his day an improved status, was held up to
such scorn. One stray, ill-chosen sentence of his, in which he
rhetorically prayed to God that no professional would ever
captain England, looked haughty and insensitive in print, and
summoned up bitter emotions from the less privileged.

> **David Foot**
> *Cricket's Unholy Trinity* (1985)

1383 The council chambers of cricket suffered their severest loss
when the wickets of these two great Englishmen fell.

> **E H D Sewell** (of Harris and Hawke)
> *Well Hit! Sir* (1947)

Hayward, T W
1384 . . . a genial and imperturbable fellow with the complexion and
robust figure of a yeoman, and the moustaches – and at the
wicket the authority – of a sergeant-major.

> **H S Altham**
> *A History of Cricket, Volume One* (1926)

1385   Coming from a stock of cricketers, he had the correctness of method instilled into him from childhood; and for soundness of ability in conjunction with excellent, though never very quick footwork, he can be ranked among the pre-eminent.

Sir Home Gordon
Background of Cricket (1939)

Headley, G A
1386   But it was to the black masses that Headley had the deepest significance. When he walked to the wicket, brisk, self-assured, and took guard in his quaintly old-fashioned, 'two-eyed' stance, he became the focus of the longing of an entire people for proof: proof of their own self-worth, their own capacity.

Michael Manley
A History of West Indies Cricket (1988)

1387   He carried, at all times, wherever he went, the hopes of the black, English-speaking Caribbean man.

Ibid.

1388   He was black excellence personified in a white world in a white sport.

Ibid.

1389   In the early days George Headley symbolised the struggle for parity, when even the wickets and the climate seemed to be against them.

Clayton Goodwin
Caribbean Cricketers (1980)

1390   He had characteristics which can be attributed to less than half a dozen in the whole history of the game.

C L R James
Beyond a Boundary (1963)

1391   George was a quiet cricketer. So quiet that you could easily underestimate him.

Ibid.

1392   George Headley, this West Indian, would be my candidate for a clinical study of a great batsman as a unique type of human being, mentally and physically.

Ibid.

Hearne, J T
1393 Hearne must be counted among the greatest quick-medium bowlers of all time.

E M Wellings
A History of County Cricket: Middlesex (1972)

1394 J T Hearne became a tradition in the Middlesex side.

Hon T C F Prittie
Middlesex CCC (1951)

1395 He became the marvel of his generation.

Ibid.

Hearne, J W
1396 Taste and discretion were the essence of his play, and its eclectic beauty was never allowed to degenerate into the merely ornate.

Hon T C F Prittie
Mainly Middlesex (1947)

1397 In entering or resigning the office of bowling, in accepting or inwardly rejecting the judgements of umpires, in benefiting from the vigilance or suffering from the indolence of fielders, he exhibited, as near as a cricketer may, a conquest over motion and emotion alike.

R C Robertson-Glasgow
More Cricket Prints (1948)

1398 Both his batting and bowling were founded on exact science, and exact science does not jump out and hit the onlooker in the eye.

Hon T C F Prittie
Middlesex CCC (1951)

Hendren, E P
1399 He brought a cockney wit and spirit of comedy to the cricket field, counterpoint to the sobriety and refinement of the Lord's atmosphere.

Ibid.

1400 His popularity was only a part of his greatness but it was the part which will be last forgotten. His very fallibility was the lucky charm hung at the end of that string of magnificent achievements.

Ibid.

1401 He loved his cricket with all his heart and soul. He did everything spontaneously and wholeheartedly and he seemed to call to us to come and play with him and to have as much fun as he was having.

Margaret Hughes
All on a Summer's Day (1953)

1402 He liked slapstick, but he knew when and at whom to throw the pie. His short, square build, busy movements, and low-geared run were made for comedy.

R C Robertson-Glasgow
Cricket Prints (1943)

1403 He had a gift for apt and spontaneous buffoonery, with the instinctive gift for timing and restraint of the accomplished clown who is sensitive to his audience and never persists beyond the moment of discretion.

I A R Peebles
Patsy Hendren (1969)

1404 He was a little man, who could have been described as roundly tubby, but that suggests a certain lack of mobility and Patsy was quicksilver in the deep field and close to the wicket alike. His face precisely revealed the man. It was an impish succession of rounded curves, the sort of face artists put on illustrations of Irish leprechauns.

E M Wellings
Vintage Cricket (1983)

Hill, C
1405 As is so often the case with the leading Australians, his success depends less upon obedience to strict canons of style than upon a full development of his own natural way of dealing with bowling of every kind.

C B Fry and G W Beldam
Great Batsmen (1905)

1406 He was a man born to lead, but by direct methods rather than finesse. He attacked frontally, never sought the flank. He would go straight through a difficulty. No situation was too difficult to face or to solve.

A G Moyes
A Century of Cricketers (1950)

Hirst, G H

1407 Stalwart as the oak, generous, and complete master of his craft, he commanded an affection and respect in all who knew him personally or by repute.

> **Diana Rait Kerr and I A R Peebles**
> *Lord's 1946 – 70* (1971)

1408 His capacity as a batsman or bowler always appeared to be equal.

> **Anthony Woodhouse**
> *The History of Yorkshire CCC* (1989)

1409 He was worshipped by players, spectators and all who came into contact with him.

> *Ibid.*

1410 In George Hirst's cricket we have, almost perfectly displayed, the outlook of the true cavalier: gay and always attacking.

> **A A Thomson**
> *Hirst and Rhodes* (1959)

1411 No bowler ever cared less whether it had rained or not.

> **E H D Sewell**
> *Well Hit! Sir* (1947)

1412 People recognised his worth not only to Yorkshire but to English cricket as well. He certainly did much for the game, by his batting and bowling and perhaps even more by the example he set to all his colleagues.

> **Sir Henry Levenson-Gower**
> *Off and on the Field* (1953)

Hobbs, J B

1413 Few have had so much power to attract to watch cricket not only those who understood the finer points of the game but also many whose knowledge of cricket was much less.

> *Ibid.*

1414 Hobbs was the master of many apparently effortless strokes, and he was so quick that often it seemed useless to try to set a field for him.

> *Ibid.*

1415   . . . was the bridge between the Classic and Modern periods.

J L Carr
Dictionary of Extra-ordinary English Cricketers (1977)

1416   In play, the salient feature of his cricket was that it seemed so unspectacular: he batted perfectly because he was the perfect batsman.

John Arlott
Book of Cricketers (1979)

1417   Alike to the expert and the casual observer he was the epitome of batsmanship. Though the game was his profession Hobbs's standard of values was always qualitative rather than quantitative.

H S Altham
A History of Cricket, Volume One (1926)

1418   Merely to see him lift or swing a bat at close quarters, to observe the flexing, tensing and relaxing of his grip on the handle was to perceive the profound sensitivity of his batting.

John Arlott
Jack Hobbs (1982) reprinted in *The Guardian Book of Cricket* (1986)

1419   We shall think of him, trim and tidy, coming out to open the innings; we shall see the twirling of the bat before each ball, the easy, perfectly poised stance at the wicket, those dancing feet move swiftly back or forward, and we shall dream of him 'burning the grass with boundaries', his bat flashing forth every stroke known to cricket.

J M Kilburn
In Search of Cricket (1937)

1420   His life is a proposition, laid out with Euclidean punctilio, that the hired hand may, through application, technical genius and stoic decency, rise as far as he cares to. His age is past and his type is extinct. The loss is cricket's. Ours too.

Benny Green
A History of Cricket (1988)

1421   He was a model for the young and a continual amazement to
       the old; yet preserved throughout an unhurried quietness, a
       steady and rooted stability, to which his brilliance was an
       adornment and not a danger.

                                                 Ronald Mason
                                              Jack Hobbs (1960)

1422   Years ago I was sitting with the late A A Milne while Hobbs
       was batting in a Test match at Trent Bridge. Milne turned to
       me and said 'The sound of his bat somehow puts me in mind
       of vintage port.'

                                                  Ben Travers
                  The Infatuee in *The Cricketer's Bedside Book* (1966)

1423   There was a wisdom so informed your bat
       To understanding of the bowler's trade
       That each resource of strength or skill he used
       Seemed but the context of the stroke you played.

                                                  John Arlott
                  To John Berry Hobbs on His 70th Birthday (1952)

1424   Like many, many others I claim that Jack Hobbs was the
       greatest batsman. He was the master on all types of pitch, his
       technique developed to overcome any difficulties.

                                                E M Wellings
                                         Vintage Cricketers (1983)

Hutton, L
1425   He brought England back to the forefront of world cricket, and
       showed to his fellow-players a perfection of technique and a
       dedicated example that were faithfully followed by his young
       disciples.

                                                 E W Swanton
                                    Sort of a Cricket Person (1972)

1426   Temperament, background, and circumstances combined to
       mould Hutton so that he is remembered as a player of superb
       and precise defence, watchful and enduring, accumulating runs
       from every mistake the attack might make, but seldom
       dominating and disrupting. But those who have had a glimpse

of the dazzling series of strokes he could produce when
impelled to do so can only wonder what his career might have
been had he played for Sussex as an amateur.

Diana Rait Kerr and I A R Peebles
Lord's 1946 – 70 (1971)

1427   His is the stern and antique figure of the gladiator, a grim
contestant, hired by the public to give them a spectacle, yet
determined that the spectacle shall be good by *his* standards,
even if it be also above the public's head.

J M Kilburn
Len Hutton (1951) reprinted in *The Observer on Cricket* (1987)

1428   Hutton was never dull. His bat was part of his nervous system.
His play was sculptured. His forward defensive stroke was a
complete statement.

Harold Pinter
Hutton and the Past in *Cricket '72* (1972)

1429   Hutton was a cautious captain. This was in his nature, and
even had it not been, the circumstances of his appointment
would have pressed him in the same direction. His caution had
its dismal aspects, particularly in the slowing of the over-rate.

Alan Gibson
The Cricket Captains of England (1979)

1430   I never much enjoyed watching Hutton bat. I was always scared
he might get out, just as mother was always scared what might
happen to the best china if she took it out of the cabinet.

Alan Gibson
Growing Up with Cricket (1985)

1431   Len was a joy to watch, even when he was scoring slowly,
because his technique was not only very good but also elegant.

Trevor Bailey
Wickets, Catches and the Odd Run (1986)

1432 Hutton's record is rich in success and he conceded class and grace to no one.

Peter Thomas
Yorkshire Cricketers 1839 – 1939 (1973)

1433 . . . left first-class cricket with a feeling of relief rather than regret. He had completed an exhausting journey.

J M Kilburn
A History of Yorkshire Cricket (1970)

Illingworth, R
1434 It is doubtful if anyone else had delved so deeply or effectively into the tactics of the various forms of the contemporary game.

John Arlott
Book of Cricketers (1979)

1435 Few players under Illingworth's command would say they were treated unfairly.

Patrick Murphy
The Spinner's Turn (1982)

1436 Flexible, shrewd, phlegmatic and resourceful – Ray Illingworth combined these qualities with an intense determination and pride.

Ibid.

1437 . . . was the ice-cold calculating brain of cricket.

John Hampshire
Family Argument (1983)

1438 He crept and shuffled rather than bobbed up to the bowling crease, ball held sinisterly, as if it were a grenade he was about to lob into an enemy trench. Here was wisdom of the hard Northern kind.

David Frith
The Slow Men (1984)

Imran Khan
1439 He has played his cricket, during a long and very illustrious career, with the bearing of a prince, hovering between over-haughtiness and innate pride.

Christopher Martin-Jenkins
Cricket Characters (1987)

1440   He never expects to be beaten or bettered.

Ibid.

1441   Of all the all-rounders who dominated world cricket in the early 1980s, Imran Khan was in several ways the most blessed.

Matthew Engel
Barclays World of Cricket (1986)

Insole, D J
1442   A resourceful captain with up-to-date ideas, he had a first-class cricketing brain and his sense of humour and lack of pomposity kept the game in proper perspective.

Christopher Martin-Jenkins
The Complete Who's Who of Test Cricketers (1987)

1443   . . . few busy men have given more honorary time to cricket.

E W Swanton
The Cricketer (1979) reprinted in *As I Said at the Time* (1983)

Intikhab Alam
1444   . . . the massive, gentle leg-spin craftsman, looked deceptively like one of Capone's bodyguards, especially when his black hair thinned away to nothing.

David Frith
The Slow Men (1984)

1445   . . . was possibly the most popular player in modern cricket.

Pat Pocock
Percy (1987)

Jackson, A
1446   He seems to have every stroke which a batsman, as opposed to a player with a bat in his hand, ought to have.

P G H Fender
The Turn of the Screw (1929)

1447   . . . the finest at his age I have ever seen.

Ibid.

1448   Men of all ages who saw him never forgot him, and a generation later they still held his banner. All those who made his acquaintance shared the desire to be regarded as his intimate friend.

David Frith
Archie Jackson (1978)

1449   His innings were invariably brief gems of style and elegance.

Jack Pollard
Australian Cricket (1982)

Jackson, F S
1450   All that Jackson did on the cricket field he did so easily that it seemed to be the only thing to do.

E H D Sewell
Well Hit! Sir (1947)

1451   Tactful and diplomatic and a man of the world, Jackson was a highly successful captain, and he was a wonderful spinner of a coin.

Sir Pelham Warner
Lord's 1787 – 1945 (1946)

1452   On the field his mind was locked in combat, off it he was the most genial of companions and opponents. He was, and looked, every inch a cricketer; every inch a captain of England.

Alan Gibson
Jackson's Year (1965)

1453   As a captain he was calm, collected, always in command; if his temper was usually even, his displeasure could be very abrupt indeed when the occasion warranted.

James P Coldham
F S Jackson (1989)

1454   He needed the stimulus of the big occasion, and was born to grace the great stages of English cricket; the county game did not always fire his imagination.

Ibid.

1455   As a batsman he never flinched and as a bowler he never
        bowled to hit the batsman. These were the unwritten laws, the
        code by which he judged others, and by which he expected
        others to judge him.

                                                            Ibid.

1456   He never did anything by halves, whether he thrashed the ball
        to the boundary or was comprehensively bowled, he played his
        stroke with a majestic flourish.

                                                            Ibid.

1457   He was always turned out, flannels, pads and boots, to
        perfection.

                                                        C B Fry
                                          Life Worth Living (1939)

1458   An excellent Englishman.

                                                            Ibid.

1459   His career overflowed with the honey of success, but it never
        spoiled him; it was still a sideline, and his departure from the
        cricket scene was to allow him to conquer with equally dazzling
        results the world of politics.

                                                    Peter Thomas
                              Yorkshire Cricketers 1839 – 1939 (1973)

Jardine, D R
1460   He was a fine cricketer and a character of granite-like texture.

                                Diana Rait Kerr and I A R Peebles
                                           Lord's 1946 – 1970 (1971)

1461   By his very 'presence' on the field, by the way his team jumped
        at the word of command, one sensed that here was a man in
        control of the situation.

                                                    Edward Docker
                                  Bradman and the Bodyline Series (1978)

1462   Alike in tactical skill and in personality, he must rank as one of
        the great captains: if he demanded much of his men, he never
        failed to give to them and to the game all that he had himself.

                                                        H S Altham
                                    Barclays World of Cricket (1980)

1463 He would not have been a popular captain with the public even without bodyline, but he would have been, in his own style, a pretty good one.

> **Alan Gibson**
> *The Cricket Captains of England* (1979)

1464 He can be a powerful friend but a relentless enemy. He gives no quarter and asks none. He is a fighter, every inch of him. He will see a job through, no matter what the consequences, and will never admit defeat.

> **Bill Bowes**
> *Express Deliveries* (1949)

1465 England's XI will be indeed fortunate if, in the future, it ever has to serve under a better man than Mr Jardine.

> **Harold Larwood**
> *Body-Line?* (1933)

1466 Jardine had a sardonic wit, but he was unlikely to choose Test cricket as a vehicle for it.

> **E W Swanton**
> *'Gubby' Allen* (1985)

1467 His personal popularity came second to that ambition.

> **Alan Hill**
> *Hedley Verity* (1986)

1468 The tribunal of history, among them scandalmongers or writers unqualified to make judgements, have vilified Jardine to a degree almost unprecedented in cricket post-mortems. It is clear that he was a maligned man and more knowledgeable critics have said that Jardine had a warmth and charm that in the long run survived a forbidding austerity.

> *Ibid.*

1469 Closer examination of his character and the testimony of those who knew him reveal that posterity has attributed to him sinister qualities which he never in fact possessed.

> **Christopher Douglas**
> *Douglas Jardine* (1984)

1470   His love for cricket was intense, passionate even, and therein lay the difficulty, it seems.

Ibid.

1471   He was a man both proud and sensitive – courageous and with a single-mindedness that must surely be an example to us all.

Sir Hubert Ashton (1958)
Quoted in *Douglas Jardine* (1984)

Javed Miandad
1472   His batting was not exactly, from the purist's point of view, a delight but from his side's point of view his improvisation was an object lesson to those who were watching.

Sunil Gavaskar
Idols (1984)

1473   Javed was a very shy and diffident character then and not the brash self-confident and cocky person he is today.

Ibid.

1474   He is an extremely volatile person.

John Arlott
100 Greatest Batsmen (1986)

1475   He has tended to symbolise the strengths and the defects of our batting in recent years – exotic strokeplay mixed up with suicidal tendencies.

Imran Khan
Imran (1983)

1476   He is a live-wire, inclined to hot-headedness, and he has too often incurred the wrath of opponents, as well as their admiration for the brilliance of his strokeplay.

Christopher Martin-Jenkins
Cricket Characters (1987)

1477   The Welsh, you see, love a true sporting star. The little Pakistani master was the cricketing equivalent of a great rugby outside-half in their eyes – and to see him take the attack apart on a sunlit afternoon at Swansea was one of sport's great joys.

Ron Jones
County Championship Review (1986)

1478 Miandad's approach has always been petty and negative.

> **Scyld Berry**
> *A Cricket Odyssey* (1988)

Jenkins, R
1479 In today's era of mass production one is happy to see someone or something that is different from the masses whether it be cricketers or anything else.

> **Roy Genders**
> *Worcestershire* (1952)

1480 He is one of the few players who are genuinely annoyed if they have to claim their insurance money for missing a game.

> *Ibid.*

1481 The more grim the conditions, the happier he is.

> *Ibid.*

1482 A true character who probably talked out as many batsmen as he bowled out, but who enjoyed his cricket and, in return, gave much enjoyment.

> **M D Vockins**
> *Worcestershire CCC* (1980)

1483 There was a determined combative approach to his cricket; workmanlike is too mundane a description because he was, too, an artist but it is an apt description for Jenkins certainly worked, and worked hard, at his game.

> *Ibid.*

Jessop, G L
1484 Gilbert Jessop was the living embodiment of that sensationalism which will always make the most direct and compelling appeal to the man who pays his shilling and wants his money's worth.

> **H S Altham**
> *A History of Cricket, Volume One* (1926)

1485 His very stance, like a panther's crouch, bespoke aggression. The secret of his hitting lay in his speed, of eye, of foot, and of hand. He combined in a unique degree strength and flexibility of shoulder, arm and wrist.

> *Ibid.*

1486   The batsman who does nearly everything a batsman ought not to do — with consummate success. The insolent unorthodoxy of his methods and the combined frequency and power of his hitting mark him as truly unique.

C B Fry and G W Beldam
Great Batsmen (1905)

1487   Here was perhaps the greatest outright hitter of all time, who was also the finest cover-point or extra cover of his day and a good enough fast bowler to be chosen once that year purely in that capacity.

C B Fry
Life Worth Living (1939)

1488   He comes into the category of phenomena. No one has ever batted in the least like Jessop.

Ibid.

1489   He crouched over his stance like a cat about to pounce; then he launched himself yards down the pitch with quick short steps and literally flung his bat at the ball, with the result that it went vastly hard and high somewhere between extra cover and long leg.

Ibid.

1490   His hitting was prodigious, but he was not a slogger.

Ibid.

1491   . . . a gentle creature, a pleasant, friendly, popular man who never lost his composure.

Brian Bearshaw
The Big Hitters (1986)

1492   Crouch he certainly did, for style meant nothing to him. Batting was a glorious gamble.

A G Moyes
A Century of Cricketers (1950)

Johnson, I W
1493 He was not quick enough to take advantage of wet pitches, but on hard, fast or crumbling pitches his bounce and mastery of flight troubled even the most skilful batsmen.

Jack Pollard
Australian Cricket (1982)

Johnston, W A
1494 A great team man and the most successful left-arm bowler Australia had ever sent to England.

Ibid.

1495 A whimsical fellow who never lost his temper, Johnston was worked so hard during the summer that he sometimes had to go straight from spinning the old ball to swinging the new.

Phil Edmonds
100 Greatest Bowlers (1989)

1496 Australians have a high opinion of this good-humoured, long-suffering likeable chap who can take it.

A G Moyes
A Century of Cricketers (1950)

Jones, W E
1497 Apparently the target weighed so heavily on his mind that when asleep at night, he would nudge his wife in bed and say, 'run up, there's three here!'

Andrew Hignell
The History of Glamorgan CCC (1988)

Kallicharran, A I
1498 . . . brilliant, entertaining and masterly batsman.

John Arlott
100 Greatest Batsmen (1986)

1499 . . . one of the most exciting of strokeplayers.

Crawford White
Barclays World of Cricket (1986)

1500 A great player and courageous individualist.

Ibid.

1501   He compensated in timing and footwork what he lacked in physical power.

Ibid.

Kanhai, R

1502   . . . a complete player on all types of wickets.

Bob Taylor
Wicketkeeping (1979)

1503   He mellowed from being an erratic but brilliant batsman to a master.

Ibid.

1504   Short, compact, with a steely resolve to score runs, he probably did more than any batsman to dispel the notion − widely believed at one time − that West Indians were flamboyant batsmen who refused to graft and build an innings against persistently accurate bowling.

Jack Pollard
Australian Cricket (1982)

1505   . . . a natural genius for batting.

Christopher Martin-Jenkins
The Complete Who's Who of Test Cricketers (1987)

1506   I shall always feel a personal debt of gratitude to Warwickshire for engaging him, not so much because of the runs he scored for them, though they have been entertaining enough in all conscience, but because I was able to see again in him what batsmen were like in the days when they still believed it was their main function in life to hit the ball hard − plus, of course, the personal panache he brought to the game.

Leslie Duckworth
The Story of Warwickshire Cricket (1974)

1507   He was sometimes a man of moods − aren't we all? − but he let the younger generation of Warwickshire players and spectators see what real batsmanship could be, and I knew that I had not dreamed there were really such batsmen once.

Ibid.

1508   An unsublimated anger in Kanhai's batting has prompted the sombre thought in more than one observer that the real, the symbolic point about cricket is to assert the power of bat over ball, of man over nature, life over death.

Donald Trelford
County Champions (1982)

Kapil Dev, R N
1509   Kapil's brand of cricket is also the attacking brand which makes him a crowd pleaser wherever he goes.

Sunil Gavaskar
Idols (1984)

1510   He is still polite, courteous to the senior cricketers and is prepared to listen to everyone. These characteristics have been difficult to find in recent years and Kapil is richly endowed with his many splendoured cricketing talents that God Almighty has showered on him.

Ibid.

1511   . . . athletic, free-flowing, honest. His stamina has been prodigious, and his movement in the air and off the seam have brought a high percentage reward.

David Frith
The Fast Men (1982)

1512   . . . an all-round cricketer of charismatic brilliance.

Christopher Martin-Jenkins
The Complete Who's Who of Test Cricketers (1987)

1513   There is something reminiscent of a wild animal in the sight of Kapil Dev on the cricket field. He is a restless figure, erect and alert, saucer eyes darting hither and thither, muscles it seems, twitching like a deer on the lookout for danger.

Christopher Martin-Jenkins
Cricket Characters (1987)

1514   If any modern cricketer has had charisma, it is Kapil Dev. India may be inconsistent under his command, but they are no longer considered to be dull.

Ibid.

Kippax, A F
1515   . . . in an era when his finesse was mistrusted by Test selectors
he left his lyrical style in the memory and assumed, in the eyes
of the world, a stature undeservedly less than major.

David Frith
Archie Jackson (1987)

1516   . . . a very free open style, and an appreciation of the purpose
for which he was given a bat and sent to the wicket.

P G H Fender
The Turn of the Wheel (1929)

1517   One always felt of him that he had enormous potentialities, yet
he did not often fulfil expectations.

Ibid.

1518   One of Australia's great right-handed batting stylists, and a
cricketer of great personal charm.

Jack Pollard
Australian Cricket (1982)

1519   Kippax's batting had a silky quality not seen in any other
player of his time or since. His leg-glancing, forward or back,
was so delicate that it had a kind of moonbeam beauty.

Ray Robinson
Between Wickets (1946)

1520   His batsmanship should have been weighted in carats, not runs.

Ibid.

Kirmani, S M H
1521   He is the best wicket-keeper in the world for the simple reason
that he has been keeping wickets to the spinners and keeping
them extremely well, throughout the seven or eight years he has
been playing Test cricket.

Sunil Gavaskar
Idols (1984)

1522   While solidity and technical finesse were the hallmarks of his work behind the wicket, when in front of the stumps Kirmani batted with gay and courageous abandon defying many of the tenets of orthodox play.

> **Ramaswamy Mohan**
> *Barclays World of Cricket* (1987)

Knott, A P E
1523   Small, perky, alert as a cat, he is unmistakable from the farthest corner of the gound, whether crouching low beside the stumps, or poised wide-eyed in front of them, handle of the bat thrust forward, as alive to possibilities of misadventure as a boy playing French cricket on a bumpy lawn.

> **John Thicknesse**
> *Barclays World of Cricket* (1980)

1524   Magnificently consistent over a remarkable period of time.

> **Bob Taylor**
> *Wicketkeeping* (1979)

1525   The game was full of long stops, headed by Alan Knott, who was nearly as agile as Evans when standing alongside the slips but was not good standing up to slow bowling.

> **E M Wellings**
> *Vintage Cricketers* (1983)

1526   Whether keeping wicket or batting, he always provided superb entertainment in a modest, very likeable manner which endeared him to fans and fellow players alike wherever he went.

> **Dudley Moore**
> *The History of Kent CCC* (1988)

1527   The sun hat, the handkerchief protruding from a pocket, the sleeves rolled down, the pieces of sticking plaster adhering to pads and clothing were his own trademarks. They irritated some people, as did the continual exercises which he did in the middle, but it never worried him – he had devised them all for a purpose.

> *Ibid.*

1528   I would say he was probably the most unorthodox player of spin bowling in the game – and the most feared.

> **Derek Underwood**
> *The History of Kent CCC* (1988)

Kortright, C J

1529   It was then only a matter of time before a 'Korty' became schoolboy slang for a really fast ball and the phrase 'as fast as Kortright' became a common-place comparison.

Anthony Meredith
The Demon and the Lobster (1987)

1530   Whether it was golf, snooker, shooting, fishing or bridge, his competitive nature always brought out the worst in him.

Ibid.

1531   To the historian Plutarch, Charles Kortright would have been the forthright, no-nonsense Roman.

Ibid.

1532   Korty matched his furious speed with a furious temper. He took strong personal dislikes to batsmen and revelled in the guise of the terrifying paceman.

Charles Sale
Korty (1986)

1533   Like many another, Kortright, it seems, did not always take kindly to being superceded in the attack.

Hon E G F French
The Cornerstone of English Cricket (1948)

1534   Kortright enjoyed being the centre of attention, but, always the sportsman, didn't like individual players being subject to criticism from the crowd.

Charles Sale
Korty (1986)

1535   Kortright's only comment when he was asked what he thought of England's attempts to play the Australian speed merchant was, 'I'd have been frightened to bowl at the modern batsmen. I'd cut 'em in half.'

Charles Bray
Essex County Cricket (1950)

1536   C J Kortright was unquestionably the fastest bowler of the last 60 years – if not, of all time.

Sir Home Gordon
Background of Cricket (1939)

1537   The fact was that not only was Kortright a holy terror as express bowler, but he revelled in being so. He took strong dislikes to certain opponents, and would let fly viciously at them.

Ibid.

1538   . . . was the most willing to hurt the batsmen, and when I said so to him long after in 1938, he agreed with a grin.

Ibid.

Laker, J C
1539   He has done what always must excite imagination. He has exemplified, in a single day, all the classical conceptions of the art of slow bowling: strict control first of length and then direction; the imparting of dangerous spin by technique superbly applied; the variation of spin with the ball that runs straight through to sow doubt as well as prompt error in the batsman; the subtle changes of flight, length and pace that will induce fatal errors of judgement; and, lastly, the cool appraisal of each batsman's temperament and resource.

Denys Rowbotham (1956)
Reprinted in *The Guardian Book of Cricket* (1986)

1540   It was with the ball that Laker made his music. All his skill was founded on the final leap into his delivery, not an exaggerated leap you understand, but a final decisive movement which was impeccably and invariably rhythmic.

Robin Marlar
Cricket Heroes (1984)

1541   Jim Laker never bowled an ugly ball, and like all great bowlers he bowled precious few bad 'uns either.

Ibid.

1542   He was a killer with the ball and his quality came not only from his action but from one of the most finely-tuned cricketing brains of his or any other generation.

Ibid.

1543   If Jim Laker is to be credited with one outstanding attribute, it
must be that of intelligence: and not merely intelligence, but
applied intelligence.

John Arlott
Cricket: The Great Bowlers (1968)

1544   His bowling was of a kind that is effective throughout the ages.

Phil Edmonds
100 Greatest Bowlers (1989)

1545   His subtle variations of flight and spin were a continued source
of delight to the connoisseur.

Trevor Bailey
The Greatest of My Time (1968)

Larwood, H
1546   Certainly he is one of the world's great bowlers. What a
wonderful action, what accuracy and stamina! I can see him
now as I write − a demon of destruction to batsmen, with all
the concentrated antagonism that a fast bowler should have.

Kenneth Farnes
Tours and Tests (1940)

1547   He was, for a certainty, the only bowler who quelled Bradman;
the only bowler who made Bradman lose his poise and balance,
departing from his set path of easeful centuries into flurried
and agitated movements.

Jack Fingleton
Brightly Fades the Don (1949)

1548   Everyone who knew him liked him, applauded his skill as a
bowler, was fascinated by the magnificent action, his masterly
control, yet because his talents were misdirected he dropped out
of the game far too soon.

A G Moyes
A Century of Cricketers (1950)

1549   It was a joy to watch him bowl, for he gave life and zest to the
conflict.

Ibid.

1550 To have seen Larwood in Australia is to have witnessed one of the greatest of all sporting occasions.

Bill Bowes
Cricket: The Great Bowlers (1968)

1551 How he ever stood the strain of bowling at such terrific speed match after match I don't know. It was amazing.

Sir Donald Bradman
My Cricketing Life (1938)

1552 The heat drained him, and the pounding over hard grounds tortured his feet and wrecked his boots. But he was there at the end, a hero to many, especially among those closest to him.

David Frith
The Fast Men (1982)

Lawry, W M
1553 His determination and powers of concentration can be paid no higher compliment than to say that they were the equal of Bradman's, but there is a limit to the number of times people want to see the ball pushed back to the bowler if there is the remotest risk that it might take a wicket.

Gerry Cotter
The Ashes Captains (1989)

1554 Lawry performed with a dourness bordering on heroism in many big matches but to many cricket buffs at the end of his career he typified the loss of decorum among Australia's top players.

Jack Pollard
Australian Cricket (1982)

Lewis, A R
1555 . . . staked no mean claim to fame with his leadership of MCC in India and Pakistan.

E W Swanton (1975)
Reprinted in *As I Said at the Time* (1983)

1556 Lewis wove episodes from the cricket skilfully into various aspects of his theme, striving to make the game more interesting and more easily intelligible to old and young.

Ibid.

1557 Darkly good-looking, with a smile which would charm a statue, Tony Lewis is a man of many talents.

Christopher Martin-Jenkins
The Complete Who's Who of Test Cricketers (1987)

Leyland, M
1558 He was aware of his own distinction in cricket but he made no parade of it and his comment on other players had to be invited before it was expressed.

J M Kilburn
Thanks to Cricket (1972)

1559 He seems to withdraw himself altogether from the conflict round him and to be engaged in some solitary meditation of his own.

Dudley Carew
To the Wicket (1946)

1560 There was no more stirring sight in cricket than that of Maurice Leyland going out to bat when his side was in difficulties. His short, square figure advancing to the wicket exuded confidence.

E M Wellings
Vintage Cricketers (1983)

1561 When Leyland began with Yorkshire they thought him a bit too dashing. He was a left-hander who liked to cut.

Alan Gibson
Growing Up with Cricket (1985)

1562 Maurice Leyland was one of the great left-handed batsmen of all time. He was the perfect Yorkshireman, too; not tall, but broad of shoulder, thick of chest, clear eyed, kindly spoken, the man of which Yorkshire dreams are made.

Peter Thomas
Yorkshire Cricketers 1839 – 1939 (1973)

1563 He did not follow the pattern of Yorkshire batsmen in that soundness and dependability was all; the soundness and dependability was there in great quantity, but there was a genius too.

Ibid

1564   He was Horatius on the tottering bridge; Hector, who alone stood between Troy and destruction. He was born to rescue.

R C Robertson-Glasgow
Cricket Prints (1943)

Lillee, D K
1565   Lillee had all the attributes required for the job – strength, stamina, height, a magnificent action and a balanced aggression that enabled him to maximise his skills of swing and subtle change of pace.

Keith Andrew
The Handbook of Cricket (1989)

1566   Few fast bowlers have had a finer physique or technique, or such a gloriously flowing action. He added edge to it; with a hostility to his opponents often theatrical and sometimes offensive. He would have been greater still without that.

John Arlott
An Eye for Cricket (1979)

1567   That aggressive streak, his piratical, insatiable appetite for more victims and his proud refusal to be dominated was always worth a wicket or two even before he took the ball in his hand.

Paul Weaver
Cricket Heroes (1984)

1568   Cricket has given Lillee the prestige of a matinee idol and financial security for life, and he has had to work tremendously hard for them.

Jack Pollard
Australian Cricket (1982)

1569   Even when he is walking back to his mark, husbanding his strength for another delivery, rubbing the ball determinedly, he gives spectators their money's worth.

Ibid.

Lindwall, R R
1570   A great fast bowler, whose exceptional pace and exciting delivery style inspired an entire generation of young fast bowlers.

Ibid.

1571 Lindwall's bowling had the beauty of power under smooth control.

J M Kilburn
Thanks to Cricket (1972)

1572 He is, of course, an artistic bowler *par excellence,* with a control of direction and of late swing which is thrilling to watch.

E W Swanton (1959)
Reprinted in *As I Said at the Time* (1983)

1573 Ray Lindwall's fast bowling changed the look of international cricket and the expression on a thousand batsmen's faces.

Ray Robinson
After Stumps were Drawn (1985)

1574 In the art of fast bowling Ray Lindwall has no peer. To me he was the greatest of them all.

Fred Trueman
From Larwood to Lillee (1983)

Lloyd, C H
1575 The West Indies left-hander is more than a cricketer, he is the personification of all that is best in sport.

John Kay
A History of County Cricket: Lancashire (1974)

1576 As an individualist he has no peer among batsmen or fieldsmen. As a team man he is ever-willing, and often anxious to escape the spotlight.

Ibid.

1577 The most amiable among men, Lloyd sometimes conceals the galvanism which is the most telling weapon in his formidable armoury.

Eric Todd
Lancashire Cricket at the Top (1971)

1578 Cricket is an art in itself and for the zest and skill with which he played it and the entertainment he has given to so many, Clive Lloyd is well worthy of the title of Master.

Gerald Hodcroft
My Own Red Roses (1984)

1579   Lloyd became captain because he seemed to hold out the promise of the best combination of a player firmly in the side on performing merit and with the greatest potential for leadership on the field, which implies tactics; and off the field, which means keeping the team together and working in harmony.

Michael Manley
A History of West Indies Cricket (1988)

1580   Lloyd did more than employ four fast bowlers. He trained and moulded his players into the most awesome fielding side in history.

Ibid.

Lock, G A R
1581   One of the most brilliant of all close to the wicket fieldsmen, and an imaginative inspiring captain.

Jack Pollard
Australian Cricket (1982)

1582   He was an orthodox slow left-arm spinner possessed of an aggression seldom found in the fastest of bowlers. Fiery, rash and quick-witted, he was quite phenomenal fielding at short-leg.

Christopher Martin-Jenkins
The Complete Who's Who of Test Cricketers (1987)

Lockwood, W H
1583   . . . great pace and break made him on certain days almost unplayable.

E B V Christian
Surrey Cricket (1902)

1584   I have the impression that Lockwood came off the pitch with abnormal rapidity after a trajectory which did not seem so fast as that of some balls sent down by his contemporaries.

Sir Home Gordon
Background of Cricket (1939)

1585   He was never likeable, and there was in his bowling a viciousness somewhat characteristic of the bad-tempered fellow he always showed himself.

Ibid.

1586   . . . was without qualification the best fast bowler I ever played
with or against.

C B Fry
Life Worth Living (1939)

Lohmann, G A
1587   . . . was perhaps the greatest medium-pace bowler England has
ever had. He had a lovely rhythmic action.

Ibid.

1588   He made his own style of bowling, and a beautiful style it was
− so beautiful that none but a decent cricketer could fully
appreciate it.

C B Fry (1901)
Reprinted in *In Celebration of Cricket* (1978)

1589   He was, indeed, the best all-round cricketer of his generation.

E B V Christian
Surrey Cricket (1902)

Lord, T
1590   The greatest and most famous name in the world of cricket
breathes its very royalty in one syllable . . . Lord's.

Peter Thomas
Yorkshire Cricketers 1839 − 1939 (1973)

1591   He was a man of handsome presence and possessed a bonhomie
which was almost irresistible.

Lord Harris and F S Ashley-Cooper
Lord's and the MCC (1914)

1592   He was in many respects a typical example of the late 18th
century entrepreneur.

Christopher Brookes
English Cricket (1978)

1593   Lord had a nose for profit, which he would shortly exercise in
the liquor trade as well as in property dealing.

Geoffrey Moorhouse
Lord's (1983)

1594   Whatever else Thomas Lord may have acquired from his family
        background and upheavals, he certainly had an astonishing
        instinct for improving his lot, ambition and the courage to
        back it.

Tony Lewis
Double Century (1987)

1595   From the moment he arrived in London, the only grass which
        Thomas Lord allowed to grow under his feet was this cricket
        ground.

Ibid.

Lyon, B H
1596   As a captain, Bev Lyon made mistakes and miscalculations. He
        never failed to keep the match alive. His approach could be as
        rakish as the angle of his familiar trilby in the morning as he
        walked briskly from the visiting team's hotel to the ground.

David Foot
Cricket's Unholy Trinity (1985)

1597   The complexities of cricket excited his shrewd, restless mind
        and he seemed to be bubbling with permanent ideas.

Grahame Parker
Gloucestershire Road (1983)

1598   He had that rare ability which makes a team greater than the
        sum of its parts. His clinical analysis of the game had long
        since reduced it to its simplest form; batting meant hitting the
        ball, bowling hitting the wicket; each game was to be won, but
        above all it was to be enjoyed by cricketers and spectators
        alike. With him on the field cricket was fun.

Ibid.

1599   His clever use of the material available to him, his infectious
        cavalier approach to the game, transmitted his own supreme
        self-confidence to the team and their cricket.

Ibid.

1600   He belonged to a different period, but his way of playing the
        game demanded the greatest courage, both individually and
        collectively.

Ibid.

1601   The sporting world has stifled his like and turned itself into a negative mediocrity.

Ibid.

1602   He had no funeral. He bequeathed his body to the Royal College of Surgeons − still looking for a positive end to the match.

Alan Gibson
Growing Up with Cricket (1985)

McCabe, S J
1603   For audacity, skill, effortless power, and courage against the bowling that beset him, no other batsman on the active list could have equalled his performance.

Ray Robinson
Between Wickets (1946)

1604   As a saver of lost causes he has no rival.

Ibid.

1605   His batting flowed like an untroubled stream, smooth and beautiful to the eye.

A G Moyes
A Century of Cricketers (1950)

1606   He could never be dull, never crude. The pictures he painted will never fade from the memory of those who saw him in his days of princely splendour.

Ibid.

Macartney, C G
1607   He was big in achievement, broad in his conception of what batting could be, rich and fertile in imagination and practice. There haven't been many better players than Charlie − none more worth watching.

Ibid.

1608   While he was there the game vibrated, for he was one of the batsmen who saw in each ball a potential four.

Ibid.

Macaulay, G
1609 He was a very passionate cricketer who did not suffer fools
gladly.

Anthony Woodhouse
The History of Yorkshire CCC (1989)

1610 As a man he was an original; fiercely independent, witty,
argumentative, swift to joy and anger.

R C Robertson-Glasgow
Cricket Prints (1943)

MacBryan, J C W
1611 He was a fighter, unafraid of whatever might come in violence
or guile.

Ibid.

1612 For six balls an over, cricket was an unrelieved battle of the
mind: in the same way as it is nowadays for another Somerset
man, Peter Roebuck. He'd have liked Roebuck, also a
Cambridge graduate who perhaps takes the game to the almost
self-defeating extreme of 'thinking about it' rather than playing
it at times with a little more instinct.

David Foot
Cricket's Unholy Trinity (1985)

McDonald, E A
1613 McDonald's action was so perfect that it was easy at times to
underestimate his speed.

Rex Pogson
Lancashire (1952)

1614 McDonald looked and was the perfect bowler. He was also a
man of moods and a difficult cricketer to placate when things
were not going right. In the mood he was masterly. Out of it he
often drove captains and comrades to despair.

John Kay
A History of County Cricket: Lancashire (1974)

1615   Like a brilliant comet he blazed across the Lancashire sky for
only six full seasons and two shortened ones, and then was seen
no more. But while the blaze lasted the light it gave was bright
indeed, and the memory of it will always be sweet.

Gerald Hodcroft
My Own Red Roses (1984)

1616   He was a handsome fellow, with strong and clear-cut features,
but saturnine and mahogany-grim; like Carver Doone, he meant
to frighten the young men with a look.

R C Robertson-Glasgow
46 Not Out (1948)

McEwan, K S
1617   Small, quiet and unassuming, McEwan was among the most
elegant of modern batsmen. Class bowling was destroyed, not
by belligerent power but the sheer range of his strokeplay.

David Acfield
Barclays World of Cricket (1987)

MacLaren, A C
1618   MacLaren was a pessimist by nature, and did not inspire his
men to believe in their own prowess; and to make your men
believe in themselves is a very important factor in cricket
leadership.

Sir Pelham Warner
Lord's 1787 – 1945 (1946)

1619   . . . conducted his entire career as though he were conducting a
cavalry charge against the forces of darkness, when in fact he
never did much more than tilt against windmills.

Benny Green
The Lord's Companion (1987)

1620   Tactically there have been few cricketers better qualified to
captain England, but he had unorthodox views when it came to
the selection of teams.

Peter Wynne-Thomas
The History of Lancashire CCC (1989)

1621   He won the devotion of many of the young players, but lacked
tact when dealing with his brother officials and some of the
committee.

Ibid.

1622 He was clean bowled on the occasion I have in mind for none, but nobody other than a giant could have made a duck so immaculately. He always played cricket as some proud Roman might have played it.

Sir Neville Cardus
A Cricketer's Book (1922)

1623 . . . a majestic batsman whose bat flowed into the ball whether the stroke was in attack or defence.

James P Coldham
F S Jackson (1989)

1624 He played in the Grand Manner. He lifted his bat for his stroke right round his neck like a golfer at the top of his full swing. He stood bolt upright and swept into every stroke, even a defensive back-stroke, with deliberate and dominating completeness. He never hedged on his stroke; he never pulled his punches. Like all the great batsmen, he always attacked the bowling.

C B Fry and G W Beldam
Great Batsmen: Their Methods at a Glance (1905)

1625 Each hit by MacLaren's bat was Quixote's lance, and the bowlers were his windmills.

Sir Neville Cardus
Cricket (1930)

1626 To see MacLaren at the wicket was like reading prose in Gibbon. The noblest Roman of them all, magnificent in his ambition and reckless in his sovereignty.

Ibid.

1627 He was excellent at producing a feeling of inferiority in the other team, but unfortunately he could produce the same effect in his own players.

Gerry Cotter
The Ashes Captains (1989)

1628   In general, for all his conversational charm as well as his
impressive bearing, there were undeniable flaws in MacLaren
the man, taking perhaps three main forms: a certain thin-
skinned haughtiness, possibly derived from having a more
mercantile background than he would have wished; a
tactlessness in human relations that had the effect of
consistently rubbing at least some people up the wrong way;
and lastly almost ubiquitously, an astonishing lack of scruples
in financial matters.

David Kynaston
Archie's Last Stand (1984)

1629   And MacLaren, surely he stood for the essential majesty in life.
Today I see him as one who transcended the cricketer's fleeting
hour; the magnificence of his play moves me now like some
reckless squandering of the dignity and spirit of man.

Sir Neville Cardus
Cricket (1930)

1630   There was a majesty and spaciousness about him which was
more than the result of talent correctly applied.

Rex Pogson
Lancashire (1952)

1631   To those who accused him of taking the game too seriously, he
would have replied that you cannot take it too seriously.

Ibid.

Mailey, A A
1632   He viewed the world at large with an impassive sense of
proportion, which means, of course, that he had a natural and
unobtrusive sense of humour.

Ben Travers
A-sitting on a Gate (1978)

1633   He treated the rush and turmoil of the modern, hurry-along-
there-please way of life with quiet impracticable practicability.

Ibid.

1634 He spun the ball till it buzzed like a bee, and released it with
the detached joy of the artist. As such he begrudged no
batsman and, if hit for six, felt that he had at least achieved
something.

Diana Rait Kerr and I A R Peebles
Lord's 1946 – 1970 (1971)

1635 It seemed that he dismissed his opponents with a wide smile
that was a googly in its own right. He was by profession
(among other professions) a cartoonist and on a wicket that
would give him a fraction of help, he could make a caricature
of any batting side.

A A Thomson
Cricket: The Golden Ages (1961)

1636 A student of character, he sized up opponents off the field
before he ever saw them bat in hand. If he judged them to be
highly strung or easygoing, vain or modest, he adopted his
bowling tactics accordingly.

Ray Robinson
Between Wickets (1946)

Majid Khan
1637 On top of his technique and the sheer eye-appeal of his strokeplay, Majid possessed the pride of the Pathan.

Tony Lewis
Playing Days (1985)

1638 In spite of the maturity of his cricket, he was, at heart, still a
small boy playing games.

Ibid.

1639 . . . calm and determined under a brimmed, fading white sun
hat, stroking the most ferocious or most cunning bowling
imperiously to the boundary.

Ibid.

Mankad, M H (Vinoo)
1640 He was the reservoir of patience and endurance.

Sudhir Vaidya
Vinoo Mankad (1969)

1641 He had absorbed the strategy of the game as naturally as breathing.

Ibid.

1642 He stoops over his bat at the crease, like a cat who has seen its deadly foe, the dog from next door.

Margaret Hughes
All on a Summer's Day (1953)

Mann, F T
1643 He was like Gulliver's sneeze among the Lilliputians.

R C Robertson-Glasgow
Cricket Prints (1943)

1644 Genial but efficient, he combined dignity with a certain jauntiness of manner and wit in a blend that made any match against Middlesex at once a task and an entertainment.

Ibid.

Marsh, R W
1645 If ever there was a cricketing desperado, at least in appearance, Rod Marsh was that man.

Keith Andrew
The Handbook of Cricket (1989)

1646 In a long-suffering race – wicket-keepers – Rodney Marsh is the one whose activities have most in common with a railway-siding buffer and a box-kite.

Ray Robinson
After Stumps Were Drawn (1985)

1647 One of the phenomena of cricket, thickset yet agile wicket-keeper whose competitive make-up has enabled him to set records that may never be broken.

Jack Pollard
Australian Cricket (1982)

1648 Not for Rodney the half-hearted dive – he goes for his catches like an Olympic swimmer on the starting platform.

Ibid.

Marshall, M D
1649 Like the modern motor-car Marshall is turbo-charged but
economical.

Christopher Martin-Jenkins
Cricket Characters (1987)

May, P B H
1650 He plays stern cricket and charming cricket.

J M Kilburn
Thanks to Cricket (1972)

1651 May, I should say, is a cavalier batsman and a roundhead
captain.

A A Thomson
Hirst and Rhodes (1959)

1652 He expresses a more elaborate personality when batting than
when speaking. The total lack of anecdote about him is
significant.

Michael Davie
Peter May and Richie Benaud (1959) reprinted in *The Observer
on Cricket* (1987)

1653 He was a good captain, and a great batsman. I suppose the
hesitations arise because he did not turn out quite as expected.
Here he was, an amateur, a classical stylist, three initials and
all, embodying a return to the old tradition – and, tactically,
playing like a canny old pro.

Alan Gibson
The Cricket Captains of England (1979)

1654 By nature he was quiet and rather reserved, not greatly given to
socialising, but kind and friendly all the same.

Gerry Cotter
The Ashes Captains (1989)

1655 On the field he seemed anything but relaxed, but still he
managed to strike a happy medium between autocracy and
democracy, being firmly in control without making it too
obvious, and working on the basis that anyone good enough to
be selected for a Test match ought not to need too manv
instructions.

Ibid.

1656 May was a fine player as well as being an extremely pleasant one; a cricketer of sensitive nature who could be as hard as nails on the field without ever slipping from the peak of sportsmanship.

Richie Benaud
Barclays World of Cricket (1987)

Mead, C P
1657 His batting was a deeply considered, rationalised technique and the first stride of a run seemed a built-in part of every stroke he made.

John Arlott
Book of Cricketers (1979)

1658 It was once said, perceptively, that Philip had no interest in batting, only in making runs.

John Arlott
County Champions (1982)

Merchant, V M
1659 . . . led almost a puritanical life, austere in his habits and conscientious in his work.

Vasant Naik
Vijay Merchant (1987)

1660 He had a technique for every kind of wicket and every kind of bowler, but against the swinging ball he was especially master.

Edward Docker
History of Indian Cricket (1976)

Milburn, C
1661 There are some cricketers who by their style and personality make a spontaneous impact on the mind of the cricket world, while others though they build up a considerable dossier of achievement remain merely names in the history books. No need surely to say into which category Colin Milburn staked a claim.

E W Swanton (1971)
Reprinted in *As I Said at the Time* (1983)

Miller, K R

1662 Miller was established as the great contemporary hero – that is not too strong a word. It was a happy fusion of technical eloquence and distinctive physical attributes, one in particular: his hair. All cricketers exhibit mannerisms but Miller's hair, and what he managed to do with it, became so intimately associated with his cricket that even in retrospect it is difficult to separate it from his play.

Mihir Bose
Keith Miller (1979)

1663 For young boys he was something out of *Boys' Own Paper,* the one cricketer likely to sustain fantasy.

Ibid.

1664 Miller enjoyed the companionship of cricket and he enjoyed the game for the game's sake. Cricket lovers recognised him as a gay cavalier and they loved him for it.

Phil Tressider
The Cricketer's Bedside Book (1966)

1665 Masculine as Tarzan, he plays lustily. Style suffuses his cricket with glowing power, personality charges it with daring and knocks bowling and convention sky-high.

Ray Robinson
From the Boundary (1951)

1666 Keith Miller is the most unpredictable cricketer I have played against. I am never quite sure what he is going to do next and I don't think he knows himself until he is about to do it.

Sir Leonard Hutton
Just My Story (1956)

1667 . . . a batsman of the blood royal, a shrewd and menacing bowler.

A G Moyes
A Century of Cricketers (1950)

1668 His fame will endure as long as cricket, for when he took the field boundary fences or ropes disappeared and spectators virtually became part of the match.

Jack Pollard
Australian Cricket (1982)

Morris, A R

1669 He is frugal, for he wastes nothing, tidy, because he puts everything in its place, especially full-tosses and long-hops.

> **A G Moyes**
> *A Century of Cricketers* (1982)

Murdoch, W L

1670 He was an ideal captain, a born tactician, a genial chief, a firm though gentle ruler, and a man of singular pluck and resource.

> **W G Grace**
> *W G – Cricketing Reminiscences and Personal Recollections* (1899)

Mynn, A

1671 He was beloved by all sorts of men, and he in return seemed to think kindly of everyone.

> **William Caffyn**
> *Seventy-one Not Out* (1899)

1672 Alfred Mynn captured hearts as well as heads. The very sight of his handsome face and magnificent figure was an attraction and his companionable manner gave him wide popularity among both players and patrons.

> **J M Kilburn**
> *Overthrows* (1975)

1673 Mr Mynn was one of the kindest-hearted men I ever met, and was as gentle in his manner as he was strong in person.

> **Richard Daft**
> *Kings of Cricket* (1893)

1674 It was as a personality of the cricket field that Alfred Mynn really shone. In old prints of XIs of the time it is his majestic figure that immediately catches the eye.

> **Patrick Morrah**
> *Alfred Mynn* (1963)

1675 Of Alfred Mynn it may be said with truth that no cricketer, with the single exception of the Champion himself, captured so completely by prowess and personality alike the hearts of his own generation.

> **H S Altham**
> *A History of Cricket, Volume One* (1926)

1676   He was a national institution; men flocked to see him wherever he played.

Ibid.

1677   How the hop-men watched their hero, massive, muscular, and
         tall,
As he mingled with the players, like a king among them all;
Till to some old Kent enthusiasts it would almost seem a sin
To doubt their county's triumph when led on by Alfred Mynn.

William Jeffrey Prowse
In Memoriam, Alfred Mynn, 1807 – 1861 (1861)

1678   With his tall and stately presence, with his nobly moulded
         form,
His broad hand was ever open, his brave heart was ever warm;
All were proud of him, all loved him. As the changing seasons
         pass,
As our champion lies a-sleeping underneath the Kentish grass,
Proudly, sadly will we name him – to forget him were a sin.
Lightly lie the turf upon thee, kind and manly Alfred Mynn!

Ibid.

Nayudu, C K
1679   He had no predecessor in Indian cricket nor has he any
successor.

Vasant Raiji
C K Nayudu (1989)

1680   One need not have a poet's eye to be captivated by the manner
in which Nayudu strode from the pavilion to the wicket.

Ibid.

1681   Nayudu held the belief that cricket was an ancient Aryan game.
He could quote sacred texts to prove it, and he played cricket
as though it were one of the battles described in the ancient
epics.

Derek Birley
The Willow Wand (1979)

1682   To know a master artist you have merely to note his gait and poise, just as to know a top-class musician you have only to hear him strike the first chord. So also with Nayudu and his cricket, you have only to see him walk to the wicket to know his class.

D N Bacha
Quoted in *C K Nayudu* (1989)

Nichols, M S
1683   Never can I recollect a greater trier than Stan Nichols.

Sir Home Gordon
Background of Cricket (1939)

1684   In a county match, if I had to have one man to play for me to save my life, pre-war it would have been George Hirst, post-war it would be Stan Nichols.

Ibid.

1685   Fast bowlers have bowled faster but few have bowled for such long spells at a time.

Charles Bray
Essex County Cricket (1950)

1686   . . . a made, rather than a natural, cricketer.

Ibid.

Noble, M A
1687   Noble studied the enemy; he also studied his own team-mates, with the result that he got the best out of them.

A G Moyes
A Century of Cricketers (1950)

1688   . . . solemn, alert competence.

C B Fry
Life Worth Living (1939)

1689   . . . a cricketer of unwavering confidence in his own ability.

Jack Pollard
Australian Cricket (1982)

Nourse, A D
1690 Almost invariably he brought a refreshing gust to the drab
ordinariness of an innings.

Louis Duffus
Giants of South African Cricket (1971)

Oldfield, W A
1691 A craftsman with a 'positional sense' so highly developed that
he could dispense with acrobatics, he made his catches and
stumpings in the most honoured tradition, without
showmanship.

G D Martineau
The Valiant Stumper (1957)

1692 Batsmen knew better than to assume from his courteous
greeting that he would be lenient with a snick or stumble.

Ray Robinson
After Stumps Were Drawn (1985)

1693 He made the art look a simple matter, a habit of champions.

A G Moyes
A Century of Cricketers (1950)

O'Neill, N C
1694 Figures cannot relay the brilliance of the spectacle when
Norman O'Neill was going well.

Colin Cowdrey
Barclays World of Cricket (1986)

1695 No one had ever seriously faulted his technique; now, however,
the flaw emerged, and it was purely psychological. He simply
became a bad starter; probably it was due to a combination of
public pressure and team responsibility on his mind.

John Arlott
100 Greatest Batsmen (1986)

O'Reilly, W J
1696 He looked as if, under necessary circumstances, he might have
founded or sacked a city.

R C Robertson-Glasgow
Cricket Prints (1943)

1697   If only one cricket ball was left in the world, and that one
       came to pieces in his hand, he would whizz down a leg-break
       with the largest fragment.

Ibid.

1698   To hit him for four would usually arouse a belligerent ferocity
       which made you sorry. It was almost like disturbing a hive of
       bees. He seemed to attack from all directions.

Sir Donald Bradman
Farewell to Cricket (1950)

1699   When bowling he completely dominated the situation. He
       roared at umpires and scowled at batsmen. There was no sign
       of veneer or camouflage when he appealed, nor were there any
       apologies or beg pardons when the umpire indicated that the
       batsmen's legs were yards out of line with the stumps.

Arthur Mailey
10 for 66 and All That (1958)

1700   Some bowlers and wicket-keepers, and others for that matter,
       are better at appealing than their mates . . . Bill O'Reilly they
       tell me was terrifying.

Richie Benaud
On Reflection (1984)

1701   . . . a constant menace to the batsmen, with his ebullient
       approach of flailing arms and scowling countenance.

Richie Benaud
Postscript to *The Complete Leg-Break Bowler* (1968)

1702   Cricket to him was something real and earnest.

Jack Fingleton
Cricket Crisis (1946)

1703   If his aged father had come to bat against him on such a
       wicket, O'Reilly would have recognised his inexorable enemies,
       the bat and pads, before recognising his own flesh and blood
       and he would have shown no mercy.

Ibid.

1704 He whose sense of humour was most marked off the field hung it up on the pavilion peg with his street clothes as he dressed for the cricket fray.

Ibid.

Palairet, L C H
1705 Everything Palairet did was gracefully done. He batted gracefully, he shot gracefully, he played golf gracefully, and he danced gracefully. He was a charming man, with a very gentle manner, and the memory of 'Coo' Palairet does not fade even with the passing of the years.

Sir Pelham Warner
Lord's 1787 – 1945 (1946)

Parker, C W L
1706 Parker may have been a trifle indolent when it came to farm work as a boy or when pretending to look for a remunerative winter's job. But the mind was active and alert. His approach to cricket, whatever the brimstone and rustic oaths, was that of the academic.

David Foot
Cricket's Unholy Trinity (1985)

1707 At this distance, it is hard to understand how his massive talents, functional and crafty as the ways of nature on the Cotswold hillsides where he ambled as an inquisitive boy, could be ignored as an England player.

Ibid.

1708 Parker was not a bowler who took kindly to fielding lapses.

E M Wellings
Vintage Cricketers (1983)

1709 No one took him lightly; he bowled with the precision of a machine and was rarely collared.

Grahame Parker
Gloucestershire Road (1983)

1710 To the end of his days he would talk unceasingly about his search for that mystery of flight which would lead him to the left-arm spinner's Eldorado.

Ibid.

1711   Perhaps he will be remembered for his sad countenance and caustic words, but at heart he was a gentle person and a devoted father.

Ibid.

1712   There was no man whom he could not make to look like a child batting with a pencil.

R C Robertson-Glasgow
Cricketing Prints (1943)

1713   In temperament he was as ironical as the fate that held him down. Slim and angular, he was a sad-eyed executioner.

Ibid.

1714   He came late into only a partial kingdom. But he was a king indeed.

Ibid.

Parkin, C H
1715   He had about him something spontaneous and infectious, an exuberant flair for the comic, which raised him at moments into the ageless tradition of laughter-makers from Shakespeare to Grock and Danny Kaye.

C S Marriott
The Complete Leg-Break Bowler (1968)

1716   Cecil Parkin was to endear himself to the Old Trafford crowds by his mischievous tomfoolery.

Benny Green
A History of Cricket (1988)

1717   His personality on the field was pervading, and he rather played up to the crowd because doing so appealed to his sense of humour.

Sir Home Gordon
Background of Cricket (1939)

1718 Parkin would try anything not just once but continually. It is difficult to set a field for a bowler who may at any time send down anything from a googly to a donkey drop, and Parkin's individualistic temperament did not always take kindly to being told so.

Rex Pogson
Lancashire County Cricket (1952)

1719 Like a music-hall comedian he knew what his audience wanted and saw that they got it.

Ibid.

Parr, G

1720 He was a nervous and choleric man, but popular with his teams. He had bright blue eyes, ginger hair, mutton-chop whiskers with moustache (or without either, according to his mood), and was not much good at administration and not very patient with those who had to do it. I would guess that he was the kind of man who, in any period, would turn out to be captain of England at something or other.

Alan Gibson
The Cricket Captains of England (1979)

1721 He was apt to be hot-tempered and difficult except with his intimates, but the professionals who made history in his great XIs all speak of him with admiration and affection.

H S Altham
A History of Cricket, Volume One (1926)

1722 In generalship, determination, and enthusiasm his contemporaries considered him a captain unsurpassed.

Ibid.

Paynter, E

1723 There was nothing wild about his batting. His defence could be as stubborn as a wall; but in his heart he thought of a runless first over as a personal affront, and of a timid draw as a moral defeat.

R C Robertson-Glasgow
Cricket Prints (1943)

1724   Eddie Paynter's career may be taken as cricket's classic example
       of Bacon's famous dictum: 'All climbing to great place is by a
       winding stair'.

                                                           Rex Pogson
                                          Lancashire County Cricket (1952)

1725   If ever he sniffed a crisis in the offing he made straight for it,
       and as often as not left his name upon it for all time, like Guy
       Fawkes.

                                                         Ronald Mason
                                          Sing All a Green Willow (1967)

1726   He will best be remembered, I think, as a Lancashire man, wiry
       as a whippet, with the humorous eyes and alert aggressive jaw
       that are part of his county's native and recognisable essentials.

                                                                   Ibid.

Peebles, I A R
1727   He had a beautifully smooth, rhythmical run-up and high
       delivery, great power of spin, and that perceptible dip at the
       end of the flight that made it difficult to judge the length. The
       best batsmen thought they were 'there', and found to their cost
       that they weren't.

                                                          E W Swanton
                                          Sort of a Cricket Person (1972)

Peel, R
1728   No man took punishment as a bowler better, and it never made
       him shorten his length or send down a wild ball, but when at
       his deadliest and congratulated afterwards one could detect no
       gleam of pleasure in his countenance.

                                                           Lord Hawke
                                   Recollections and Reminiscences (1944)

1729   He was immensely talented as a player, firmly independent in
       character and susceptible to temptations in the way of life of
       professional cricketers of his time.

                                                          J M Kilburn
                                   A History of Yorkshire Cricket (1970)

1730   He was never a tired or dispirited bowler, never a reluctant
       batsman, never a fielder trying to avoid involvement.

                                                                   Ibid.

1731 The great actor Henry Ainley, forever a rabid Yorkshire enthusiast and member, considered the highlight of his life was when as an established idol on the stage, he carried Peel's bag from station to ground.

Peter Thomas
Yorkshire Cricketers 1839 – 1939 (1973)

Pilling, H
1732 A happy man indeed, capable of translating his happiness to the crowds.

Eric Todd (1973)
Reprinted in *The Guardian Book of Cricket* (1986)

Pilling, R
1733 Quiet and unostentatious though he was, he took the fastest bowling with consummate ease and astonishing quickness. It mattered not whether the bowling was fast or slow, he crouched over the wicket with his nose close to the bails, snapping the ball with unerring certainty, whether it came from the leg side or the off side.

W G Grace
W G – Cricketing Reminiscences and Personal Recollections (1899)

1734 . . . went so far as to declare himself incapable of keeping wicket otherwise than right up to the stumps.

G D Martineau
The Valiant Stumper (1957)

Pollock, R G
1735 His very nature is magnetic, that smile and that apparent disregard of a tense situation, gives him a personality which warms and appeals.

Peter Pollock
Giants of South African Cricket (1971)

1736 His footwork shamed Fred Astaire, his power was Hammond at his best and his temperament was as cool as that of the county marshall who knows that the film-script determines his survival.

Ibid.

1737   The power and range of his strokes and the grandeur of some
of his most famous innings have confirmed him as a batsman
who would have adorned any age.

Michael Melford (1970)
Quoted in *From Bradman to Boycott* (1981)

Ponsford, W H
1738   There was no showmanship in Ponsford's batting and he
appeared to give no thought to the scoring rate, only to his job
of subduing and carving up the bowling.

Jack Pollard
Australian Cricket (1982)

Procter, M J
1739   . . . the greatest match-winner in the history of the club.

Grahame Parker
Gloucestershire Road (1983)

1740   Mike Procter strode in, head up to take on the world.

Ibid.

1741   Few can deny that fast bowling the Procter way is both
ruggedly attractive and brutally efficient, the latter always being
the major criterion.

Peter Pollock
Giants of South African Cricket (1971)

1742   Perhaps the greatest compliment that can be paid Michael John
Procter is that friend and foe alike enjoy his cricket and when
that sometimes involves being on the fiery end of a mean
bouncer, his personality and character triumphs in the severest
test of all.

Ibid.

Ramadhin, S
1743   There is almost a kind of magic in the very name 'Ramadhin'.
It seems redolent of mystery and guile.

R E S Wyatt
Three Straight Sticks (1951)

1744 Sonny Ramadhin's little eyes would wrinkle in amusement as his victims groped and prodded.

E W Swanton (1974)
Reprinted in *As I Said at the Time* (1983)

1745 Ramadhin, stoical of manner, with his twinkle-toed approach and magical twirl of the arm, seemed to mesmerise all and sundry.

Michael Manley
A History of West Indies Cricket (1988)

1746 He was so small and exercised such magical powers that one thought of him rather as a concert violinist than as a sporting combatant.

David Frith
The Slow Men (1984)

Randall, D W
1747 What will become of him? Oh God of cricket, let it be good, for he has given much to your game.

Robin Marlar
Barclays World of Cricket (1980)

1748 If Derek had only learned to remain still, instead of giving his celebrated imitation of a cat on hot bricks as each ball is bowled, he would never have been out of the England side, especially if one also takes into account his enormous value in the field.

Trevor Bailey
Wickets, Catches and the Odd Run (1986)

Ranjitsinhji, K S
1749 No Englishman could have batted like Ranji. 'Ranji,' said Ted Wainwright once, ''e never made a Christian stroke in his life.'

Sir Neville Cardus
The Summer Game (1929)

1750 He combines an Oriental calm with an Oriental swiftness − the stillness of the panther with the suddenness of its spring.

A G Gardiner
Pillars of Society (1913)

1751   Something of the languidity of the Orient and a playfulness
        akin to jugglery tincture his batting, at times somewhat
        unpleasantly conveying the impression that he merely toys with,
        rather than attempts to master, the bowling.

                                                          A E Knight
                                               The Complete Cricketer (1906)

1752   Ranji, like Saladin in *The Talisman* with black magic in his silk
        wrists which could cut a silk handkerchief in two with a flicker
        of the scimitar.

                                                       Denzil Batchelor
                                                          C B Fry (1951)

1753   At his best Ranjitsinhji was a miraculous batsman. He had no
        technical faults whatever; the substratum of his play was
        absolutely sound.

                                                              C B Fry
                                                   Life Worth Living (1939)

1754   Ranjitsinhji is usually either dismissed as a genius, very
        unorthodox in his methods and quite unaccountable to the
        accepted laws of style, or he is buried under a heap of vague
        epithets of wonder.

                                               G W Beldam and C B Fry
                                  Great Batsmen: Their Methods at a Glance (1904)

1755   He does nothing blindly. He thinks about the game, starts a
        theory, and proceeds to find out what use it is. Some of his
        strokes were discovered by accident.

                                                              C B Fry
                                                         Cricket (1903)

Rhodes, W

1756   It was my grandfather who first told me about him. He once
        walked the 30 miles to Bradford to see Rhodes play and he
        never forgot it.

                                                       Michael Parkinson
                                                      Cricket Mad (1969)

1757   That valiance of character, the tenacity of purpose would
        conquer any difficulty in the world.

                                                          A A Thomson
                                                 Cricket My Pleasure (1953)

1758   Wilfred studies the game more than a financier ever studied the stock market.

Bill Bowes
Express Deliveries (1949)

1759   The most famous of all Yorkshire cricketers.

John Callaghan
Yorkshire's Pride (1984)

1760   Rhodes was as conservative with the use of words as he was with the meanness of giving away runs. Cricket was not fun.

Peter Thomas
Yorkshire Cricketers 1839 – 1939 (1973)

1761   Many players adored him; others resented him, but no captain failed to realise that whatever Wilfred said, he meant well for Yorkshire.

Ibid.

1762   In first-class cricket Rhodes never served an apprenticeship; he came as a master-craftsman, his talent beyond question, his technique already polished.

J M Kilburn
A History of Yorkshire Cricket (1970)

Rice, C E B
1763   Clive Rice has been not only a major cricketer but a major influence on the game.

Matthew Engel
Barclays World of Cricket (1986)

1764   The epitome of the modern, hard-headed, hard-hatted professional, and the single-minded leader of two of the era's most formidable non-national teams.

Ibid.

Richards, B A
1765   Once in two or three generations there comes a virtuoso batsman who beguiles even his opponents; such is Barry Richards.

John Arlott
Book of Cricketers (1979)

1766   He appeals to the aesthetic sense because of the innate elegance
of his movement, the sensitivity with which he harnesses the
ball's course, such a princely style as makes the batting of some
Test players seem workaday stuff.

Ibid.

1767   He strolls where others must hustle.

Ibid.

1768   . . . a complex, shadowy and sometimes misunderstood
cricketer, certainly the most unrepentant mercenary among the
many overseas stars who have dominated the professional game
in England.

Peter Walker
Cricket Conversations (1978)

1769   A man who is upset by failure yet who outwardly seems
indifferent, even bored, in the daily chore of the playing of the
game.

Ibid.

Richards, I V A
1770   He is a fallible genius. He flirts with the record book when, we
suspect, he could monopolise it. His cricket, always potent and
often pure, is unwaveringly instinctive.

David Foot
Viv Richards (1979)

1771   When Viv goes out to bat he doesn't walk, he swaggers,
moving his hips and shoulders with an air of authority that is
saying he is better than any bowler he is going to face.

Jack Simmons
Flat Jack (1986)

1772   The Richards career, brimming though it is with stunning
statistics, will surely survive in the end as a parade of
unforgettable images.

Hugh McIlvanney
Viv Richards (1985) reprinted in *The Observer on Cricket*
(1987)

1773 Even when his looks, his sense of theatre and his dazzling technical brilliance are taken into account, the extent to which Richards can electrify his audiences, the way he can stir responses only rarely touched by sport, remains extraordinary.

Ibid.

1774 . . . bats with the passionate intensity of a murderer rather than the cool rationality of an assassin.

Peter Roebuck
Slices of Cricket (1982)

1775 In all he does Richards has style. He possesses that elusive ability to appear in complete command despite overwhelming evidence to the contrary.

Ibid.

1776 From the moment Viv comes down the pavilion steps a long and forceful innings seems inevitable.

Clayton Goodwin
Caribbean Cricketers (1980)

1777 Proud as a peacock, handsome as a prince, strong as a horse, Viv Richards was for the best part of ten years recognised as the best batsman in the world. That is a big statement.

Christopher Martin-Jenkins
Cricket Characters (1987)

Richardson, T
1778 There was no position a fast bowler could aspire to that he did not attain again and again, and his records are without parallel.

A A Lilley
Twenty-four Years of Cricket (1912)

1779 Richardson was the most indispensable man on the side.

E B V Christian
Surrey Cricket (1902)

1780 No other fast bowler ever showed such consistency, and having to bowl mainly on The Oval enhanced the credit he deserved.

Sir Home Gordon
Background of Cricket (1939)

Roberts, A M E
1781   . . . crashing in like an educated bull.

> **David Frith**
> *The Fast Men* (1982)

1782   'A cold killer' is how one county player referred to him − in awe rather than revulsion.

> *Ibid.*

1783   His success comes from speed, combined with excellent control and the ability to change his pace without changing his action. He is a complete fast bowler.

> **Fred Trueman**
> *From Larwood to Lillee* (1983)

Robins, R W V
1784   No cricketer ever brought to the game a more propitious mixture of devotion, enthusiasm, knowledge and humour.

> **Diana Rait Kerr and I A R Peebles**
> *Lord's 1946 − 1970* (1971)

1785   However big the crowd or serious the occasion there is something about the cricket of Walter Robins which suggests half-holidays and kicking your hat along the pavement. Perky is the word.

> **R C Robertson-Glasgow**
> *Cricket Prints* (1943)

1786   He has all the spirited violence of jazz, its jerk and starts, its nervous ecstasies and emotional supercharge. He has its erratic measure and its lack of rounded, classical finish. He has, in fact, all of its virtues and some of its faults.

> **Hon T C F Prittie**
> *Mainly Middlesex* (1947)

1787   To his own aggressive play he added an audacity and originality as captain which has never been surpassed in the history of English county cricket.

> **Hon T C F Prittie**
> *Middlesex CCC* (1951)

1788 He has left his imprint on a whole generation who saw in him the very essence of cricket's greatest charm, its unpredictability.

Ibid.

1789 Robins was one of the best captains in the game, a leader of infinite dash combined with resourcefulness.

E M Wellings
Vintage Cricketers (1983)

1790 Cricket did not make the best use of Walter Robins after his playing days had ended. He should have joined the Allens and Warners in cricket government, but I cannot imagine that such a forthright character was ever very well in with the establishment.

Ibid.

Ryan, F P
1791 There were times when he did not spin, nor did he toil.

Andrew Hignell
The History of Glamorgan CCC (1988)

1792 Apparently after one lengthy drinking session after a day's play, he forgot where the team were staying and returned to the ground to sleep under the covers!

Ibid.

Sandham, A
1793 There can be no question that no cricketer in recent times has received international honours *less* commensurate with his sterling worth than Sandham.

Louis Palgrave
The Story of The Oval (1949)

1794 To watch Sandham at his best, was like fluttering over the illustrated pages of a book on *The Art of Batsmanship*.

Ibid.

Sellers, A B
1795 At times almost a caricature of the Yorkshireman he wanted to be, once he had found his feet he drove his side with hostility: overaweing, and all but demolishing, many of their opponents.

John Arlott
An Eye for Cricket (1979)

1796   A controversial figure in the politics of Yorkshire cricket, many accused him of living in the past. An outspoken personality, forthright in his views, he perhaps bore much of the blame for some of the club's unwise actions.

Anthony Woodhouse
The History of Yorkshire Cricket (1989)

1797   He was never up to county class as a batsman but his qualities of leadership and sheer guts meant that his position in the side was never questioned.

Ibid.

1798   Sellers became a captain of distinction because he played an essential part willingly and to a degree 'beyond the call of duty'.

J M Kilburn
Cricket: The Great Captains (1971)

1799   He has the perfect attitude to the game. He respects it and enjoys it equally.

R C Robertson-Glasgow
Cricket Prints (1943)

1800   He came to the county side as a batsman of determination, a fieldsman of inexhaustible energy and a captain of passionate devotion to duty.

J M Kilburn
A History of Yorkshire Cricket (1970)

1801   He was essentially of the team as distinct from being with the team. Their interests and their welfare were his and however scathing he might have had to be in the private dressing-room his public identification was always with his players.

Ibid.

Shackleton, D
1802   . . . became one of the most successful seam bowlers of the day with an economy of action which allowed feats of stamina unsuspected in a frail frame.

E W Swanton
A History of Cricket, Volume Two (1962)

1803   It is doubtful if any single player has done quite so much for any county in the last ten years as this quiet, grinning, tireless north country man has done for his adopted Hampshire.

John Arlott
Book of Cricketers (1979)

Shaw, A
1804   No more accurate bowler ever lived.

H S Altham
A History of Cricket, Volume One (1926)

1805   Wherever he went, and especially in his long service with Notts, Shaw's name stood for hard work, clean living and straight dealing.

Ibid.

Shrewsbury, A
1806   If ever there was a batsman who never took a risk it was Arthur Shrewsbury. He should have been permanent president of any or all Anti-Gambling Societies.

E H D Sewell
Well Hit! Sir (1947)

1807   A dignity and grace characterised the man and his cricket.

A E Knight
The Complete Cricketer (1906)

1808   The Champion had been asked to name the greatest batsman with whom he had been associated in the 50 years of his unique cricketing life. With a stroke of his silvery beard and an inimitable twinkle of those bright eyes from behind their bushy brows, he had, with a little persuasion, agreed that he himself should be considered *hors concours*, but as regard the *proxime accessit* his answer came quick and decided: 'Give me Arthur!'

H S Altham
A History of Cricket, Volume One (1926)

1809   Shrewsbury was the most modest and unassuming of men, but he played the game with intense earnestness and seriousness.

Sir Pelham Warner
Cricket Reminiscences (1920)

Simpson, R B

1810 . . . owes his great success to a rigorous dedication to cricket allied to great natural ability.

Christopher Martin-Jenkins
The Complete Who's Who of Test Cricketers (1987)

Sims, J M

1811 A truly great character. He spoke out of the side of his mouth, and often most amusingly.

E M Wellings
Vintage Cricketers (1983)

1812 A grey-haired, grey-visaged veteran with round shoulders and the mournful expression of a man upon whom fate has just played a rather nasty trick and who is expecting another one any minute now.

Barry Norman
County Champions (1982)

1813 In the field he was not so much inactive as virtually motionless.

Ibid.

1814 Jim Sims was what a leg-spinner ought to look like – lugubrious, deeply and pessimistically philosophical, an Eeyore among bowlers.

Ibid.

Small, J

1815 Here lives John Small
Makes bat and ball
Pitch a wicket, play at cricket
With any man in England.

John Nyren
Quoting shop sign in *The Young Cricketer's Tutor* (1833)

1816 His life was like his innings, long and good,
Full ninety summers he had death withstood.
At length the ninetieth winter came, when (fate
Not leaving him one solitary mate)
The last of Hambledonians, old John Small,
Gave up his bat and ball, his leather, wax and all.

Pierce Egan
Book of Sports and Mirror of Life (1832)

Smith, C I J
1817   Smith brings back memories of provincial music halls, of
whelks, and pints of old and mild.

Kenneth Gregory
In Celebration of Cricket (1978)

1818   However great the impression made by his bowling, and
however obvious his chances and potentialities as a Test player
of the near future, primarily it was Smith's batting that caught
the eye and stirred the imagination of the cricket public.

Hon T C F Prittie
Mainly Middlesex (1947)

1819   Smith has this unique distinction − that, save when he is
actually protecting his person, he hits at every single ball sent
down to him!

Ibid.

1820   Big Jim has already bequeathed a rich legacy to the game and
to those who watch it; a legacy of great, spinning sixes, of
rocketing mis-hits and spreadeagling stumps, of a pleasant and
unspoiled personality behind whose mask lurks a kingly humour
and a sense of the ridiculous.

Ibid.

Snow, J A
1821   . . . has been one of cricket's enigmas, appearing to lose
interest when play becomes quiet, and giving the impression −
incomprehensible to some − that there is more to life than
cricket.

David Frith
The Fast Men (1982)

1822   He left observers wondering what might have been had he
awoken every morning of his playing life with nothing on his
mind but the ambition to bowl out all ten opponents before
sunset.

Ibid.

1823   His temperament when bowling was also in keeping with the 'spaghetti western' anti-hero — mean, moody and essentially a loner who was permanently at odds with the establishment, sometimes with, but often without a cause.

Trevor Bailey
From Larwood to Lillee (1983)

1824   In full cry, John Snow bowling was one of the finest sights in cricket: genuine pace, a brooding hostility, and that lovely flowing action.

Ibid.

1825   Like most fast bowlers, John had a volatile temperament and fire in his belly.

Fred Trueman
From Larwood to Lillee (1983)

Sobers, G St A
1826   Nobody in cricket has given me more sheer delight than Sobers. His brilliance has been breathtaking.

Jack Fingleton
Fingleton on Cricket (1972)

1827   Some centurions struggle, go slow and fast in patches, have their lucky streaks, possibly bog down in the 90s and emerge, at last, gasping at the three-figure mark. There was nothing like this about Sobers. He just flowed on and on, his technique and strokeplay on a pedestal.

Ibid.

1828   Ye gods, how I envy him! It was enough for him, it seems, to think of becoming this multi-headed cricketer to achieve it. His body was so obedient to his whim that he didn't really notice.

Ted Dexter
Garfield Sobers (1966) reprinted in *The Observer on Cricket* (1987)

1829   He was the most complete of cricketers in that he was supreme in all the skills of batting, bowling and fielding.

Keith Andrew
The Handbook of Cricket (1989)

1830   In addition, his personality, his grace of movement and his open-mindedness on matters other than cricket gave him an aura that could only be associated with greatness, whether it be as an athlete or in any other walk of life.

Ibid.

1831   There have been many great cricketers, but none has ever displayed such a vast range of talents before such a wide audience without ever losing his intense passion for the game.

Trevor Bailey
Sir Gary (1976)

1832   The greatest all-round player the world has ever seen, he was happy to stand or fall by his belief that cricket, even at Test level, should be entertaining.

Ray Illingworth
Captaincy (1980)

1833   A genius, an ultimately professional player himself, Sobers lacked the one quality that might have rescued his leadership. Insight is not easy to define, indeed, it involves a paradox.

Michael Manley
A History of West Indies Cricket (1988)

1834   Sobers, the professional, assumed that all professionals were like him, that is to say, able to give absolutely of themselves regardless of circumstance, sometimes despite injury and irrespective of interpersonal relationships. Sobers could do this because he was unique.

Ibid.

1835   John Kennedy once wrote of courage as 'grace, under pressure'. Sobers had all of that but under pressure he had something else: the capacity to counterattack and to direct his riposte to the precise requirement of the situation.

Ibid.

1836   He had shown the capacity to lead a strong side effectively; but he had not shown the capacity to lift a weak or an ageing side to performances beyond those which came naturally.

Ibid.

Spofforth, F R
1837   What was this Spofforth, called the Demon yet,
For men forget, but cannot all forget?
A tall, lean, wiry athlete inly lit
With mind, and saturnine control of it.

John Masefield
Eighty-five to Win in *The Bluebells and Other Verses* (1961)

1838   His pace was terrifically fast, at times his length excellent, and
his break-backs were exceedingly deceptive. He controlled the
ball with masterly skill, and if the wicket helped him ever so
little was almost unplayable.

W G Grace
W G – Cricketing Reminiscences and Personal Recollections
(1899)

1839   Spofforth earned his soubriquet of 'The Demon', not because
he was fast, but because he was difficult.

C B Fry
Life Worth Living (1939)

Spooner, R H
1840   'Reggie' Spooner won the heart of Neville Cardus, the writer as
a schoolboy even trying to style his hair to match Spooner's.
When Spooner failed to score, Cardus says that he wandered
the streets, sad and inconsolable.

Peter Wynne-Thomas
The History of Lancashire CCC (1989)

1841   Everything that Spooner did at the wicket was a model of ease
and grace, but his particular glory was the off-drive.

Rex Pogson
Lancashire County Cricket (1952)

1842   The charm of Spooner's cricket was a true reflection of the
man himself; modest, friendly, sincere.

Ibid.

Statham, J B
1843   Lithe, sinewy and destructive, Statham came along to add lustre
to both Lancashire and England cricket in an age when it was
dominated by professionals.

John Kay
A History of County Cricket – Lancashire (1974)

1844   His captain's word was his command, and when it came his
        own turn to be a captain he asked nothing of his men he was
        not prepared to give himself.

                                                              Ibid.

1845   The direct approach can be classed as Statham's cricketing
        creed, and he lived by it.

                                                              Ibid.

1846   Essentially an honest, hard-working bowler, Brian played
        cricket the right way, keen to win and hating to lose.

                                                  Fred Trueman
                                        From Larwood to Lillee (1983)

Steel, A G
1847   The greatest amateur bowler England has possessed, the
        conjunction of the mental and the physical giving him fecundity
        of artifice.

                                                     A E Knight
                                        The Complete Cricketer (1906)

Stephenson, J W A
1848   He did really tear his hair, he did really leap off the ground
        like some figure in a mad Frederick Ashton cricketing ballet.

                                                  Dudley Carew
                                            To the Wicket (1946)

1849   In the field his acrobatics only seemed extraordinary when he
        first came to light, and before it was realised that such efforts
        were the spontaneous manifestations of one with a unique
        passion for the game.

                                                  E W Swanton
                             A History of Cricket, Volume One (1962)

1850   For here is a cricketer to whom the game was the best thing in
        life; who kicked cynicism and smugness violently aside; who
        evidently and unashamedly thought cricket 'fit to employ all the

heart and the soul and the senses for ever in joy'; who could and would bowl all day with a sort of ferocious accuracy; who danced with delight when he flattened a stump, slapped umpires on the back, ran three when the book said two, and was probably known by his first name to the sparrows in the deep-field.

R C Robertson-Glasgow
Cricket Prints (1943)

Stoddart, A E
1851   One's difficulty is that Mr Stoddart became great in what may be called the transition stage of batsmanship. He led a host of followers as far as the very banks of Jordan, and then he declined himself to enter the promised land.

Philip Trevor
The Lighter Side of Cricket (1901)

Stollmeyer, J B
1852   In Jeffrey Stollmeyer cricket has a batsman whose stroking of the ball so charms the eye that, even if no runs result, it gives pleasure to onlookers who otherwise are not content without fours or sixes.

Ray Robinson
The Glad Season (1955)

Strudwick, H
1853   Strudwick seemed to bubble over with life. His energy, good-humour and speed were as great after a boiling day in the sunshine as when he first walked onto the pitch.

Sir Henry Levenson-Gower
Off and on the Field (1953)

Surridge, W S
1854   His drive and his bubbling enthusiasm made Surrey into a ruthlessly efficient side and undoubtedly put him among the outstanding county captains of history. Not the least of his achievements was the way in which he made the most of his own limited talent with bat and ball.

E W Swanton
A History of Cricket, Volume Two (1962)

1855   His infectious enthusiasm inspired the whole side. No one
bothered about individual performances and averages; these
were merely achieved in the course of events.

Norman Preston
Cricket Heroes (1959)

1856   A true leader, Surridge was always the boss. He would never
tolerate any sign of slackness.

Ibid.

Sutcliffe, H
1857   Herbert Sutcliffe made himself an integral part of Yorkshire
cricket. He served its cause and honoured its traditions, but he
was not a passive accepter. He elevated the cause and enlarged
the traditions.

J M Kilburn
Thanks to Cricket (1972)

1858   He lived a corporate life in splendid isolation.

Ibid.

1859   Proficiency demands concentration of the highest order, and
Herbert had more of this than anyone else I know.

Sir Leonard Hutton
Just My Story (1956)

1860   It is impossible not to learn something from close association
with a man of outstanding talent.

Sir Leonard Hutton
Herbert Sutcliffe (1978) reprinted in *The Observer on Cricket*
(1987)

1861   He was a dandy cricketer!

Alan Gibson
Growing Up with Cricket (1958)

1862   He had established a personal authority which demonstrated
itself in a total confidence in his abilities.

Gerald Howat
Cricket's Second Golden Age (1989)

1863   He had style in everything − cricket, dress and manner − and
Len Hutton would be his most apt pupil.

Ibid.

1864   Sutcliffe flourished hardily at times; the ordinary lean patches
of crude disappointment that attend most mortal batsmen did
not seem to encumber him, and even if they had I cannot see
them disturbing that classic equipoise.

Ronald Mason
Sing All a Green Willow (1967)

1865   Sutcliffe, steel-nerved, oaken-hearted, cool-headed, did not
waste time looking back on his triumphs, but built warily for
the future.

Ibid.

Tait, J R
1866   Tait was a flamboyant amateur with a somewhat cavalier
approach to batting, believing that any bowler whom he did not
hit for at least three boundaries an over was getting off lightly!

Andrew Hignell
The History of Glamorgan CCC (1988)

1867   The comment was once made that according to all the rules of
batsmanship, he was not a batsman at all. But he made runs
and when he did, the spectators were thrilled and the bowlers
demoralised as neither knew what was going to happen next.

Ibid.

Tate, M W
1868   Maurice Tate did not play cricket; he lived in it.

John Arlott
Cricket Heroes (1959)

1869   It was as if bowling had been implanted in him at birth, and
came out − as the great arts come out − after due digestion,
at the peak of greatness which is not created − but only
confirmed − by instruction.

Ibid.

1870   For Maurice Tate it was who personified Sussex cricket, and
throughout a long precious exciting day he seemed always to be
at the centre of things.

Gerald Brodribb
Maurice Tate (1976)

1871 His anguished appeals to the fates to deal more kindly with him were part and parcel of the man's character; there was no moaning about it, no self-pity, only an intense, concentrated mental and physical urge to destroy.

A G Moyes
A Century of Cricketers (1950)

1872 I regard him as the least fortunate of bowlers.

Sir Home Gordon
Background of Cricket (1939)

Tayfield, H J
1873 On the field ambition and sheer courage – even vanity and near foolhardiness – were so blended in him that anything less than notable success appeared to him as abject failure.

Charles Fortune
Giants of South African Cricket (1971)

Taylor, R W
1874 Bob Taylor was the only wicket-keeper fully worthy of the title by the start of the '80s.

E M Wellings
Vintage Cricketers (1983)

Tennyson, L H
1875 Over all, the Hon L H (later Lord) Tennyson presided with contagious geniality and optimism.

E W Swanton
A History of Cricket, Volume Two (1962)

1876 . . . of the amazing flair and equally surprising vagaries.

John Arlott
Hampshire Handbook (1970)

Titmus, F J
1877 And while he wheeled away and captured more wickets for Middlesex than anyone in their history, he formed a commentary in himself on the nature of our game.

Phil Edmonds
100 Greatest Bowlers (1989)

1878   Throughout his long career he has characterised the best
qualities in the game.

Trevor Bailey
The Spinners' Web (1988)

Trueman, F S

1879   Some men have bowled a cricket ball faster than Trueman, but
none has done so with more gusto. As much as anything his
triumphs have been based on sheer belligerence.

Geoffrey Moorhouse
Fred Trueman (1956) reprinted in *The Guardian Book of
Cricket* (1986)

1880   Fred Trueman was the kind of fast bowler he had created for
himself; a larger-than-life-sized figure compounded in the
imagination of a boy from the fancies, facts, loyalties, cricket,
reading, traditions and all other influences of a semi-rural,
semi-industrial area of South Yorkshire in the 1930s.

John Arlott
Fred (1971)

1881   The bowling energy and fierce pace of youth matured to a
semi-instinctive, but also extremely shrewd, technique in
handling the fast bowling machine that was a body perfectly
constructed for precisely that purpose. For a decade − again
much longer than the peak period of even the best of the kind
− he was, when the fire burned, as fine a fast bowler as any.

Ibid.

1882   Trueman's cricket drew response from both student and the
simpler spectator. His bowling gave satisfaction through its
vigour and by its sophistication. Greatness was in him and it
was not obscured.

J M Kilburn
A History of Yorkshire Cricket (1970)

Trumper, V T

1883   Victor Trumper had the greatest charm and two strokes for
every ball.

C B Fry
Life Worth Living (1939)

1884   But never have I felt the pride of life to open and to flow more grandly and sweetly and graciously than I feel it today as I call back to mind the batsmanship of Victor Trumper.

Sir Neville Cardus
Good Days (1934)

1885   Many great players have illustrated the game of cricket: of Trumper, more than anyone, it may be said that he adorned it.

Alan Gibson
Jackson's Year (1965)

1886   But then no rules, no generalisations can ever be applied to Trumper. He will always be the most enchanting, and most maddening, cricketer of them all.

Ibid.

1887   In Victor Trumper we have seen the very poetry and heard the deep and wonderful music of batsmanship.

A E Knight
The Complete Cricketer (1906)

1888   With luxuriant masterfulness, yet with the unlaboured easy naturalness of a falling tear, or rather of showers from the sunny lips of summer, he diverted the ball in every conceivable direction which his genius willed.

Ibid.

1889   He has no style, and yet he is all style. He has no fixed canonical method of play, he defies all the orthodox rules, yet every stroke he plays satisfies the ultimate criterion of style – minimum of effort, maximum of effect.

G W Beldam and C B Fry
Great Batsmen: Their Methods at a Glance (1905)

1890   There is a love – and usually a sadness – at the heart of a cult. Victor Trumper was the first tragic hero of Australian cricket.

David Frith
Archie Jackson (1987)

1891   He was not gauche, but he was shy. He loved cricket, and he
enjoyed himself hugely, though without vainglory, when he was
batting. But he did not love what have been called the
attendant glories of the cricket field.

Philip Trevor
Cricket and Cricketers (1921)

1892   Of course, he was a perfect timer of the ball; yet as he played
some of his strokes I could not tell whether it was forearm or
wrist which he was using more.

Ibid.

1893   He was very kind-hearted; he was very generous, and generous
in thought as well as in deed. If he was not simple he was the
greatest actor who ever lived, and personally I do not think he
was an actor at all.

Ibid.

1894   Trumper entranced the eye, inspired his side, demoralised his
enemies, and made run-getting appear the easiest thing in the
world.

H S Altham
A History of Cricket, Volume One (1926)

1895   As he walked past me he smiled, patted the back of his bat and
said: 'It was too good for me.' There was no triumph in me as
I watched the receding figure. I felt like a boy who had killed a
dove.

Arthur Mailey
10 for 66 and All That (1958)

Turnbull, M J
1896   Turnbull adopted a cavalier approach and led from the front,
being at his best when others were failing or when quick runs
were needed, mixing textbook strokes and the unorthodox in an
effort to dishearten the bowlers. Off the field he led with a cool
authority, insisting that the professionals made an appointment
if they wanted to see him, and ensuring that the amateurs
always travelled in first-class accommodation and did not mix
with the professionals!

Andrew Hignell
The History of Glamorgan CCC (1988)

1897 For one so young his knowledge of the game was unique, and I
regarded him as one of the most astute captains of my time.
His quick and alert brain was working every minute of a game.

J H Morgan
Glamorgan County Cricket (1952)

Tyson, F H
1898 Like a meteor which flashes across the sky, creating an
unforgettable impression and then vanishing, so Frank burst on
to the first-class cricket scene.

Fred Trueman
From Larwood to Lillee (1983)

1899 Tyson falls into the particularly modern pattern of the
sportsman who, by taking thought, has added a cubit to his
athletic stature.

John Arlott (1955)
Reprinted in *Arlott on Cricket* (1984)

1900 Frank Tyson brings back the day of the demon bowler to
cricket. By sheer speed he subdues batsmen, splinters stumps,
silences barrackers, sways Test rubbers.

Ray Robinson
The Glad Season (1955)

1901 He could not recall a time when he did not want to bowl as
fast as humanly possible.

David Frith
The Fast Men (1982)

Underwood, D L
1902 Bowling quicker than the famous slow left-handers of the past
and so flighting the ball less, he relies all the same on the old-
fashioned virtues – length, subtle change of pace and just
enough movement to beat the bat or find its edge.

R L Arrowsmith
A History of County Cricket – Kent (1971)

1903 . . . the nearest approach to a babbling brook that it is possible
to find on a cricket field once he takes charge of an end.

Alan Knott
Stumper's View (1972)

1904   Of all the left-armers I have faced on a wet, helpful pitch, Derek was the closest to being unplayable.

Trevor Bailey
The Spinners' Web (1988)

1905   A quiet, naturally modest man with a generous spirit (though the last never applied to his bowling), he serves as proof that it is possible to reach the very top in sport and still remain completely unspoiled.

Ibid.

1906   He bowls like a god, but talks like a civil servant.

Michael Davie
The Packer Revolution (1977) reprinted in *The Observer on Cricket* (1987)

Valentine, A L
1907   As he bowls in the sunshine, some hidden power is suggested by flashes from his spectacles, from a gold chain bracelet on his right wrist and from his teeth, bared in an expectant grimace.

Ray Robinson
The Glad Season (1955)

1908   . . . imparting a ferocious tweak to the ball which, they said, hissed through the air before breaking sharply off the pitch.

Michael Manley
A History of West Indies Cricket (1988)

Verity, H
1909   Verity counted cricket both a privilege and an obligation and bowling a subject for serious study.

J M Kilburn
A History of Yorkshire Cricket (1970)

1910   Cavalier cricket even in wartime seemed to Verity unwarranted and undignified. It was beyond his understanding.

Alan Hill
Hedley Verity (1986)

1911 He was a Yorkshireman who had made up his mind that he would play for Yorkshire. He kept that aim in view all the time, he worked, as all cricketers who are determined to succeed have to work, and he gained the reward he earned.

Herbert Sutcliffe
For England and Yorkshire (1935)

1912 He is a scholarly bowler; graduating, to judge by his rather inquiring attitudes, in science and experimental philosophy rather than in any romantic faculty.

R C Robertson-Glasgow
Cricket Prints (1943)

1913 He treated his colleagues and opponents alike with respect and admiration but he never failed to strive to prove that he was the better man.

John Kay
Cricket Heroes (1959)

1914 Bowling to him was never a job to be undertaken lightly. Almost every ball he bowled was sent down with a purpose.

Ibid.

1915 He left behind him not a story but a legend of a man who played the game as it should be played, accepted success modestly, and bore failure with dignity. He was the kind of man I should have liked to be.

Ibid.

Viswanath, G R
1916 It has been his single aim to entertain, at the same time enjoying himself during a well-played innings and this is the reason why he has been such a popular cricketer.

Sunil Gavaskar
Idols (1984)

1917 . . . a batsman of considerable character who has probably been overshadowed by the record books.

John Arlott
100 Greatest Batsmen (1986)

Voce, W

1918   Burly, swarthy, he had begun as a slow bowler, but soon made his name as a distinctly awkward fast left-arm bowler whose pounding run to the wicket was filled with menace.

David Frith
The Fast Men (1982)

1919   Voce is, in his way, a very fine attacking bowler, but he has not that command of the ball which you look for in the absolute top class. You cannot be quite certain what he is going to do − nor is he always quite certain himself.

A W Carr
Cricket with the Lid Off (1935)

1920   . . . discovered a method of attack that found out the batsman's weaknesses and made him vulnerable, but batsmen, who for years have had things their own way, cried aloud their condemnation.

G H M Thurlow
Truth (1934) quoted in *Cricket with the Lid Off* (1935)

1921   . . . the one central character of the whole explosive saga to survive, somehow, the traumatic after-events.

David Frith
The Fast Men (1982)

Wadekar, A L

1922   His record had never been even remotely approached by any other captain of India, nor was likely to be in the forseeable future. A capable and conscientious skipper who had played the game according to his lights.

Edward Docker
History of Indian Cricket (1976)

1923   Like all Indian captains he placed his faith in the Oriental virtue of patience.

Ray Illingworth
Captaincy (1980)

1924   Not the type of personality of which legends are made. Containment, rather than aggression, was his style and it did not make for riveting cricket.

Ibid.

Walcott, C L
1925 Few batsmen have been able to match Clyde Walcott's power and majesty.

> **Trevor Bailey**
> *The Greatest of My Time* (1968)

Walters, C F
1926 He walked to the wicket like a free man, one going out to a hard, but agreeable task.

> **R C Robertson-Glasgow**
> *More Cricket Prints* (1948)

1927 . . . a glorious batsman and a most charming personality.

> **Roy Genders**
> *Worcestershire County Cricket* (1952)

1928 The facility with which he stroked the ball through the outfield masked the speed at which the ball travelled, a sign of immaculate timing.

> **M D Vockins**
> *Worcestershire CCC* (1980)

Walters, K D
1929 He is said to have frequently gone in to bat not knowing his team's score, dropping his cards to grab his bat and cap.

> **Jack Pollard**
> *Australian Cricket* (1982)

Wardle, J H
1930 Wardle's powers of spin, in any form, were exceptional and he had the physical resources to permit long spells of bowling.

> **J M Kilburn**
> *A History of Yorkshire Cricket* (1970)

1931 He was more inclined to thrive on success than to rise to a challenge and an urge towards the spectacular tended to obscure appreciation of team needs.

> *Ibid.*

Warner, P F
1932   Among the figures that challenge oblivion in the long vistas of
the game – W G, with his black beard and MCC cap, Ranji in
his fluttering sleeves of silk – few surely were more familiar,
none certainly was better loved, than that of 'Plum' Warner,
the 'Happy Warrior', in his Harlequin cap.

H S Altham
A History of Cricket, Volume One (1926)

1933   He was a great captain. His methods were gently persuasive
rather than fire-eating, but no tactician ever exceeded his
shrewdness and his alert grip of the momentary situation, nor
his knowledge of the foibles of friend and foe alike.

Diana Rait Kerr and I A R Peebles
Lord's 1946 – 1970 (1971)

1934   His own cricket set an example of grit and determination, and
he was an optimist who could visualise eventual victory in the
most forbidding circumstances.

E M Wellings
A History of County Cricket – Middlesex (1972)

1935   No heartier cricketer than Pelham Warner ever chose a bat.

C B Fry
The Book of Cricket (1899)

1936   . . . a golden treasury of all that ever happened, or was likely
to happen, in the game of cricket.

Ibid.

1937   He was a cricketer who made himself good enough to hold his
own among those more naturally talented than he.

Gerald Howat
Plum Warner (1987)

1938   He was a born leader of men and proved one of the
outstanding captains in the game's history. His readiness to
identify and encourage young cricketers paved the way for
several distinguished careers.

Ibid.

Washbrook, C
1939 His square-cut was like the quick fall of a headsman's axe,
clean and true.

Margaret Hughes
All on a Summer's Day (1953)

1940 In the final estimate of Washbrook's batting it will probably be
reckoned that he fell somewhere short of greatness.

Gerald Hodcroft
My Own Red Roses (1984)

Wasim Bari
1941 Loose-limbed and very quick, he is a bouncy character with a
wiry strength which enables him to keep going all day.

Alan Knott
Stumper's View (1972)

Weekes, E D
1942 . . . whose ferocity all but concealed a superb technique.

Michael Manley
A History of West Indies Cricket (1988)

Wellard, A W
1943 Wellard was a pragmatist: he liked to do what he could do
best. That meant the hitting of sixes, crude and crashing,
insensitive to the inner torment of the bowler.

David Foot
Sunshine, Sixes and Cider (1986)

Wells, B D
1944 He was a natural clown at a time when cricket on the county
circuit was still a game of character and characters.

Nico Craven
Waiting for Cheltenham (1989)

1945 If he was batting, running between the wickets could be
devastating to all concerned; he would run without calling, call
without running or else change his mind in mid-wicket.

Grahame Parker
Gloucestershire Road (1983)

1946   He may have batted like an engine shunting trucks but his
bowling was something different. He was a top-class off-spinner
with a bewildering run-up which could vary from nought to
seven yards as the whim took him.

Ibid.

Whittington, T A L
1947   As befits a solicitor, he was normally unruffled by peculiar
events on the field and he led with a calm assurance.

Andrew Hignell
The History of Glamorgan CCC (1988)

Willis, R G D
1948   Few top cricketers have lived on their nerves as much as he did.

Gerry Cotter
The Ashes Captains (1989)

Woods S M J
1949   Everyone loved Sam, for the whole world's manliness and
generosity seemed to have gathered into his heart.

R C Robertson-Glasgow
46 Not Out (1948)

1950   Everything about him was bountiful: his shoulders, his smile,
the thrust of his bowling arm, the playful swing of his bat, his
drinking capacity, and the warmth of his heart.

David Foot
From Grace to Botham (1982)

1951   He was very fast in those days and a bit wild when he wasn't
concentrating.

David Foot
Sunshine, Sixes and Cider (1986)

1952   He never noticeably grieved too much about a defeat; a rebuke
to a pro (or amateur) was tactfully handled.

Ibid.

1953   He was the greatest character in the history of Somerset cricket,
as big a celebrity, around the Blackdown Hills, the Quantocks,
the Mendips and Poldens, as Grace himself.

Ibid.

Woolley, F E

1954   The most graceful of the efficient, and the most efficient of the graceful.

I A R Peebles
Woolley – The Pride of Kent (1969)

1955   Nobody was ever bored by what Frank Woolley did or said on a cricket field.

C S Marriott
The Complete Leg-Break Bowler (1968)

1956   But the appeal of his batsmanship lies in something more than its beauty: it reflects, in its unruffled ease, a singularly gracious, and, in its challenging power, a gallant personality.

H S Altham
Frank Woolley (1938) reprinted in *The Observer on Cricket* (1987)

1957   There was an extraordinary negligence about his batting, as though his thoughts were elsewhere, but what terrible things he did to bowlers!

Michael Meyer
Summer Days (1981)

1958   None of my many heroes, then or since, has matched Woolley for excitement and romance. To describe him in terms of modern batsmen, he combined the grace of Graveney with the power of Dexter – or, if you are too young to have seen them, the grace of Gower with the power of Botham.

Ibid.

1959   . . . there was all summer in a stroke by Woolley, and he batted as it is sometimes shown in dreams.

R C Robertson-Glasgow
Cricket Prints (1943)

1960   He never showed off; it was an attitude of which he was incapable even as a youngster, but it pleased him always to give pleasure, and he left the game before that power in him had diminished. For that reason, he will always be remembered in Kent as a man who retained his youth until his fifties.

I A R Peebles
Woolley – The Pride of Kent (1969)

1961 In Woolley's batsmanship there is radiance, but never a light that is garish.

Sir Neville Cardus
Days in the Sun (1924)

1962 I hold it better to have seen Frank's swing
And let its fragile beauty magnify
My own poor discord, joyous graceful thing,
Than to have reaped all Painting's harmony.

M C J Allom and M J Turnbull
Frank Woolley

1963 When he walked in for the last time something went out of cricket which could never be recaptured.

E W Swanton
A History of Cricket, Volume Two (1962)

Worrell, F M
1964 In every respect he was a magnetic personality who through his mature and inspiring captaincy of the West Indies brought pride and success to the wayward talents of its players.

Keith Andrew
The Handbook of Cricket (1989)

1965 There was no Future, there was no Past.
The Present was all that mattered to him.

Undine Giuseppe
Sir Frank Worrell (1969)

1966 As Shakespeare said − some men in their lives play many parts. Worrell was one of the few to do it all at the same time.

Clayton Goodwin
Caribbean Cricketers (1981)

1967 Frank Worrell, a proud and strong-minded man, had grown up increasingly restless under the unyielding racial hierarchy that was Barbados society.

Michael Manley
A History of West Indies Cricket (1988)

1968   Worrell had entered the world of tactics and strategy and
shown that he was master of their equations. He had been
tested in the fire of adversity and shown that he could handle
this with icy self-control and unfailing dignity. Most of all, he
had penetrated a realm that defies analysis: leadership.

Ibid.

1969   Frank Worrell turned West Indies from being the most
magnificent group of individual cricketers in the world into a
close-knit team. No one else could have done it.

Richie Benaud
On Reflection (1984)

1970   . . . whose back-lift was as nobly upright as his character.

A A Thomson
Cricketers of My Times (1967)

Wright, D V P
1971   For years there was no bowler in the world against whom the
best batsmen felt less secure, none who was more likely to
produce a ball which left them helpless.

R L Arrowsmith
A History of County Cricket – Kent (1971)

1972   . . . whom fortune never easily favoured; whose brave efforts
seemed to be put forth when he was on the losing side and who
was genuinely reckoned a potential match-winner without ever
quite fulfilling this potential.

A A Thomson
Cricketers of My Times (1967)

Wyatt, R E S
1973   Outwardly he always gave an impression of unruffled calm and
an enviable self-control. But his apparent indifference to the
reactions of the crowd was vaguely resented; he was considered
cold and humourless.

Gerald Pawle
R E S Wyatt (1985)

1974 Dour as he was on the field where he has rarely been known to smile, in the pavilion his great charm and knowledge of the game is there for all to partake. Cricket is Bob Wyatt's whole life and he has given his whole life to the game.

Roy Genders
Worcestershire County Cricket (1952)

Yardley, N W D
1975 He was a true gentleman in an age when dedicated professionalism was only beginning to give way to winning at any cost.

Anthony Woodhouse
The History of Yorkshire CCC (1989)

1976 Would be recognised as one of England's best post-war skippers but for one endearingly human failing: he was too nice.

Ray Illingworth
Captaincy (1980)

1977 To him winning was important but not all-important, striving took precedence over achievement and discipline was the acceptance of obligations.

J M Kilburn
A History of Yorkshire Cricket (1970)

Zaheer Abbas
1978 He smiled like the normally solemn choirboy who knew that he had the top note − with purity and grandeur.

David Foot
Zaheer Abbas (1983) reprinted in *The Guardian Book of Cricket* (1986)

INDEX
OF
AUTHORS

A

Acfield, D I 1617
Ainslie, R St J 717
Allen, D R 319
Allom, M C J 1962
Alston, R 1007
Altham, H S 69, 73, 987, 1014, 1049, 1087, 1253, 1305, 1306, 1384, 1417, 1462, 1484, 1485, 1675, 1676, 1721, 1722, 1804, 1805, 1808, 1894, 1932, 1956
Ames, L E G 549, 554, 1109
Andrew, K V 5, 573, 574, 581, 610, 1059, 1066, 1095, 1130, 1565, 1645, 1829, 1830, 1964
Andrews, W H R 334, 352, 650
Anonymous 208, 209, 211, 366, 405, 501
Arlott, J 74, 80, 153, 204, 220, 255, 306, 395, 408, 469, 497, 540, 552, 579, 760, 761, 778, 788, 883, 909, 937, 955, 956, 1053, 1069, 1099, 1100, 1103, 1116, 1117, 1118, 1133, 1163, 1416, 1418, 1423, 1434, 1474, 1498, 1543, 1566, 1657, 1658, 1695, 1765, 1766, 1767, 1795, 1803, 1868, 1869, 1876, 1880, 1881, 1899, 1917
Arrowsmith, R L 996, 997, 1050, 1147, 1151, 1213, 1214, 1241, 1242, 1902, 1971
Ashley-Cooper, F S 1591
Ashton, Sir H 1471
Aumonier, S 121, 132, 133, 423, 480, 526, 569, 570, 723, 724, 798

Ayckbourn, A 9, 125, 382, 692, 746, 764, 765

B

Bacha, D N 1682
Bailey, T E 314, 523, 572, 623, 624, 625, 649, 779, 854, 897, 899, 900, 926, 984, 985, 1029, 1030, 1038, 1096, 1156, 1199, 1200, 1211, 1232, 1233, 1275, 1276, 1431, 1545, 1748, 1823, 1824, 1831, 1878, 1904, 1905, 1925
Balcon, Sir M 330
Baloch, K H 986
Bange, W 747
Barker, R 349, 1191, 1194
Barnes, S 1187, 1188, 1189, 1190
Barrie, Sir J M 313
Batchelor, D 773, 1752
'Beachcomber' 17
Bearshaw, B 1491
Bedser, A V 518, 520, 1025, 1088
Beginner, Lord 828
Beldam, G W 450, 1304, 1405, 1486, 1624, 1754, 1889
Belloc, H 234
Benaud, R 1656, 1700, 1701, 1969
Benson, E F 398
Bentley, E C 1315
Berry, S 874, 1272, 1362, 1478
Betjeman, Sir J 749

Billington, M 152, 193
Birley, D 655, 656, 683, 839, 855,
    1076, 1104, 1105, 1681
Birmingham Post 1235
Blake, W 430, 485
'Blazer' 582
Blofeld, H C 106, 120, 1057, 1137,
    1138
Blunden, E 6, 273, 975, 976
Bose, M 378, 379, 865, 868, 869,
    870, 871, 1662, 1663
Bowen, E E 715
Bowen, R 232, 1028
Bowes, W E 1464, 1550, 1758
Box, C 166
Boycott, G 259
Bradman, Sir D G 413, 698, 831,
    1551, 1698
Bray, C 1166, 1167, 1168, 1535,
    1685, 1686
Brearley, J M 612, 613, 614, 637
Bright-Holmes, J 532
Brodribb, G 732, 1870
Brookes, C 1592
Brown, I 99
Bucknell, E 966
Bullett, G 4
Byron, Lord 159, 182

C

Caffyn, W 1671
Callaghan, J 917, 918, 919, 1077,
    1078, 1759
Cameron, J 23
Cardus, Sir N 51, 53, 113, 117, 136,
    140, 176, 216, 223, 441, 451, 460,
    506, 602, 676, 696, 756, 791, 795,
    798, 811, 838, 850, 886, 915, 1171,
    1622, 1625, 1626, 1629, 1749,
    1884, 1961
Carew, D 54, 66, 169, 425, 808, 911,
    1124, 1173, 1559, 1848
Carr, A W 658, 659, 667, 840, 1919

Carr, J L 605, 1225, 1312, 1415
Carroll, L 751
Castle, D 320, 321, 322, 323, 737,
    738, 739
Castlerosse, Lord 841
Chadwick, A E 157
Chesterfield, Lord 77
Chesterton, G K 181
Christian, E B V 433, 434, 719, 990,
    1293, 1583, 1589, 1779
Christie, P 809
Clarke, J 1160
Clay, J C 212, 834
Close, D B 329
Cobbold, W N 677
Cochrane, A 254, 256, 411, 517, 550
Cohen, M 112
Coldham, J D 668, 1369
Coldham, J P 48, 84, 603, 878, 912,
    913, 1374, 1375, 1381, 1453, 1454,
    1455, 1456, 1623
Compton, D C S 789
Constantine, Sir L N 41, 345, 483,
    484, 543, 578, 674
Cooke, A 141
Cotter, G 752, 1040, 1110, 1111,
    1112, 1148, 1149, 1158, 1297,
    1368, 1553, 1627, 1654, 1655, 1948
Couch, A 288, 289
'Country Vicar' (R L Hodgson) 235,
    704, 785
Cowdrey, C S 328
Cowdrey, M C 1361, 1694
Craven, N 65, 527, 533, 962, 1944

D

Daft, R 1316, 1673
Darwin, B 1291, 1296, 1308, 1309,
    1310
Davie, M 1652, 1906
Davies, D 146
Denness, M H 356, 357, 358
de Selincourt, H 60, 90, 266

H

I

J

Y